D0103502

foliage

david joyce

foliage

dramatic and subtle leaves
for the garden

Trafalgar Square Publishing

To Ruth Rosenberg,
with love and admiration

Half-title: The uncoiling frond of the tree fern, *Dicksonia antarctica*.

Title page: The hard materials of a contemporary garden are softened by the textures and colors of foliage plants and the movement of trees in the wind.

Above: The fan-like leaves of the maidenhair tree (*Ginkgo biloba*), a living fossil virtually unchanged over a period of more than 200 million years.

Opposite: Leaflets of the honey bush (*Melianthus major*), with sidelighting distorting their glaucous blue-gray color but underlining their jagged pattern.

Editorial Director: Jane O'Shea
Creative Director: Mary Evans
Design: Paul Welti
Project Editor: Carole McGlynn
Editorial Assistant: Helen Desmond
Production: Julie Hadingham
Picture Research: Nadine Bazar
Picture Assistant: Sarah Airey
Indexer: Michèle Clarke

First published in the United States of America in 2001 by
Trafalgar Square Publishing,
North Pomfret, Vermont 05053

Printed and bound in Germany by Monheim GmbH

Copyright © Text David Joyce 2001
Copyright © Design & Layout Quadrille Publishing Ltd 2001

All rights reserved. No part of this book may be reproduced, stored in a retrieval system or transmitted in any form or by any means, electronic, electrostatic, magnetic tape, mechanical, photocopying, recording or otherwise, without prior permission in writing of the publisher.

The right of David Joyce to be identified as the author of this work has been asserted by him in accordance with the Copyright, Design and Patents Act 1988.

ISBN 1-57076-187-6

Library of Congress Catalog Card Number: 00-105134

contents

introduction

The new and lively interest in plants with ornamental foliage continues to gather momentum. The distinctive and unusual characteristics of these plants appeal to gardeners at a time when ideas of garden design have become much freer. Foliage plants are also attractive because their effect is long-lasting and they can be exploited in ways that have many practical advantages. The interest in foliage marks an important shift in the way we look at plants. Most gardeners have at some time suffered from leaf blindness brought on by the dazzle of flowers, but there is now a wide acceptance that the rivalry between the ornamental qualities of foliage and flowers is false. It is true, however, that gardeners still find it much more difficult to get information about foliage than they do about flowers. In particular, what has been missing, it seems to me, is an approach that frees the appreciation of the ornamental qualities of foliage from the technical language of botanical description.

My aim in writing this book is to draw attention to interesting leaf characteristics that are appealing aesthetically and of real garden value, and to present them in a way that any gardener can understand. The formula I have adopted is to provide simple descriptive labels for distinctive aspects of leaf shape and size, leaf texture and leaf color, backing these with a selection of strong images that show the characteristics described. This approach has also been extended to include the stance and poise of plants, for it is so often not leaves seen individually but the way they are presented that counts in the setting of a garden. Under each label I have listed a personal selection of plants that show relevant characteristics, and these plants are among those described briefly in Selected Foliage Plants (pages 126–151). There are comments throughout on the use of plants in gardens and in particular in the chapter, The Garden (pages 108–125).

Whorls of tree fern fronds in the setting of a subtropical rainforest are a reminder that leaves came before flowers and remain highly ornamental features of many plants.

Before being seduced by the ornamental qualities of foliage it as well to remember that leaves play a vital role in the life of plants and of all living things. Leaves are the organs through which plants "breathe" and they house the green pigment chlorophyll that is the key to the conversion of solar energy into sugars. Although on close analysis certain elements are consistent in the structure of leaves, the formula is expressed in countless different ways that catch the imagination of scientists and gardeners alike.

Categories of foliage

There are a few broad distinctions between different kinds of leaves. One great divide in flowering plants is that between monocotyledons (monocots) and dicotyledons (dicots). These two groups,

An autumnal jigsaw of aspens (*Populus tremuloides*) and spruce (*Picea glauca*) in the mountains of Montana vividly contrasts deciduous and evergreen, broad-leaved and coniferous.

equally widespread throughout the world, are distinguished at the seedling stage, the dicots having two seed leaves, the monocots, probably descended from dicots, only one. The distinction persists when the true leaves develop. In monocots, such as grasses, the true leaves have parallel veins, and are usually narrow and elongated. The leaves of dicots are very much more varied in shape and the veins are netted.

Another important difference is that between evergreen and deciduous plants. Leaves have a limited lifespan, except in the case of annuals, shorter than the life of the plant. There is no one moment in the year when evergreens shed their leaves, the shedding process being spread out, with individual leaves commonly lasting three to five years. Deciduous plants shed their leaves annually as a way of surviving a winter period of low temperatures, or, as in some tropical plants, to survive a seasonal dry period.

Several other broad distinctions can be made. Conifers, unlike most broad-leaved plants, have needle- or scale-like leaves. Ferns, which are not flowering plants but bear spores, have a life cycle with alternating generations, the dominant generation producing fronds, which not only play the usual role of leaves but also carry spores on the undersides (many ferns produce sterile and fertile fronds). It is these spores when shed that give rise to the sexually active generation, but the organisms (prothalli) are so small that they usually go unnoticed.

Foliage variety

Although these broad distinctions are important, they do not explain the astonishing diversity of plants found in almost every corner of the world except the high snow-bound summits of mountains and the permanently frozen expanses of polar regions. In searing desert, freezing tundra, sea coasts sprayed by salt-laden gales, and lush swamps, there are plants that manage the processes of transpiration and photosynthesis just as there are in temperate woodland, alpine meadow, or open prairie. Each species is, in its own way, a demonstration of one of the grand themes of biology, evolution by natural selection. In addition to being enormously varied, the adaptations made by plants to particular environmental conditions are often highly complex. Some of the most easily appreciated are to be seen in the leaves of plants, whether in the tiny rosetted clusters of compressed alpines, the vast fans of palms, or the fleshy armored blades of large succulents. These diverse leaf forms have an intrinsic interest, but many also have ornamental values that translate effortlessly to garden settings.

Gardens have been enriched over several centuries by the finds plant hunters have made throughout the world. The great flood of introductions in the nineteenth and early twentieth centuries has slowed, but there is still a trickle of new introductions, augmented by the reintroduction of plants that have been lost in cultivation. Yet another source of new foliage plants are those raised in cultivation. These are sometimes chance sports, spotted by someone with a keen eye for the garden-worthiness of, say, an interestingly variegated form. Sometimes they are the result of a planned breeding program. Gardeners are simply spoiled for choice.

Plant selection

The plants illustrated and described in this book are a selection from the many species and cultivated plants with ornamental foliage. Most are hardy enough to stand some degree of frost. Many are very hardy. Some, however, are tropical and subtropical plants that show no resistance to frost at all. Tender exotics with foliage of dramatic and unusual beauty often have a very powerful aura that is strong enough for them to create a tropical atmosphere wherever they are grown. This has helped to make some of them popular plants in cooler regions of the world, where they are often used in summer bedding, or treated as container plants that can be moved outdoors for several months of the year but otherwise need the protection of a frost-free environment. Some exotic bedding plants such as the castor oil plant (*Ricinus communis*) may be shrubs and perennials, but they are raised annually and disposed of when the beds are dismantled. Others, such as cannas, are lifted at the end of the summer season and stored in a dormant state until planted out the following year.

Above: Even in nontropical parts of the world, a luxuriant summer garden filled with foliage plants such as palms, bananas, and cannas can suggest the languid heat of the tropics and the subtropics. Quite hardy plants such as cordylines and phormiums may be used to supplement the authentic vegetation of hot and humid places.

An indication of hardiness and a guide to cultivation is given in the Selection entries (pages 126–151), where plants are listed alphabetically within broad categories. Trees and shrubs have been amalgamated to avoid duplicating entries for certain genera and because the distinction between large shrubs and small trees is somewhat artificial. Bulbous plants, although commonly treated as a separate group, are herbaceous perennials, and the small number with sufficiently distinctive foliage have been included in the broader category.

The use of botanical names throughout may dishearten some gardeners. If a generally accepted common name exists, it is given as well, but there are many plants that do not have a common name, and there are some common names that cause confusion because they are attached to two or even more plants. The advantages of a logical and internationally accepted way of naming plants outweigh all the disadvantages of unfamiliar language. It is often the pronunciation that is most daunting. Take courage. Other gardeners and nursery staff know the problems—and quite a lot of those who seem to be on top of botanical Latin are only bluffing.

Opposite: The remarkable adaptations plants have made to different growing conditions accounts for the great diversity of leaf forms, colors, and textures. There are foliage plants for every kind of garden. Here the biennial gray-green thistle *Onopordum acanthium* dominates a sunny dry garden with its gaunt spininess.

Conclusion

Many of the foliage plants that lend themselves to illustration are dramatic in form and arresting in color. I am a strong advocate of their use. But I should add as a corrective that the gardens that most appeal to me have their character determined by plants that are quiet and undemonstrative. They include good grays such as the artemisias, evergreen trees and shrubs such as the Portugal laurel (*Prunus lusitanica*) and phillyreas, deciduous shrubs and trees that are as beautiful for their spring freshness as they are for their brilliance in the fall, elegantly understated ferns, grasses and bamboos, not to mention numerous herbaceous plants that have flowers of very great beauty but also well-formed delicate or dignified foliage that is pleasing before and after the flowers have come and gone. The current fashion for plants that gesture extravagantly may pass, but I am confident that many other good foliage plants will be with us for a long time.

leaf shape and size

A brief description of the essential structure of a leaf and its role in photosynthesis is no preparation for the range of leaf sizes and shapes. The many forms leaves take can be put down to evolutionary processes that have resulted in plants that survive in bleak tundra, salt-sprayed coasts, the gloom of tropical forests, and countless other habitats. But gardeners have also played a role, for the ornamental value of different leaf shapes and sizes has long been recognized, and plants have been selected and bred to increase the variety available. You can see this highlighted in the numerous cultivars of the Japanese maple (*Acer palmatum*), a species that has shown a phenomenal capacity to produce different leaf forms that are very distinctive in shape, size, and color.

In broad terms the leaf is part of the unique and consistent character of a plant and as such is a valuable aid in identification. However, variability, even on a single plant, can be puzzling. The format of lobed foliage, for instance, is often very elastic. The leaves of many oaks (*Quercus*), to take an example, conform to recognizable patterns, and yet the lobing and indentation can be highly idiosyncratic. In the case of several perennials, especially rosette-forming plants like mulleins (*Verbascum*), the basal leaves are different in character from those carried on the branching stems. Difference may also be age related, a common trait in the eucalypts. The juvenile leaves of the Tasmanian blue gum (*Eucalyptus globulus*) are almost heart-shaped, stem-clasping, and very blue. But if the tree has a chance to keep growing, this foliage is replaced after two or three years by long, sickle-shaped pendent leaves that are deep green.

These puzzles only confirm that it is their wide variety that makes the size and shapes of leaves so interesting. Not only are the shapes often very beautiful in themselves, but they make attractive contrasts when set against one another and, where the range is well used, there is a richness of textures and shadows that lifts the garden out of the ordinary.

Right: The eastern redwood (*Cercis canadensis*) is a deciduous shrubby tree bearing bright pink pea flowers in late spring. The heart-shaped leaves of "Forest Pansy" glow red before developing their purple summer tones.

Left: The leaves of the horned holly (*Ilex cornuta*) are almost rectangular in shape and prominently spined. "Rotunda" is a compact female cultivar that bears long-lasting red berries provided there is a male nearby.

SELECTION simple geometry

TREES & SHRUBS *Amelanchier lamarckii • Arbutus unedo • Betula pendula • Buxus sempervirens "Rotundifolia" • Camellia japonica • Cornus alba • Cotinus coggygria • C. "Flame" • Cotoneaster horizontalis • Elaeagnus × ebbingei "Gilt Edge" • E. pungens "Maculata" • Eucalyptus globulus* (juvenile) *•Euonymus fortunei "Emerald Gaiety" • Fothergilla major • Hamamelis virginiana • Ilex cornuta • Ligustrum lucidum • L. ovalifolium • Phillyrea latifolia • Photinia "Redstart" • Prunus sargentii • Prunus laurocerasus "Rotundifolia" • Rhododendron falconeri • R. sinogrande • Salix "Boydii" • Sorbus aria "Lutescens"*

CLIMBERS *Hedera helix "Little Diamond" • Trachelospermum jasminoides*

PERENNIALS *Bergenia ciliata • Darmera peltata • Galax urceolata • Nymphaea* hybrids *• Pelargonium "Blazonry" • Sedum sieboldii "Mediovariegatum" • Stachys byzantina*

ANNUALS & BIENNIALS *Tropaeolum majus*

FERNS, PALMS, & CYCADS *Adiantum venustum • Cyrtomium falcatum • Onoclea sensibilis • Osmunda regalis*

EDIBLE PLANTS Orach

Many plants have leaves that can be described, at least approximately, in terms of familiar geometric shapes. As with other leaf shapes, these are not intrinsically ornamental, but the more or less literal appropriation of them by the vegetable world can be eye-catching and the shape repeated many times and combined with other features often helps to make a plant highly ornamental.

Many leaves are rounded, but in the majority of cases the leaf stalk or petiole that attaches it to the plant gets in the way of the circle being completed. You see this, for example, in zonal and fancy-leaved pelargoniums, some admittedly with lobed or scalloped margins. In these pelargoniums, banding, sometimes in several colors, as with "Blazonry" or "Dolly Vardon," underlines the circular shape. Widely grown and highly variable plants often have forms selected for their rounded leaves. An example of this on a small scale is the very slow-growing, broad-leaved form of the common box, *Buxus sempervirens* "Rotundifolia." None of these selected forms is likely to have the chance of showing off its round leaves in the dramatic way that water lilies (*Nymphaea*) can. Whether seen against silky or ruffled water, the glossy and sometimes mottled disks make handsome patterns well before the sumptuous flowers emerge.

Right: There are several purple-leaved forms of the smoke bush (*Cotinus coggygria*). In this case, a rim of frost defines the near oval shape of the leaves.

Instead of being attached at the side, some leaves are joined to the leaf stalk at the center. The most familiar example of peltate leaves, as those attached in this way are called, are found in the nasturtium (*Tropaeolum majus*). This easy trailing annual is a really beautiful foliage plant, and you can use it that way very effectively, as a filler in a new garden, in moist and reasonably fertile soil, even in light shade. It will produce fewer leaves, but will flower profusely if grown in rather poor, dry soil. More aristocratic plants with peltate and rounded leaves include two moisture-lovers, the sacred lotus (*Nelumbo nucifer*) and the umbrella plant (*Darmera peltata*). The leaves of both are dished at the center, and those of the lotus have an undulating margin. Generous lobing and heavily veined texturing attract attention to the umbrella plant, but it makes its point, too, by the impressive way it stacks large rounded leaves.

You would expect the oval to be a common shape, but it is usually distorted by stretching and swelling at one end or the other. This is also true of the ellipse, a flattened circle and, strictly speaking, the shape of an angled section across a cone. Of course, examples can be found, but it is often some other characteristics that make the leaves interesting. The strawberry tree (*Arbutus unedo*) has oval leaves, but what they are best remembered for is their glossy evergreen leatheriness. One of the most impressive is *Rhododendron falconeri* whose large leaves are approximately elliptic and up to 14in/35cm long; they hang like a ruff of dark green paddles, fuzzy brown on the underside, below trusses of creamy flowers.

Right: The nasturtium (*Tropaeolum majus*) is a climbing and trailing annual, but the plants grown are often compact cultivars. The smooth mid-green leaves, attached to the leaf stalk underneath and slightly off-center, are almost circular, with a wavy margin.

Left: A margin of frost obscures the jagged outline of the segments of this holly fern (*Cyrtomium falcatum*). The broad outline of its fronds, like that of many ferns, is triangular to lance-shaped. This hardy species tolerates exposure to full sun better than most ferns.

Few plants make sharply angled leaf shapes, but allowing for a degree of rounding, the triangle and the diamond are common enough shapes, diamonds cropping up several times in the ivies. The triangle is a familiar format for the fronds of ferns. In the kitchen garden you can find it, miniaturized, in the young leaves of claytonia, a winter salad that can be used as a cut-and-come-again crop. Orach, spinach-like whether raw or cooked, is a plant on a quite different scale, growing to about 6ft/1.8m. The red form, with its purplish triangular leaves and red stems, is very decorative. Rectangles and squares are rare, but, with a bit of imagination, you can find a four-angled shape in the leaves of the horned holly (*Ilex cornuta*).

Left: The deciduous woodland shrub *Disanthus cercidifolius*, which needs lime-free soil, has broadly heart-shaped blue-green leaves. There are small red-pink flowers in the fall, but a much greater effect is made by the intense scarlet and purple of the foliage before leaf fall.

SELECTION hearts and kidneys

TREES & SHRUBS *Ballota acetabulosa • Betula maximowicziana • Cercis canadensis "Forest Pansy" • C. siliquastrum • Corylus avellana "Aurea" • Disanthus cercidifolius • Physocarpus opulifolius "Dart's Gold" • Populus lasiocarpa • Rhododendron orbiculare • Tilia cordata*

CLIMBERS *Hedera hibernica "Deltoidea" • Vitis coignetiae*

PERENNIALS *Asarum europaeum • A. hartwegii • Bergenia cordifolia • Brunnera macrophylla • Caltha palustris • Epimedium x rubrum • Farfugium japonicum "Argenteum" • Glechoma hederacea "Variegata" • Heuchera sanguinea • Hosta "Frances Williams" • H. "Sum and Substance" • Houttuynia cordata "Chameleon" • Myosotidium hortensia • Pelargonium dichodrifolium • Ranunculus ficaria "Brazen Hussy" • Rheum "Ace of Hearts" • Sanguineria canadensis • Saxifraga fortunei • Tellima grandiflora • Viola riviniana Purpurea Group*

In the sixteenth and seventeenth centuries, herbalists relied heavily on the Doctrine of Signatures, reading a plant's inner virtues in its outward appearance. The classic example is the lungwort (*Pulmonaria officinalis*). Because in their shape and white spotting the leaves bear a resemblance to the lung, they were valued in the treatment of consumption. Although we are now struck by the cranky arbitrariness of the doctrine, we still often find ourselves referring to parts of the body when we are describing plants.

Two organs commonly used to define the shape of leaves are the heart and the kidney. In the botanical specific epithets of plants *cordatus* (also *cordata* and *cordatum*) means heart-shaped and comes up frequently; less common is *reniformis* or *reniforme*, meaning kidney-shaped. Given the great variability of leaf shapes within a species, and even in a single specimen, there are pitfalls in describing foliage in precise anatomical terms. The leaves of the Judas tree (*Cercis siliquastrum*), the bloodroot (*Sanguinaria canadensis*), or the semi-evergreen perennial *Saxifraga fortunei* are often described as heart- to kidney-shaped or kidney-shaped to round. Even where there is no anatomical ambiguity, the shapes themselves may be stretched, usually lengthwise, and modified by scalloped or serrated margins.

The heart or kidney shape of leaves can help to underline other foliage qualities or work with them to make a strong impression. Color makes a difference, as in a purple-leaved form of the eastern redbud (*Cercis canadensis* "Forest Pansy") or the yellow-leaved hazel (*Corylus avellana* "Aurea"). And when the shrub *Disanthus cercidifolius* takes on its lovely autumn color, differences in hue and intensity from one leaf to another make their heart outline conspicuous. Scale is another important factor. The red-veined hearts of *Populus lasiocarpa*, up to 1ft/30cm long and unusually large for a poplar, demand to be noticed. Presentation counts, too. The leaves of *Rhododendron orbiculare* are not large, but are held in a rigid horizontal way that draws attention to their shape.

You can turn to perennials for other examples. The pick of the ornamental rhubarbs for the smaller garden is *Rheum* "Ace of Hearts." Its airy sprays of pale pink or cream flowers are themselves attractive, but it is the heart-shaped leaves that catch the eye. The shape is boldly defined; they are deeply furrowed by red veins, and you may get a tantalizing glimpse of the purplish

Right: The evergreen kidney-shaped leaves of asarabacca (*Asarum europaeum*) make a richly colored ground cover in shade. The greenish-purple bell-shaped flowers of this perennial are tucked among the leaves.

Below: The foliage of the barrenworts (*Epimedium*) is held on wiry stems and forms an elegant cover 6-12in/15-30cm above ground level. The leaflets of *E.* x *rubrum*, toothed and heart-shaped at the base, are tinged copper-red in spring.

underside. The large, rather pointed heart-shaped leaves of *Brunnera macrophylla* are best when showing off variegation or spotting. Several popular hostas with heart-shaped leaves are variegated, the best of them to my mind being *H.* "Frances Williams." But among the hostas with heart-shaped leaves some of the loveliest are plain. "Plain" is, though, an inadequate term to describe the veined luster of *H.* "Royal Standard," the puckered blue-green of *H. sieboldiana* var. *elegans*, or the thickly textured lime-green of *H.* "Sum and Substance."

Is it pure chance that the kidney shape crops up in the leaves of several waterside plants? These include the glossy kingcup or marsh marigold (*Caltha palustris*) and the less hardy *Farfugium japonicum*, with forms that are white variegated ("Argenteum") and yellow spotted ("Aureomaculatum"). The kidney-shaped basal leaves of the vanilla-scented winter heliotrope (*Petasites fragrans*) and other butterburs might be thought useful ground cover, but these plants are not content until they have colonized the damp areas of whole landscapes. Plants with kidney-shaped leaves are, in fact, found in a wide range of habitats. European ginger (*Asarum europaeum*), is a low woodland carpeter. Many hybrid pelargoniums, derived from species found in southern Africa, have more or less kidney-shaped leaves. An unusual example is *Pelargonium dichondrifolium*, whose small, neat leaves smell of lavender when bruised.

Much smaller hearts are those carried profusely as the leaflets on the wiry stems of barrenworts such as *Epimedium* x *rubrum*. The shape shows up particularly well in the spring and the fall when the leaves are flushed red, but not all to the same extent. With its shining golden flowers, the lesser celandine (*Ranunculus ficaria*) is a low-growing beauty regarded as a weed by fastidious gardeners; its heart-shaped leaves are glossy, deep green, and variably marked, but in the cultivar "Brazen Hussy" they are a beautifully polished chocolate brown.

SELECTION eggs and spoons

TREES & SHRUBS *Berberis thunbergii • Carpinus betulus • Catalpa bignonioides • Crataegus persimilis "Prunifolia" • Idesia polycarpa • Myrtus communis • Paulownia tomentosa • Rhamnus alaternus "Argenteovariegata"*

CLIMBERS *Actinidia kolomikta • Hedera canariensis "Gloire de Marengo" • Hydrangea petiolaris • Schizophragma hydrangeoides*

PERENNIALS *Bergenia "Beethoven" • B. "Rosi Klose" • Raoulia australis • Saxifraga paniculata • Sedum spathulifolium "Cape Blanco"*

EDIBLE PLANTS Corn salad

In colloquial speech leaves are rarely described as egg-shaped. After all, the egg is three dimensional. But in botanical descriptions the case is very different, and large numbers of plants are said to have ovate leaves – that is, egg-shaped with the leaf stalk attached at the broadest end. Others are described as obovate, again egg-shaped, but with the broadest point at the tip. There is a certain amount of give and take in the use of these descriptions, and the shapes can be modified in various ways. For example, ovate leaves are often heart-shaped at their broadest end and have an extended taper at the tip. Both heart base and extended tip can be seen in the handsome leaves of the deciduous tree *Idesia polycarpa*.

Left: The deciduous shrub *Berberis thunbergii* and the purple-leaved f. *atropurpurea* have egg- to spoon-shaped leaves, the tip the broadest part. The foliage of the purple form turns intense red in the fall.

On the face of it, the egg shape does not seem to warrant special mention, but what makes it worth featuring is that it crops up so often among good foliage plants. You can see it in several climbers. The chameleon transformations of *Actinidia kolomikta* come and go on an ovate leaf that is finished with a pretty tip. The leaves of the highly decorative ivy, *Hedera canariensis* "Gloire de Marengo," are as much as 10in/25cm long and patterned in silvery gray and white. In the self-clinging *Hydrangea petiolaris*, the well-shaped leaves merge to form a dark green curtain that shows off the flat-topped clusters of creamy white flowers. The shape occurs in other categories of plants, too. A large-leaved example among woody plants is the Indian bean tree (*Catalpa bignonioides*), in the form "Aurea" one of the most handsome foliage plants in the lime-green to yellow range.

From an egg to a spoon is not such a radical shift, if you imagine the tapered end elongated to form a handle. Lawn perfectionists will know well the ground-hugging spoon-shaped leaves of the common daisy (*Bellis perennis*). The cultivated forms are grown for their pincushion flowerheads, but in the winter garden their fresh green makes a good edging. One of the hardiest salad vegetables, corn salad or lamb's lettuce, has a similar leaf. These summer-sown plants can be cut to come again, their little spoon leaves, mild in flavor, offsetting bitter tastes in winter salads.

The spoon or spathulate shape is found in a number of sedums, but the plant with a name that describes the leaf, *Sedum spathulifolium*, holds them so tightly in fleshy rosettes that it is difficult to get any sense of the leaves as spoons. Some of the loveliest of the alpine saxifrages, including the highly variable *Saxifraga paniculata*, are as interesting for their foliage as for their flowers, making rosettes of tongue- or spoon-shaped leaves that are silvered by limy encrustations. For lovers of carnivorous plants, an intriguing miniature is *Drosera spatulata*, which greedily extends tiny spoons, covered with sinister dewy hairs. The show auriculas (*Primula auricula*) are mainly grown for their curious, beautiful flowers and given protection so that their meal and circle of white paste are not spoiled. A dusting of meal also makes the gray tongue-shaped leaves conspicuous.

Plants with spoon-shaped leaves that really do add to the garden include several elephants' ears. A large example is *Bergenia* "Beethoven," while smaller and one of the best in flower is "Rosi Klose." The hostas cannot accurately be described as having spoon-shaped leaves, but when they are of heart to ovate shape, as many are, and held up on long leaf stalks to catch the light, they look to me like a clutch of spoons splaying artistically from an upright drainer.

Left: The fast-growing evergreen Italian buckthorn (*Rhamnus alaternus*) and its white-variegated cultivar "Argenteovariegata" have leathery leaves of variable form; the basic egg shape sometimes stretches to an oblong.

straps and ribbons

In searching for straps and ribbons to contrast with rounded leaves, the first place to look is among the grasses and grass-like plants, all of which have the parallel veining typical of monocots (plants that begin life as a single seedling leaf). After years of neglect, grasses are in the limelight, lavishly massed in landscape gardening, the epitome of good taste in mixed beds, and much favored in gardens planted on ecological lines. Grasses have their limitations, but many are highly effective at adding light texture to the garden, and among the best are plants with elegantly arching strap-like foliage or more sinuous ribbon leaves.

Near ground level the fluttering sunny liveliness of Bowles' golden grass (*Milium effusum* "Aureum") wakens shady corners of the garden in spring. On a quite different scale, a match for *Gunnera manicata* and other giant perennials, *Miscanthus sacchariflorus* stands tall at the waterside, its pennants still beautiful when they are bleached and rustling dryly. The striped variegation in some of these grasses subtly underlines their arching or undulating linearity. It is very striking in a real moisture-lover for shallow water, *Glyceria maxima* var. *variegata*, and in a relatively well-behaved form of gardener's garters (*Phalaris arundinacea* var. *picta* "Feesey"). Buff and bronze in the gold variegation of *Hakonechloa macra* "Alboaurea" help to make it a lovely soft clump of layered ribbons, good at the front of a bed and outstanding as a container plant. Like other grasses, maize or corn is wind-pollinated, so growing it in a block gives it the best chance of a good

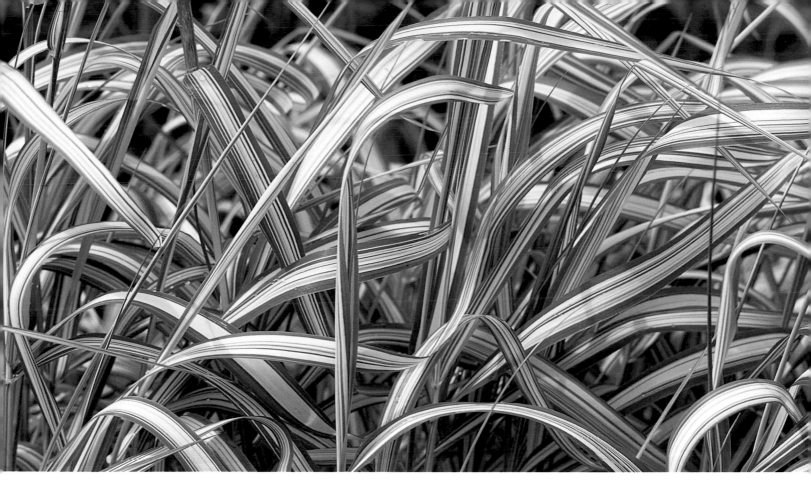

Above: Because of its sinuous animation and the clean brightness of its ribbons, "Feesey" is an immediately appealing form of gardener's garters (*Phalaris arundinacea* var. *picta*). The standard version is highly invasive, but this is superior and slower-growing.

Top left: A stand of silver banner grass (*Miscanthus sacchariflorus*) suggests a thicket of subtropical bamboos. The arching blades are about 1in/2.5cm wide but up to 3ft 3in/1m long, and these pliant straps rustle and flutter in the slightest breeze.

Left: The narrow shiny straps of the lilyturf *Ophiopogon planiscapus* "Nigrescens" are melodramatically dark, although the bases of leaves often show a hint of green. Sprays of mauve bells among the spidery tufts are followed by clusters of shiny black berries.

crop, and you have a pleasing little forest, 8ft/2.5m or more high, full of wavy-margined tapering leaf straps and ideal as a quick filler. The purely ornamental forms include the white-variegated *Zea mays* "Variegata," only about 3ft/90cm high, but with bold foliage to break up large blocks of flower color in bedding schemes.

The foliage of many bulbs dies shabbily, but I am pleased to see the strap-like leaves of some bulbs in their early stages. The snowdrop *Galanthus elwesii* is a vigorous species with relatively broad gray-bloomed straps that often have a twist to them. The onions (*Allium*) are vexing when the leaves die as the flowers reach their prime, but *A. karataviense* is a superb foliage plant for a sunny, well-drained position, each bulb usually producing a pair of broad gray-green purple-tinted straps that are still in good condition as the flowers develop. There are also non-bulbous members of the lily and daffodil families with attractive strap-shaped leaves. The South African clivias are unfortunately not frost-hardy, but where they can be grown they make a dense, richly evergreen cover of strap-shaped leaves. Evergreen African blue lilies such as *Agapanthus africanus* make dense clumps of rich green straps, but the deciduous species and hybrids of agapanthus are more hardy.

Some of the best-known members of the agave family have succulent foliage, but there are others with leaves that are rigid and spiky, or leathery and strap-like. Several of the smaller New Zealand flaxes (*Phormium*) have arching rather than sword-like leaves, and the straps of *Yucca flaccida* are much laxer than those of most of its relatives. The New Zealand cabbage palm (*Cordyline australis*), a monocot of tree-like proportions, makes a spiky head of leathery straps, the lower ones hanging as a fringe.

There are several ferns with undivided leaves, those of the hart's-tongue fern (*Asplenium scolopendrium*) being the most strap-like of all. In their general outline and arching growth, the fronds of *Blechnum penna-marina* are also strap-like, but they are deeply fringed by the divisions, particularly close on the sterile fronds. Mrs. Frizell's lady fern (*Athyrium filix-femina* "Frizelliae") is an amusing curiosity, with rounded lobes alternating along the short fronds so they seem like stiff ribbons of green tatting.

arrows
and lances

There are not many ornamentals with leaves of arrowhead shape, but they are striking enough to stand out in any garden. What helps to make them conspicuous is their season or the special conditions in which they thrive. The most eye-catching of the lords and ladies in the winter garden is *Arum italicum* subsp. *italicum* "Marmoratum." The dark, glossy, arrow-shaped leaves are veined with green ivory. Several other perennials with arrow leaves are waterside plants, so there is a good chance of seeing their leaves against an uncluttered background. However, the glossy bright green arrows of the arum lily (*Zantedeschia aethiopica*) are so well-defined, even when the edge is wavy, that they are easily picked out among other foliage.

The lance may be a less familiar ancient weapon, but it crops up even more frequently than the arrow in descriptions of leaf shape. When a leaf is said to be lanceolate or lance-shaped, the image conjured up is of the lance's metal blade, several times longer than wide, broadest near the base, and tapering to a fine tip. It is the image that is also evoked when leaves are described as willow-like, as they frequently are, for among the willows (*Salix*) the lance shape is common. You can see the tapered shape in the silvery-leaved *S. alba* var. *sericea* and in other forms of the white willow planted for their strongly colored winter shoots. It is telling, too, in weeping willows such as *S.* x *sepulcralis* "Chrysocoma." This has become a cliché at the edge of water in large gardens, but what can match it for its outline and the graceful movement of its long branchlets, for which the tapered leaves are so appropriate? The coyote willow (*S. exigua*) is another beautiful species, growing well on free-draining soil. Its narrow tapered leaves, silvered and silky at first, move freely on drooping stems to make a light and airy large shrub or small tree. Note that, as with almost all the lance-shaped leaves, these willow leaves are pliable, not rigid and war-like.

The weeping form of the willow-leaved pear (*Pyrus salicifolia* "Pendula") continues the silver theme. This is a much stiffer plant than the weeping willows, but it makes a pleasing small tree when trained up on a single stem. An alternative for a dry garden is *Elaeagnus* "Quicksilver," which has the advantage of small but very fragrant flowers hiding among the scaly tapered leaves. In many species of eucalypt, the rounded and stem-clasping juvenile leaves give little hint that the mature leaves will be narrow and tapered. The lance-shaped mature leaves of *Eucalyptus perriniana*, like those of many other species, hang in a docile way on slender stalks, giving the trees their drooping elegance – and also avoiding the full heat of the midday sun. In some of these eucalypts – *E. globulus* is an example – a slight curve gives the leaves a sickle shape.

Lance-shaped leaves in perennials often go unnoticed, but they can make a strong impact, as they do in large clumps of the ginger lilies (*Hedychium*) and in a few hostas, especially *Hosta lancifolia*. The lance-shaped leaf may also go unrecognized in many of the bamboos, but the beauty of most of these woody grasses relies on a profusion of slender tapered leaves swaying freely in a light breeze.

Top: Caladiums are tropical tuberous plants with thin arrow- or heart-shaped leaves that often combine green and white with pink or red.

Right: The crumpled spears or arrows of the perennial *Arum italicum* subsp. *italicum* "Marmoratum" unroll in late fall to stand through winter, their ivory veins gleaming in pallid light.

Below: The glaucous or glossy green mature leaves of the snow gum (*Eucalyptus pauciflora* subsp. *niphophila*) are lance- to sickle-shaped.

Left: *Imperata cylindrica* "Rubra" is sometimes known as blood grass for the dark red-purple staining of its narrow upright blades. In a cool climate it does not usually flower, but in warmer conditions it can become a weed through self-seeding.

SELECTION swords and blades

TREES & SHRUBS *Cordyline australis* • *C. australis* Purpurea Group • *C. indivisa* • *Yucca filamentosa* • *Y. filamentosa* "Bright Edge" • *Y. gloriosa* • *Y. whipplei*

PERENNIALS *Astelia chathamica* • *Canna* hybrids • *Crocosmia* "Lucifer" • *C.* x *crosmiiflora* "Solfatare" • *Dianella tasmanica* • *Eryngium agavifolium* • *E. proteiflorum* • *Iris* "Florentina" • *I. pallida* "Argentea Variegata" • *I. laevigata* "Variegata" • *I. pseudacorus* "Variegata" • *Libertia ixioides* • *Phormium tenax* • *P. tenax* Purpureum Group • *P.* "Sundowner" • *Sisyrinchium striatum* "Aunt May"

GRASSES *Imperata cylindrica* "Rubra"

The arsenal of the plant world is formidable. Stiff sword- or knife-like leaves of the kind produced by many monocots seem to be, like needles, thorns, and spines, yet further additions to the armory. Some plants with blade-like leaves certainly are well defended. The succulent *Agave americana* has large fleshy leaves that are jagged and toothed along the margins and fearsomely spined at the tip. Many yuccas, too, have bayonet or dagger tips to their leaves, a fact that is reflected in the common names of several species. There are, however, many plants that in their appearance convey the clangor of war, but are in reality much more docile than they seem. To the gardener it can be a relief that these plants are easy to handle, even though their clumps of stiff swords or blades make jagged accents that contrast strongly with small-leaved and lax growers that move easily in a breeze.

The New Zealand cabbage palm (*Cordyline australis*) is one of the few trees with sword-like leaves that can be grown in temperate gardens. The central leaves of the jagged tuft are held upright, but as they age they become increasingly straplike and hang down. A more impressive foliage plant where the climate is mild enough, *C. indivisa*, has broader leaves that follow the same progression. Although not tree-like, the saber-rattling New Zealand flax (*Phormium tenax*) can make clumps up to 10ft/3m high, so it is suitable for emphatic statements in garden or landscape. A few of the leaves in the plain or purple-leaved form (*P. t.* Purpureum Group) may arch or bend over, but they are generally much more rigid than those of the numerous hybrids, often strikingly variegated, that have been introduced recently.

On a smaller scale, some of the best sword-like foliage is readily found among the rhizomatous irises. The orris root (*Iris* "Florentina") is itself a good gray-green foliage plant, but its perfection lies in the ghostly beauty of its pale gray flowers. Another good gray-green is *Iris pallida* subsp. *pallida*, but more eye-catching are the white-striped fans of *I. p.* "Argentea Variegata." All these irises like sun and good drainage. Their equal at the waterside is *I. laevigata* and its brightly variegated form *I. l.* "Variegata." The yellow-flowered common flag (*Iris pseudacorus*) also thrives in shallow water, its stiff, rather narrow blades making good verticals in a wildlife garden. It is on the coarse side, but the yellow-striped *I. pseudacorus* "Variegata" has a subtle beauty, tender yellow as the fans emerge but eventually turning green in

summer. If you dislike variegation, the striped forms of the irises might bring you around because, even when the color contrast is startling, it does not clash with the form of the leaf. It works just as well in the iris-like leaves of *Sisyrinchium striatum* "Aunt May," which are striped with cream.

"Aunt May" is a good example of a plant in which foliage and flowers are perfectly matched. You find other examples among the montbretias. In *Crocosmia* "Lucifer" a jagged leafy base gives point to the horizontal or arching sprays of flame-red flowers. I like these happy combinations very much, but I also relish the mainly foliage effects of several stiff grasses. The upright blades of *Imperata cylindrica* "Rubra" stained with red stir the imagination, for you might well think that someone mortally bloodied has stumbled through the garden.

Above: The fanned swords of *Iris pallida* "Variegata" seemed sharpened to a creamy-yellow edge. The crinkled flowers are soft blue but eclipsed in ornamental value by the foliage.

Left: *Yucca glauca* gives a confusing message, its stiletto blades surrounded by the wispy curls of marginal threads.

Left: The Montezuma pine (*Pinus montezumae*), a Mexican species that can make a large domed tree, has chimney-brush heads of long needles, usually gathered in sets of five.

SELECTION needles and threads

CONIFERS *Cedrus atlantica* Glauca Group • *C. deodara* • *C. libani* "Sargentii" • *Juniperus rigida* • *Larix kaempferi* • *Picea breweriana* • *P. pungens* "Hoopsii" • *Pinus aristata* • *P. montezumae* • *P. mugo* "Mops" • *P. patula* • *P. sylvestris* "Beuvronensis" • *P. wallichiana* • *Pseudolarix amabilis* • *Taxus baccata* • *T.* x *media*

PERENNIALS *Armeria maritima* • *A. juniperifolia* • *Dianthus erinaceus* • *Equisetum telmateia*

GRASSES *Carex buchananii* • *C. comans* • *C.* "Frosted Curls" • *Festuca punctoria* • *F. glauca* "Elijah Blue"

ANNUALS & BIENNIALS *Bassia scoparia* f. *trichophylla* • *Nigella damascena*

EDIBLE PLANTS Dill • Fennel

In the northern hemisphere, vast tracts of inhospitable terrain are still covered by conifers. Much of their success in surviving harsh conditions can be attributed to their needle or scale-like foliage. Needles have the same components as other leaves, but their long thin shape has many advantages where the climate is harsh. Needles shed snow readily and hold little sap, so the risk of damage by freezing is minimized. They also have relatively few breathing pores or stomata, and those they do, arranged in lines, are set deep and usually protected by wax. The rate of transpiration is slow, and relatively little moisture is lost in the process. Despite living where winters can be bitterly cold, most conifers are evergreen, although the last stands of trees in the most northern reaches of Siberia are of the Dahurian larch (*Larix gmelinii*) which, like other larches, loses its leaves annually.

Many conifers make beautiful large trees, enjoyed for their overall shape and color, and valued for their usefulness in creating year-round shelter. Their size counts against them in the smaller garden, but they have a natural grace that is often lacking in their numerous dwarf and slow-growing versions. The pines (*Pinus*) come to the top for the ornamental value of their needles, which in most species are produced in bundles of two, three, or five. Several compact pines such as *P. mugo* and its various dwarf forms have short, rather stiff needles. Appearance does not always give a good idea of the way the needles feel in the hand. The bristle cone pine (*P. aristata*), a shrub or small tree native to the southwestern United States, looks like it has prickly foliage, but it is so soft that this conifer is sometimes known as the foxtail pine. There are, astonishingly, living specimens of this pine more than 4,000 years old. The most showy pines have long drooping needles. The Bhutan pine (*P. wallichiana*) is an elegant Himalayan species, while the Mexican weeping pine (*P. patula*) and the Montezuma pine (*P. montezumae*) are more tender.

In other conifers it is often the growth pattern that makes the needle-like foliage. The temple juniper (*Juniperus rigida*) and the Brewer spruce (*Picea breweriana*) are weeping, while the Japanese umbrella pine (*Sciadopitys verticillata*) has its stiff needles arranged like the ribs of an umbrella. In numerous other cases, as with forms of the white fir (*Abies concolor*) and the Colorado spruce (*Picea pungens*), it is foliage color that counts.

Several shrubs, including heathers (*Erica*) and rosemary (*Rosmarinus officinalis*), have narrow linear leaves, but often their shape is overlooked. In the burning bush (*Bassia scoparia* f. *trichophylla*), an annual that turns from green to intense red or purple in late summer, the individual linear leaves count only in that they contribute to the general impression of a highly colored dwarf conifer.

Far more conspicuous on account of their leaves are low plants, including grasses, that make tufts of very narrow leaves. The thrift *Armeria juniperifolia* and the pink *Dianthus erinaceus* are both examples of small tufted plants equipped to endure the rigors of life at high altitudes. Larger than these are stiff, clump-forming grasses such as the blue *Festuca glauca* "Elijah Blue." In the leather-leaf sedge (*Carex buchananii*), the apparently cylindrical leaves (they are actually three-angled) are more like burnished knitting needles.

If narrow leaves are not held stiffly, they look more like threads than needles. The sedges provide a few examples. The silvery green strands of *Carex* "Frosted Curls" twist as they arch over, the hair-like leaves being seen to good effect in pot-grown plants. The foliage of plants with divided leaves that are reduced to mere threads is sometimes described as feathery, but this suggests far too much bulk to be an adequate description of plants such as love-in-a-mist (*Nigella damescena*) or fennel (*Foeniculum vulgare*).

Above: The Mexican weeping pine (*Pinus patula*) is a graceful medium or small tree, with drooping bright green needles up to 12in/30cm long, usually clustered in sets of three.

Left: The horsetails (*Equisetum*), a group of plants that evolved very early, are similar to ferns in that they produce spores, not seed. They include some almost ineradicable weeds, so it may be wise to treat *E. telmateia* as a container plant.

notches and lobes

The lobed or notched outline to the foliage is an attractive and common feature in many plants. It is, though, almost entirely confined to the dicots, the plants that begin with two seedling leaves and whose true leaves are crisscrossed by a network of veins. The parallel veins of the monocots seems to be too single-minded for what in the dicots can sometimes take on a baroque extravagance. The significance to the plant of lobed or notched foliage is not self-evident, but it is said that it creates turbulence that affects the temperature at the surface of the leaf and as a result influences the rate of transpiration and the amount of water lost in the process.

Top: The tulip tree (*Liriodendron tulipifera*) is a tall-growing deciduous species native of eastern North America. It is remarkable for the distinctive lobing of its leaves and the green and orange flowers that give it its common name.

Left: In the fall the green lobed foliage of oak-leaved hydrangea (*H. quercifolia*) turns magnificent shades of bronze and purple just as the conical white flowerheads take on a pink flush.

Above: *Vitis* "Brant" is like the grapevine (*V. vinifera*), with three- to five-lobed leaves. In summer there are clusters of small edible blue-black grapes that ripen shortly before the leaves color richly; the veins remain green or yellow-green.

In some plants the lobing is highly variable, as in the leaves of the white mulberry (*Morus alba*), the source of food for silkworms. On a single tree there may be leaves that are nearly heart-shaped and unlobed, some that are three-lobed, and others that have a mitten shape, one small lobe extending like a thumb from the main outline. The mitten shape also crops up in the foliage of a North American tree, *Sassafras albidum*. But on a single specimen of this tree, you might also find unlobed leaves and, most frequently, leaves consisting of three forward-pointing lobes. A much greater variability in the lobing is found in some cultivars of coleus (*Solenostemon*). What is so astonishing with these is that, although individual leaves are so different in outline, there is enough consistency for them to seem part of the same whole.

Many of the most regular of the lobed leaves are hand-like or fan-shaped, to which I refer later (see pages 36-37). Of those remaining, many are so distinctive that they give the plants carrying them a unique character. On a small scale, one of the prettiest is *Vancouveria hexandra*, with leaflets consisting of three angular lobes. Another delightful small perennial is *Tiarella wherryi*, with ivy-like leaves, in "Bronze Beauty" tinted red. Several perennials with handsomely lobed leaves relish copious moisture. In *Astilboides tabularis* and *Darmera peltata* the lobing completes leaves of rounded shape. One of the most unusual perennials for its foliage is *Amicia zygomeris*, with leaflets that are arranged in pairs and inversely heart-shaped, but with a bite out of each tip.

The maples *(Acer)* are among the best-known trees and shrubs with lobed leaves. In many cases the five to seven lobes are arranged in a fan, but some are more sparsely lobed. One of the snakebark maples, *A. pensylvanicum*, is an example with three-lobed leaves that are rich yellow in the fall. After the maples the oaks (*Quercus*) are the most widely planted trees and shrubs with lobed leaves. Two American species with deeply lobed leaves are the pin oak (*Q. palustris*) and the red oak (*Q. rubra*). The oak reference comes up in descriptive names of other trees and shrubs, an outstanding example being the oak-leaved hydrangea (*Hydrangea quercifolia*). Like the above two species of American oak, it reaches its peak of beauty when the lobed leaves color in fall.

The tulip tree (*Liriodendron tulipifera*) remains for me one of the most appealing plants with unusual leaves. They have been described imaginatively as saddle-shaped, a description that fails to take account of numerous variations. Its ultimate size limits the tulip tree's usefulness as a garden plant, whereas the ivies with very distinctive lobing can be fitted easily into a small garden. *Hedera helix* "Duckfoot" is a favorite container plant, and for a climber I would keep on the same theme with the bird's-foot ivy (*H. h.* "Pedata"), which has a long central toe.

toothed, jagged, and prickly

SELECTION

TREES & SHRUBS *Acer japonicum "Vitifolium" • Berberis calliantha • Camellia japonica • Cercidiphyllum magnificum • Fothergilla gardenii • Fraxinus angustifolia "Flame" • Ilex x altaclarensis "Golden King" • I. aquifolium "Ferox" • I. aquifolium "Handsworth New Silver" • I. cornuta • I. x meserveae • Lavandula dentata • Mahonia japonica • Melianthus major • Olearia macrodonta • Osmanthus heterophyllus • Quercus coccifera • Sorbus aria "Lutescens" • Tilia henryana • Yucca gloriosa • Zelkova carpinifolia • Z. serrata*

CLIMBERS *Actinia kolomikta • Parthenocissus henryana • P. tricuspidata*

PERENNIALS *Acaena saccaticupula "Blue Haze" • Acanthus spinosus Spinossisimus Group • Agave americana "Marginata" • A. parryi • Astilbe hybrids • Astilboides tabularis • Artemisia ludoviciana "Valerie Finnis" • Astrantia major "Sunningdale Variegated" • Bergenia stracheyi • Cynara cardunculus • Echinops ritro "Veitch's Blue" • Epimedium x perralchicum "Frohnleiten" • E. perralderianum • E. x rubrum • Eryngium agavifolium • E. proteiflorum • Geranium x magnificum • Glaucidum palmatum • Gunnera magellanica • Helleborus argutifolius • H. foetidus • Heuchera micrantha var. diversifolia "Palace Purple" • Kniphofia caulescens • Lamium maculatum "White Nancy" • Ligularia przewalskii • L. "The Rocket" • Meconopsis horridula • Pachyphragma macrophyllum • Plectranthus forsteri "Marginatus" • Podophyllum hexandrum • Rheum palmatum "Atrosanguineum" • Rodgersia podophylla • Tellima grandiflora • Tolmiea menziesii "Taff's Gold" • Trollius europaeus • Waldsteinia ternata*

ANNUALS & BIENNIALS *Eryngium giganteum "Silver Ghost" • Lunaria annua "Alba Variegata" • Onopordum acanthium • Silybum marianum • Solenostemon*

FERNS, PALMS, & CYCADS *Cyrtomium falcatum*

EDIBLE PLANTS Balm, lemon • Mint (*Mentha suaveolens* "Variegata") • Parsley, broad-leaved

---

Countless plants have leaves with smooth edges, or to use a botanical term, their leaves are entire. But a highly distinctive feature of many other plants is the way the margins of their leaves are serrated, armed with prickles, cut, or slashed. The value to the plant of the very varied leaf shapes that result from these different margins is not always obvious. Even the prickliness of plants such as the Kermes oak (*Quercus coccifera*) is not a totally effective defense against grazing animals, as you can see from the topiary work of goats in the Mediterranean region. You can, though, be more confident about the ornamental value of minuscule teeth, serrations, or extravagant cutting. In many cases it is the margin of the leaf that catches the eye and lends a plant its unique character.

Perhaps it is only as we are shuffling through the beautiful debris of autumn that we take in the fact that the leaves of the hornbeam (*Carpinus betulus*), for instance, have irregular teeth, while those of many other trees are much more evenly spaced, even fastidiously so, as they are in the Caucasian elm (*Zelkova carpinifolia*). Low light and variable fall coloring, however, do make it easier to appreciate the outlines of leaves, finely scalloped in the case of the Katsura tree (*Cercidiphyllum japonicum*), a ripple of flame along the edge of the leaflets in the case of the climber *Parthenocissus henryana*.

It is when leaves are at and below eye level that we can easily focus on their outlines. The finish can be nicely understated, as it is in the lustrous leaves that show off the sophisticated flowers of camellias. More assertive are the spiny teeth of the Corsican hellebore (*Helleborus argutifolius*), a shrub-like evergreen perennial that makes an impressive clump with or without its green flowers. The hollies (*Ilex*) are more seriously prickly, so gardeners often prefer forms that are

Top: The weighty leaves of the succulent *Agave americana*, tipped and edged with sharp spines, form impressive rosettes. There are several yellow-variegated forms including "Marginata," shown here.

Right: Backlighting shows up the bristle-like teeth of *Tilia henryana*, a slow-growing Chinese species of linden that eventually makes a tree more than 65ft/20m high.

more or less spineless, such as *I.* x *altaclarensis* "Camelliifolia." The hedgehog holly (*I. aquifolium* "Ferox") and its variegated forms have taken prickliness to a silly extreme, but it is true that hollies with spines are usually the most glittering, the stiff waving of the margins between spines making a complex reflecting surface. *Desfontainea spinosa* and *Osmanthus heterophyllus* have holly-like leaves. So, too, does *Itea ilicifolia*, lovely against a sheltering wall, where the glossy leaves, edged with tiny sharp teeth, become a background for tassels of tiny honey-scented flowers in late summer.

Far more dramatic than hollies and their lookalikes are numerous plants with jagged and gashed leaves. The effect sometimes results simply from the division of prickly leaves into numerous leaflets, as it is with the mahonias. In the sunny dry garden there is nothing that quite matches the honey bush (*Melianthus major*), a subshrub that can be treated as herbaceous. Its compound leaves with boldly toothed leaflets make a grand fugue with complex counterpoint in blue-gray. Some of the most impressive plants with jagged foliage are large-leaved perennials, in many cases the cutting of the leaves multiplying the effect of lobing. You see this in great moisture-lovers such as *Gunnera manicata*, ligularias, and *Rheum palmatum*. Of the grand perennials that are sometimes described as sculptural, my favorite is the cardoon (*Cynara cardunculus*) which, with the magnificent biennial thistle *Onopordum acanthium*, is a quick and sure cure for blandness in the garden. One can love the bragging, even aggressive, posture of these plants, but find pleasure, too, in a less demonstrative selection of perennials. Lamiums, tellimas, tiarellas, and tolmieas are the sort of plants that win you over by the refinement of their leaves, color contrasts often pointing up the quality of the finish at the margins.

Above: *Eryngium agavifolium* is an evergreen South American species of the thistly perennials with a rosette of well-armed, limply sword-like leaves. From it rises a branched stem with cone-shaped green-white heads.

SELECTION compounds

TREES & SHRUBS *Ailanthus altissima • Aralia elata "Variegata" • Choisya ternata • C. "Aztec Pearl" • Fraxinus angustifolia "Flame" • F. excelsior "Jaspidea" • F. pennsylvanica "Summit" • Gleditsia triacanthos f. inermis • G. triacanthos "Rubylace" • Koelreuteria paniculata • Lotus berthelotii • L. hirsutus • Mahonia japonica • Melianthus major • Meliosma veitchiorum • Nandina domestica • Pterocarya fraxinifolia • Rhus glabra • R. x pulvinata "Red Autumn Lace" • R. typhina "Dissecta" • Robinia pseudoacacia "Frisia" • R. pseudoacacia "Umbraculifera" • Rosa glauca • Sambucus nigra "Guincho Purple" • Sorbus aucuparia "Aspleniifolia" • S. sargentiana • S. reducta • S. vilmorinii*

CLIMBERS *Clematis armandii • C. montana var. rubens • Jasminum officinale "Fiona Sunrise" • Wisteria brachybotrys "Shiro-kapitan" • W. sinensis*

PERENNIALS *Acaena microphylla "Kupferteppich" • A. saccaticupula "Blue Haze" • Artemisia "Powis Castle" • Astilbe species and hybrids • Dicentra eximia • Epimedium x rubrum • E. x perralchicum "Frohnleiten" • Erodium chrysanthum • E. manescaui • Ferula communis • Helleborus argutifolius • H. foetidus • Oxalis adenophylla • O. enneaphylla • O. tetraphylla "Iron Cross" • Paeonia cambessedesii • P. mlokosewitschii • Polemonium caeruleum "Brise d'Anjou" • Rodgersia pinnata "Superba" • Thalictrum aquilegiifolium • T, flavum subsp. glaucum • Trifolium pratense "Susan Smith" • T. repens "Purpurascens Quadrifolium" • Waldsteinia ternata*

FERNS, PALMS, & CYCADS *Adiantum pedatum • Blechnum penna-marina • Cycas revoluta • Dicksonia antarctica Dryopteris erythrosora • Polypodium vulgare • Polystichum munitum*

EDIBLE PLANTS *Angelica • Strawberry, alpine, "Baron Solemacher"*

Left: The leaves of the evergreen shrub *Mahonia japonica* are up to 18in/ 45cm long and consist of paired spiny leaflets with a single one at the tip. Red coloring is brightest in full sun and on poor soil. The yellow flowers in winter are strongly scented.

Right: In *Trifolium repens* "Purpurascens," chocolate clover leaflets in threes are picked out by their green rims.

A great many plants – woody and herbaceous, including even some ferns – have simple leaves that are complete in themselves. Others have leaves that are made up of separate leaflets. One way to think of these compounds is as simple leaves that are so deeply lobed that the blade has been broken up into several leaf-like components. It is not always easy to be certain that a leaf is compound, but at least on a shrub or tree a clue is provided by the presence of a leaf bud at the junction of the leaf and the twig or stem to which it is attached. On a compound leaf there are no separate buds for each leaflet, but you should be able to detect a bud at the axil where the leaf's midrib meets the stem.

There are three principal ways in which the leaflets of a compound leaf can be arranged. The most common is with the leaflets attached on each side of the leaf's midrib. You see this in some of the simplest ferns, such as the common polypody (*Polypodium vulgare*) or the sword fern (*Polystichum munitum*). On a quite different scale, you get this in the common ash (*Fraxinus excelsior*) and the tree of heaven (*Ailanthus altissima*). Botanists call the arrangement pinnate, from the Latin for a feather, *pinna*. Another version of the compound leaf is an elaboration of the pinnate arrangement, each leaflet itself being divided into leaflets. In the temperate garden, aralias provide the most dramatic examples of bipinnate leaves, as these compounds are called. They may be up to 4ft/1.2m long, and their extravagant effect can be heightened by variegation. The arrangement is common, too, in many ferns, where dense repetition of the leaflets (the correct term in the case of ferns is pinnae) creates some of the most delicate foliage effects. The third arrangement has the leaflets radiating from a central point, so that in many cases they seem like the fingers of a hand. Hand-like or palmate shapes deserve a discussion of their own (see pages 36-37), but a few curiosities, including leaflets in threes or fours, are dealt with here.

There seems to be no simple explanation for plants having compound rather than "ordinary" leaves. Compound leaves are probably, though, an advantage to early successional trees that shoot up where there are gaps in the forest. They need to get ahead before they are shaded out by competition from other plants and instead of investing energy in developing woody branches, they rely on compound leaves – in effect, disposable branches – while making rapid vertical growth.

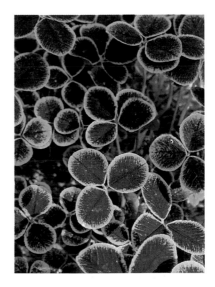

The tree of heaven (*Ailanthus altissima*), the Kentucky coffee tree (*Gymnocladus dioica*), and various species of sumac (*Rhus*) are all examples of temperate trees or shrubs with compound leaves that are fast-growing colonizers of open ground. Another advantage of compound leaves may be suggested by acacias and other trees of savanna and near-desert areas. When they shed their leaves in the dry season, they also shed the twigs that would otherwise be a source of water loss.

It is not surprising that some trees and shrubs with pinnate leaves rank as weeds, seeding freely and shooting away quickly. This is exactly the way the tree of heaven behaves, so you may find it difficult to appreciate it as a seed-bearing mature specimen. It is, however, one of the deciduous trees that can be cut back regularly, and then the low framework of branches will produce very decorative large compound leaves. They make a bold effect, as does the foliage of many other pinnate-leaved trees and shrubs. Mahonias, with the advantage of winter flowers, and sumacs, spectacular in fall color, are widely planted, but other less usual plants are worth considering. The rare *Meliosma veitchiorum* is an arresting tree with a distinctive stance, and its large leaves, consisting of up to eleven deep green leaflets, have conspicuous red leaf stalks.

Boldness is not the only virtue of pinnate foliage. Several of the mountain ashes (*Sorbus*) have leaves of delicate and ferny beauty that becomes radiant with fall coloring. A good choice for a small garden is *S. vilmorinii*, a deciduous shrub or small tree that rarely exceeds 5ft/1.5m. The low suckering shrub *S. reducta* has less refined foliage, but is an even smaller plant. Its trails of pea-like blossoms make the Chinese wisteria (*Wisteria sinensis*) a superb spring-flowering climber, but the lax pinnate leaves complete the impression of a vigorous but graceful plant.

Below: The large leaves of the stag's horn sumac (*Rhus typhina*), with prettily notched drooping leaflets, demand attention when they assume their brilliant fall colors.

Above: The cycads are evergreen palm-like plants that represent an early stage in the evolution of seed-bearing plants. The best-known example is the Japanese sago palm (*Cycas revoluta*), which has whorls of glossy dark green leaves composed of numerous narrow leaflets.

The fact that leaves are compound can easily be overlooked in some low-growing plants. The heart-shaped leaflets of epimediums, held on wiry stems, are banked up, making effective ground cover and also hiding their compound structure. The arrangement of leaflets is, however, apparent in many small plants. The pinnate leaves of the New Zealand burrs (*Acaena*) or *Dicentra eximia*, the more complex compounds in ferns, and the threesome of toothed leaflets in the alpine strawberry, all make lovely contrasts of texture with more rounded or linear leaves.

Some miniatures with compound leaves deserve close scrutiny. The clovers provides the classic model of a compound leaf with three radiating leaflets. In *Trifolium pratense* "Susan Smith" the leaflets are brightened by gold veining, while in *T. repens* "Purpurascens Quadrifolium" the chocolate-centered leaflets are in lucky sets of four. The folding leaflets of *Oxalis tetraphylla* "Iron Cross" make an even more striking arrangement in fours, a dramatic mahogany band covering each leaflet at the center. And several of the really dwarf oxalis have beautifully furled flowers over gray compound leaves that fold down like little umbrellas.

Right: The honey bush (*Melianthus major*) is a shrub often treated as perennial, the old growths being cut down annually to make way for new blue- to gray-green leaves composed of serrated leaflets.

Left: The numerous forms of the Japanese maple (*Acer palmatum*) offer many variations on the hand shape. In some cases there is a palm with five fanned lobes, as here, but the lobes can be cut almost to the leaf stalk and the digits may be very narrow and finely cut.

SELECTION # hands and fans

TREES & SHRUBS *Acer japonicum* "Vitifolium" • *A. palmatum* "Osakazuki" • *A. platanoides* "Crimson King" • *A. rubrum* • *A. shirasawanum* "Aureum" • *Aesculus hippocastanum* • *A. x neglecta* "Erythroblastus" • *x Fatshedera lizei* • *Fatsia japonica* • *Kalopanax septemlobus* • *Liquidambar styraciflua* • *Lupinus arboreus* • *Platanus x hispanica* • *P. orientalis* • *Ricinus communis* "Impala"

CLIMBERS *Hedera helix* "Buttercup" • *Parthenocissus henryana* • *P. quinquefolia* • *Passiflora x caerulea-racemosa* • *Vitis vinifera* "Incana" • *V. vinifera* "Purpurea"

PERENNIALS *Alchemilla alpina* • *A. conjuncta* • *A. mollis* • *Anemone tomentosa* • *Astrantia major* "Sunningdale Variegated" • *Farfugium japonicum* • *Geranium macrorrhizum* • *G. palmatum* • *Heuchera americana* • *H.* "Pewter Moon" • *Kirengeshoma palmata* • *Pelargonium* "Bird Dancer" • *Peltiphyllum peltata* • *Rodgersia aesculifolia* • *R. podophylla*

FERNS, PALMS, & CYCADS *Chamaerops humilis* • *Trachycarpus fortunei* • *T. wagnerianus*

EDIBLE PLANTS Fig

Two-leaf structures result in shapes that suggest, often dramatically, an open hand or a spread fan. In the case of the horse chestnut tree (*Aesculus hippocastanum*), the leaves are compound, a palmate framework of ribs radiating from a central point supporting separate leaflets. The leaves of the many maples (*Acer*), on the other hand, have a palmate shape based on radiating lobes. In the perennial lady's mantle (*Alchemilla mollis*), even a lightly scalloped margin gives the impression of an open fan.

Do not insist on anatomical accuracy when you are looking for hand shapes, for plants have a way of being approximate in the number of digits they produce. Among the most arresting of hand-shaped leaves are those of the evergreen shrub *Fatsia japonica*. The strongly ribbed dark green leaves invariably have supernumerary lobes, sometimes a grand total of eleven. But the effect is still of gesturing hands, grabbing attention and protesting a tropical provenance, although this plant from Korea and Japan is in fact hardy enough for many temperate gardens. The common fig is another plant with hand-like foliage, although the leaves are often missing a digit or two. Even where it is difficult to ripen the fruit satisfactorily, the fig is worth growing for its bold foliage carried on knobbly gray stems. In the vegetable garden, many of the squashes and pumpkins have attractively lobed leaves and, in the case of some zucchini, the depth of the cutting readily suggests splayed fingers.

Extravagant fan shapes are associated with several tropical plants, especially palms. Two tropical-looking palms are in fact hardy enough for many temperate gardens. *Chamaerops humilis*, the only

Right: Several palms, including the Chusan palm (*Trachycarpus fortunei*), shown here, and the dwarf fan palm (*Chamaerops humilis*), the two most commonly grown in cooler regions, are distinctive for the fanned arrangement of leaflets or segments.

European palm and usually well under 10ft/3m high, has narrow leaflets that are slightly limp toward the tips, making more than two-thirds of a circle. The Chusan palm (*Trachycarpus fortunei*), of oriental origin, is capable of making a much more substantial tree, topped by large rattling fans, sometimes over 4ft/1.2m across. The blue hesper palm (*Brahea armata*) will not stand frost, but can be pot-grown and moved indoors or out, where its cool waxy fans make an unusual contrast to tropical greens.

Strong fan shapes, creating dramatic shadows when side lit, are found in numerous perennials, especially moisture-lovers. It is hardly adequate to describe the giant leaves of *Gunnera manicata* as fans, but plants that do well in similar conditions include rodgersias, with fanned leaflets, in *Rodgersia aesculifolia* strongly suggesting the leaf of a horse chestnut. Like so many plants of the bog garden, their flowers are interesting, but it is their vigor expressed in dramatic foliage that makes an indelible impression.

In the end, though, you may feel that hand and fan shapes are more appealing when they are refined rather than dramatic. In the woodland perennial *Kirengeshoma palmata*, the light green lobed leaves are of an understated elegance that perfectly matches the unusual and subtle flowers. The appeal of the lady's mantle lies in the quiet harmony of soft green leaves, the lovely fan shape generously repeated, and the frothy green flowers. Not surprisingly, its daintier small relatives such as *Alchemilla conjuncta* have an irresistible charm. The refined fan-shaped leaves of maples put them in the first rank of foliage plants. The leaves are exquisite when unfurling in spring, handsome in their summer fullness, and splendid in the brilliance of their fall colors, even when they are no more than a sumptuous litter.

Above: Castor oil plant (*Ricinus communis*) is naturalized in many parts of the tropics and subtropics. In cooler parts of the world it is usually grown as an annual, particularly in its red-leaved forms, such as "Impala."

feathers and filigree

Ferns have no flowers to fall back on, but must please by the beauty of their fronds alone. In the majority of cases these are composed of a blade that is divided into many leaflets or pinnae, a first division of the frond often being divided again, sometimes more than once. During the short nineteenth-century craze for ferns, collectors were galvanized by bizarrely divided fronds, but in the long period of neglect that followed, many of these forms were lost to cultivation. It is no bad thing that the revival of interest in ferns is based on their value as good garden plants, since they are among the very best in shade and in moist conditions. The Himalayan maidenhair fern (*Adiantum venustum*), the male fern (*Dryopteris filix-mas*), and the soft shield fern (*Polystichum setiferum*) or its numerous cultivars all produce fronds that make telling contrasts with simple geometric shapes or jagged outlines. What places these and many other ferns in the first rank of foliage plants is their feathered grace and delicacy.

The conifers are a more surprising category of plants in which to find feathery foliage. This does not apply to those with needles, but rather to conifers with sprays of scale-like leaves. The best Lawson cypresses (*Chamaecyparis lawsoniana*) show this well, the fan-like leaf sprays, gray-blue in the case of "Pembury Blue," leaning out and drooping. But for soft-textured plume-like foliage in the conifers, there is nothing to equal a form of the Japanese cedar, *Cryptomeria japonica* "Elegans." Although this will eventually develop into a small tree, it retains soft juvenile foliage throughout its life. The effect is especially beautiful in the fall and winter, when the foliage turns purplish bronze.

Lacy and wispy foliage is found in the cut-leaf versions of several broad-leaved shrubs and trees. An astonishing number of variations of the fan-shaped leaf, sometimes cut and nibbled away to a skeletal fragment, are found in the Japanese maple (*Acer*

Top: The feathery leaves of *Ferula communis*, a giant unscented fennel, make a large mound. After years of gathering strength, the plant sends up a sturdy stem bearing rounded heads of small yellow flowers.

Above: Cold soggy winters do not suit *Artemisia* **"Powis Castle" and many other gray-leaved plants, but the finely divided leaves of this shrubby perennial gleam with its sterling qualities in full sun on well-drained soils.**

Left: The filigree silveriness of cotton lavender (*Santolina chamaecyparissus***) intensifies when this compact evergreen shrub is grown in hot dry conditions. It has yellow button flowers in summer.**

palmatum). Purple in the Dissectum Atropurpureum Group and green in the Dissectum Viride Group, the overall effect of their low soft mounds lies somewhere between lace and hair. The stag's horn sumac (*Rhus typhina*) has large pinnate leaves, and in "Dissecta" the shredded leaflets make a provocatively lacy effect, especially when the foliage flames in the fall. An elder, *Sambucus racemosa* "Sutherland Gold," is another shrub with lacy foliage, and in this case the cut compound leaves are an eye-catching yellow-green. The cut-leaf versions of several trees have the advantage of making a light canopy, a point worth considering if you are planting in a small or medium-sized garden where trees creating heavy shade could be a problem. A good example is a silver birch, *Betula pendula* "Laciniata." The fern-leaved beech (*Fagus sylvatica* var. *heterophylla* "Aspleniifolia") is a very beautiful tree, although not suited to a small garden, and a rather similar purple-leaved form, *F. s.* "Rohanii" has the advantage of making a less weighty statement in the landscape than most of the purple-leaved beeches.

There is, it has to be said, something a bit contrived about the cut-leaved forms of shrubs and trees. This is not something I feel about the filigree foliage of many beautiful perennials with much-divided and cut leaves. Some of these, like the silvery *Dicentra* "Langtrees," are little plants with a daintiness that holds the attention of the most critical scrutinizing eye. Others, such as a purple-leaved form of Queen Anne's lace, *Anthriscus sylvestris* "Ravenswing," make a more general effect of fine open texture. The best are as ravishing as the finest ferns and have the advantage of offering a broader range of foliage color and, in some cases, good flowers.

leaf flowers

In the many adaptations assumed by plants, leaves are sometimes modified to take on specialized functions. The tropical bromeliad family, which includes the pineapple (*Ananas*), also has numerous perching or epiphytic species in which the leaf bases overlap to form tanks or flowerpots that trap falling water and debris that then serve as reservoirs of moisture and food. The tendrils by which the sweet pea attaches itself to supports are in fact modified leaves, as, too, are the spines of cacti, which rely on their succulent green stems to carry out photosynthesis and transpiration. More gruesomely ingenious are the leaf traps of the flesh-eating pitcher plants such as the North American species of *Sarracenia*. The leaves of some plants, notably the hen-and-chicken fern (*Asplenium bulbiferum*) and the perennial thousand mothers (*Tolmiea menziesii*) can produce miniature versions of the parent plant.

The bracts that in some plants are found at the base of a flower or flowerhead, are also modified leaves. They can be scale-like and austerely functional, simply protecting the flowers, but they can also be very much more flamboyant, in some plants their size and coloring helping to attract pollinators to the small and inconspicuous flowers that they surround. In the garden they attract the eye, too. One of the most sensational introductions to Western gardens from China at the beginning of the twentieth century was the dove or handkerchief tree (*Davidia involucrata*). In late spring the branches of mature specimens appear to be hung with hundreds of laundered handkerchiefs pegged out to dry. A pair of white bracts of unequal size surrounds each flowerhead. More conventional flower-like arrangements are produced by the bracts of various dogwoods, including the North American flowering dogwood (*Cornus florida*) and the Asiatic *C. kousa*. The branches are loaded with a prodigious display of white and in some cases pink "flowers," the small true flowers packed into a head forming a central boss.

In the aroid family, which includes *Arum* as well as the tropical flamingo flower (*Anthurium*), the bracts around the flowers are often very conspicuous and curiously petal-like. The flowers themselves are tiny and stacked on a spike-like structure known as the spadix (common names such

Opposite: *Salvia sclarea* var. *turkestanica*, sometimes known as Vatican sage, is a form of biennial clary, which in its second year is topped by stiff stems packed with the delicately colored bracts that surround the small flowers.

Right: The stems of the sea holly *Eryngium* x *oliverianum* are metallic blue with purple tints, as are the spiny ruffs surrounding the cones of small flowers. This perennial makes a long-lasting effect in sunny gardens.

Below: The insignificant flowers of several Asiatic and North American species of dogwood (*Cornus*) are surrounded by showy bracts. A fine example is the large deciduous shrub *C. kousa* var. *chinensis*. The bracts turn almost white before coloring red-pink.

as lords-and-ladies for *Arum* species suggest its resemblance to a male member). The bract or spathe that in some aroids extravagantly envelops the spadix makes the "flower." The spathe of the arum lily (*Zantedeschia aethiopica*) is a white swirling funnel, while most of the arisaemas have curiously hooded and striped spathes. That of *Arisaema sikokianum* is mysteriously dark with faint striations leading to a white throat surrounding a white club-like spadix.

An ornamental advantage of bracts is that they are usually long-lasting. It is this quality that makes many spurges (*Euphorbia*) such useful garden plants and the poinsettia (*E. pulcherrima*) a popular container plant at Christmas in the northern hemisphere. The shrubby *E. characias* subsp. *wulfenii*, for example, has the much reduced flower parts like little eyes cupped by bracts that are fused together to make a single structure. Although the scarlet sage (*Salvia splendens*) is often maligned for its relentless intensity, the fact that the bracts remain colorful after the flowers have fallen is an advantage in bedding schemes. Long-lasting bracts are a feature of several other sages too and give the flower spikes of *S. nemorosa* and *S.* x *superba* their rich coloring. Some of the sea hollies (*Eryngium*) have such long-lasting bracts that their stems are often cut for winter drying. The small flowers are stacked to form a cone that sits at the center of lacy or jagged and prickly bracts which, in the best forms such as *E. alpinum* "Blue Star," are an intense metallic blue or silver gray.

Left: Mother-of-thousands, one of the common names of *Soleirolia solerolii*, suggests the expansionist tendencies of this dwarf evergreen perennial. The tiny leaves make a bright mat.

Below: The dune manzanita (*Arctostaphylos pumila*) is a Californian prostrate species of these lime-hating evergreen shrubs. Its tiny leaves are downy and spoon-shaped.

SELECTION giants and miniatures

TREES & SHRUBS LARGE: *Acer macrophyllum* • *Aralia elata* • *Betula maximowicziana* • *Catalpa bignonioides* • *Magnolia grandiflora* • *M. macrophylla* • *Paulownia tomentosa* • *Populus lasiocarpa* • *Rhododendron rex* • *R. sinogrande* • *Rhus typhina* • *Tilia americana*
SMALL: *Arctostaphylos pumila* • *Buxus microphylla* • *Calluna vulgaris* • *Cotoneaster horizontalis* • *Erica carnea* • *Hebe ochracea* "James Stirling" • *Ulmus parvifolia* "Frosty"

CONIFERS SMALL: *Cupressus cashmeriana* • *Picea mariana* "Nana"

CLIMBERS LARGE: *Vitis coignetiae* • *Wisteria sinensis* SMALL: *Hedera helix* "Duckfoot"

PERENNIALS LARGE: *Acanthis mollis* Latifolius Group • *Agave americana* "Marginata" • *Astilboides tabularis* • *Canna* hybrids • *Cynara cardunculus* • *Darmera peltata* • *Gunnera manicata* • *Ligularia* "Gregynog Gold" • *Lysichiton americanus* • *Nymphaea* hybrids • *Petasites japonicus* var. *giganteus* • *Phormium tenax* • *Rheum palmatum* "Atrosanguineum"
SMALL: *Aquilegia flabellata* var. *pumila* • *Artemisia schmidtiana* "Nana" • *Gunnera magellanica* • *Hosta venusta* • *Oxalis enneaphylla* • *Raoulia australis* Lutescens Group • *Saxifraga* x *irvingii* "Jenkinsiae" • *Sedum spathulifolium* • *Soleirolia soleirolii*

GRASSES LARGE: *Arundo donax* • *Indocalamus tesselatus* SMALL: *Festuca punctoria*

ANNUALS & BIENNIALS LARGE: *Onopordum acanthium* • *Verbascum olympicum*

FERNS, PALMS, & CYCADS LARGE: *Cycas revoluta* • *Dicksonia antarctica* • *Osmunda regalis* • *Musa basjoo* • *Trachycarpus fortunei* SMALL: *Blechnum penna-marina*

EDIBLE PLANTS LARGE: Angelica SMALL: Mint (*Mentha requienii*) • Thyme (*Thymus serpyllum* "Minimus")

The full range of leaf size is represented at one extreme by a palm, *Raphia farinifera*, which has leaves up to 65ft/20m long. At the other are minuscule duckweeds and numerous mat-forming plants, of which mind-your-own-business (*Soleirolia soleirolii*) is a familiar example. The size of the plant, however, is not in itself a guide to leaf size. The General Sherman, a specimen of the big tree or giant redwood (*Sequoiadendron giganteum*), is reckoned to be the the world's largest living thing, and yet the leaves of this species are not much more than 1/4in/5mm long.

Large flat leaves are good at trapping the light's energy, but water loss increases with high rates of transpiration, and broad leaf surfaces are vulnerable to wind damage. It is not surprising, therefore, that huge leaves are so often found on tropical plants growing in moist, sheltered, and shady conditions. Even in temperate forests, trees and shrubs have sun and shade leaves, the shade leaves being larger, thinner, and usually a darker green than those in sun. Among the most remarkable of the large-leaved plants from temperate regions are perennials that thrive in really squelchy ground. The South American *Gunnera manicata* is the most impressive, a clump at the water's edge creating

an atmosphere of primeval tropicality. The deeply veined, lobed leaves, up to 5ft/1.5m across, are strongly supported on massive bristly stems. How surprising that a diminutive relative, *G. magellanica*, has leaves less than 4in/10cm long. Other large-leaved perennials for really moist ground include the skunk cabbages (*Lysichiton*) with paddle-like leaves, tall grasses such as *Arundo donax*, the round-leaved *Astilboides tabularis*, jagged ligularias, and the royal fern (*Osmunda regalis*).

Using real tropical or sub-tropical plants is an option in temperate gardens, although you may have to grow plants such as the Japanese banana (*Musa basjoo*) and the tree fern *Dicksonia antarctica* in pots and overwinter them under glass. In summer they can supplement the effect of hardier large-leaved plants such as the Chusan palm (*Trachycarpus fortunei*), the New Zealand flax (*Phormium tenax*), and *Indocalamus tesselatus*, an extremely large-leaved bamboo. In bedding schemes there is nothing to match the luxuriant effect of cannas, which can be planted out annually as large foliage and flowering plants.

Above: Massive prickly leaf stalks and giant leaves up to 6ft/1.8m across make *Gunnera manicata* the ultimate perennial for moist conditions. The green-brown flowers are packed in a curious cone-shaped spike.

The relatively large scale of their leaves makes *Acer macrophyllum*, *Betula maximowicziana*, *Magnolia macrophylla*, and *Populus lasiocarpa* interestingly distinct from closely related species of trees and shrubs. Some of the most useful large-leaved trees and shrubs are those that can be cut back on a regular basis (see page 154). Hard pruning and generous feeding result in particularly large leaves on the tree of heaven (*Ailanthus altissima*), the Indian bean tree (*Catalpa bignonioides*), and the foxglove tree (*Paulownia tomentosa*).

Plants with small leaves are often well adapted to living in harsh environments. Some have dispensed with leaves completely, as have almost all the cacti. A reduction in the scale of plants and in the size of their leaves is very marked in alpine plants. In the garden the refinement of Kabschia saxifrages and other miniatures is best appreciated when specimens are grown in a trough, raised bed, or dry-stone wall.

Larger plants with a dense cover of small leaves are useful as background. Conifers such as the common yew (*Taxus baccata*) with small scale- or needle-like leaves that respond well to regular trimming make valuable hedging and topiary plants. Some small-leaved plants like *Buxus microphylla* "Green Pillow" develop into tight shapes without trimming. These small balls and domes, and also mats of miniature leaf rosettes like those of the raoulias, hold for me a real fascination. But I also like small leaves with more air about them, particularly when they are part of a complex overall pattern, as they are in *Cotoneaster horizontalis*.

leaf texture

Plants are constantly engaged in a difficult balancing act. To convert light energy into food, they must transpire, but during that process they inevitably lose water. In order to minimize this loss, plants growing in difficult conditions, with high temperatures and low rainfall, and where wind can be desiccating, frequently have specially adapted leaves. Some are succulent, some have leathery leaves, and others have leaves covered to some extent with protective hairs that deflect light and provide insulation. At another extreme, plants living in areas of high rainfall may have glossy leaves, commonly with a drip tip, which encourage excess water from torrential showers to flow away promptly. These adaptations, often much more complex than these generalized observations might suggest, all contribute to a surprising range of foliage textures, in some cases wonderfully lustrous, in others sensuously tactile, suggesting to the hand as well as to the eye luxurious fabrics.

Given that these are adapations to particular sets of conditions, it is perhaps surprising that so many different textures can be brought together in the same garden. It says something of the tolerant character of many plants that glittering hollies (*Ilex*), gray-leaved lavenders (*Lavandula*), fleshy sedums, leathery strawberry trees (*Arbutus*), fine-leaved maples (*Acer*), and heavily pleated hostas can all be assembled in a fairly small space. These contrasts are certainly something to strive for, because a garden in which the texture of the foliage is only slightly differentiated is tiresomely bland.

This chapter is essentially concerned with textures that result from the different surface qualities of leaves. But it is worth remembering that there are other ways to enrich the garden's texture, especially by using foliage of different size and shape (see pages 12-43) and finding places, too, for those plants where the underside of the leaf, revealed perhaps by a breeze, has a different texture from the upper surface (see page 87).

Right: Enlargement reveals the heavy quilting and fine hairiness of the tactile leaves of the perennial *Geranium renardii*.

Left: Knobbly flower spikes, still at bud stage, stand out against the polished dark green leaves of *Prunus laurocerasus* "Otto Luyken," a compact form of the evergreen cherry laurel.

glitter and sheen

SELECTION

TREES & SHRUBS *Acer monophyllum* • *Arctostaphylos uva-ursi* • *Aucuba japonica* "Lance Leaf" • *Buxus sempervirens* • *Camellia japonica* • *C.* x *williamsii* • *Choisya ternata* • *Daphne laureola* • *Elaeagnus pungens* "Maculata" • *Eriobotrya japonica* • x *Fatshedera lizei* • *Griselinia littoralis* • *Ilex* x *altaclarensis* "Camelliifolia" • *I. aquifolium* "Handsworth New Silver" • *I. cornuta* • *I. crenata* • *I.* x *meserveae* • *Ligustrum lucidum* • *Liquidambar styraciflua* • *Mahonia aquifolium* • *Myrtus communis* • *Osmanthus heterophyllus* • *Phillyrea latifolia* • *Pieris formosa* var. *forrestii* "Wakehurst" • *Prunus laurocerasus* "Otto Luyken" • *Rhododendron rex*

CONIFERS *Pinus patula*

CLIMBERS *Hedera helix* "Ivalace" • *Trachelospermum jasminoides*

PERENNIALS *Acanthus mollis* Latifolius Group • *Arum italicum* subsp. *italicum* "Marmoratum" • *Asarum europaeum* • *Bergenia* "Sunningdale" • *Caltha palustris* var. *palustris* • *Galax urceolata* • *Heuchera micrantha* var. *diversifolia* "Palace Purple" • *Hosta lancifolia* • *Lysichiton americanus* • *Nymphaea* hybrids • *Pelargonium* ivy-leaved hybrids • *Pontederia cordata* • *Ranunculus ficaria* "Brazen Hussy"

GRASSES *Carex morrowii* "Fisher's Form" • *Fargesia nitida* • *Indocalamus tesselatus* • *Phyllostachys viridiglaucescens* • *Semiarundinaria fastuosa* • *Uncinia rubra*

FERNS, PALMS, & CYCADS *Asplenium scolopendrium* • *Cycas revoluta* • *Polystichum aculeatum*

EDIBLE PLANTS Chard

Flowers undoubtedly provide gardeners with an extraordinary range of colors, but for the most part, their petals are matte. It is shiny leaves that enliven the garden with their innumerable fragments of reflected light.

Glossy evergreens come into their own in the muted winter garden, though large evergreens that cast perpetual shade can be a problem in gardens where space is limited. A neglected large shrub or small tree that can be trained up on a single stem is the Chinese privet (*Ligustrum lucidum*), which in late summer has panicles of white flowers against its lustrous dark green foliage. It is still easy to appreciate why the cherry laurel (*Prunus laurocerasus*) was such a success when it was introduced to northern gardens in the sixteenth century, but there are now many other shade-tolerant shrubs to give variety. Some are small leaved, like the magically scented sweet box (*Sarcococca*). Others, like camellias, combine outstanding foliage and flowers. In several mahonias,

Right: The lax evergreen shrub x *Fatshedera lizei*, the result of a cross between an ivy and a *Fatsia*, has hand-like glossy leaves. There are several variegated forms, including the yellow-splashed "Annamieke."

Below: A perennial for the margins of a pool or a sunny moist border, the arum lily (*Zantedeschia aethiopica*) makes an impressive clump of arrow-shaped and satin-shiny leaves.

glossiness adds a metallic sheen to seasonal changes of color, while in numerous shrubs, such as forms of *Elaeagnus pungens*, the gloss enhances the radiance of a sunny variegation. You can see this also in the many variegated hollies (*Ilex*), but the plain-leaved forms have enough glitter to make the most appealing hedges. Many conifers have either matte or conspicuously waxy foliage, but the Mexican weeping pine (*Pinus patula*) makes a striking exception. In this frost-hardy species, the light green lax needles hang in clusters, looking like wonderfully lustrous but straight-haired scalps. I reserve a special enthusiasm for the bamboos, for the slightest breeze reminds you of their glittering leafy cascades.

Few perennials can have more presence than bear's breeches (*Acanthus mollis*), which makes an imposing clump of glossy, dark green, and lobed leaves. The lighter foliage of the crown imperial, one of the most impressive of spring-flowering bulbs, provides a striking contrast. A shiny whorl of lance-shaped basal leaves is matched by a tuft of leaf-like bracts, crowning the cluster of bells. It is a shame that its foliage is so briefly in its prime and needs to be overtaken by other growth as it withers.

Several waterside plants are splendidly glossy. Those to grow in shallow water include the pickerel weed (*Pontaderia cordata*) and the arum lily (*Zantedeschia aethiopica*). The arum lily will also grow in the sort of boggy conditions that suit the skunk cabbages (*Lysichiton*), plants that have large, shiny, paddle-like leaves, which develop as the yellow or white flower-like spathes go over. However, for waterside luster in the spring, nothing can quite match the kingcup or marsh marigold (*Caltha palustris*), shiny in leaf and in golden flower. The giant marsh marigold (*C. palustris* var. *palustris*), which reaches out more boldly from the margins, is just as glossy in leaf, but has fewer flowers. You can complete the pool with the shiny pads of water lilies (*Nymphaea*), whose gleaming disks are a contrast to the rippling surface of broken water.

The lustrous *Hosta lancifolia* and metallic *Heuchera micrantha* var. *diversifolia* "Palace Purple" are the sorts of plants with tufts and clumps of shiny foliage that become important incidents in the flickering patchwork of dappled light. I want plenty of these in a garden, but I value, too, the gleam of low plants like asarabacca (*Asarum europaeum*), which enhances their value as good ground cover.

leaf texture **glitter and sheen** | 47

SELECTION tough and leathery

TREES & SHRUBS *Arbutus unedo • Arctostaphylos manzanita • Buxus sempervirens • Cordyline australis • Daphne laureola • Eucalyptus pauciflora subsp. niphophila • E. perriniana • Fatsia japonica • Ilex* x *altaclarensis "Camelliifolia" • Magnolia grandiflora • Mahonia japonica • Olea europaea • Rhododendron yakushimanum • Skimmia japonica • Viburnum tinus*

CONIFERS *Araucaria araucana • Pinus mugo*

CLIMBERS *Hedera colchica "Dentata"*

PERENNIALS *Bergenia cordifolia "Purpurea" • B. "Sunningdale" • Helleborus argutifolius • H.* x *sternii "Boughton Beauty" • Phormium cookianum • P. "Sundowner" • P. tenax • Saxifraga* x *urbium*

FERNS, PALMS, & CYCADS *Asplenium scolopendrium • Blechnum chilense • Cycas revoluta • Polystichum munitum • Trachycarpus fortunei*

EDIBLE PLANTS Fig • Rosemary • Bay laurel

You might think that to describe the leaves of a plant as leathery is to condemn it as ornamentally handicapped. While leathery foliage is certainly no guarantee of beauty, there are numerous examples of plants where the character of the leaves goes with other qualities to make an overall impression that is pleasing. Tough, somewhat thickened, and often strongly fibrous leaves certainly help plants survive in difficult conditions, especially where they are battered by strong, sometimes salt-laden winds, and have to extract a living from dry and poor soils.

Above: The standard version of the hart's-tongue fern (*Asplenium scolopendrium*) is an evergreen shuttlecock of tough, strap-shaped fronds. This bird's-eye view of Crispum Group shows the tightly waved frond margins of a distinguished variant.

Right: The elephants' ears (*Bergenia*) owe their common name to the round shape and leathery texture of their weather-resistant leaves. An appealing feature of "Sunningdale" and other cultivars is the rich coloring of the leaves in the fall and winter.

Left: The Corsican hellebore (*Helleborus argutifolius*) is an evergreen perennial with clawed leathery leaves, consisting of three sharply toothed leaflets. Apple-green cup-shaped flowers complement the foliage in spring.

It is among evergreens that you expect to find some degree of leatheriness, for these leaves have to last. It is not, however, that the leaves are kept indefinitely. Gardeners are often dismayed by the amount of litter that needs to be cleared up from under evergreens, which shed leaves piecemeal rather than over a short period, as deciduous plants do. There is certainly an astonishing toughness about the leaves of many conifers. Characterful broad-leaved trees and shrubs of the Mediterranean region include the olive (*Olea europaea*) and the mastic tree or lentisk (*Pistacia lentiscus*). Another is the strawberry tree (*Arbutus unedo*), one of several species in which the shape of the limbs, their peeling and colorful bark, and the glossy leathery leaves are all of a piece. This species, unusual for a member of the heath family, is tolerant of alkaline soils. In this respect the bearberries and manzanitas (*Arctostaphylos*) are more typical ericaceous plants. Where conditions are suitable the Californian *A. manzanita* is an arresting shrub or small tree, but its smooth red-brown limbs attract more attention than the leathery leaves.

The eucalypts tease by changing tack as they mature. The juvenile leaves, often distinctly gray-blue, rounded, and opposite, give way, unless the plants are coppiced, to longer, often sickle-shaped, alternate leaves. Although tough and leathery, rustling drily as it moves in the wind, the mature foliage and the patterned or gray-white bark of eucalypts complete the impression of unconventional elegance that these trees so often convey.

Palms and cycads tend to hold their leaves longer than many other evergreens, so it is not surprising that they are tough and leathery. The sago palm (*Cycas revoluta*) is very slow growing, the long, deeply cut dark green leaves radiating from the top of a short sturdy trunk. In China the tough leaves of the Chusan palm (*Trachycarpus fortunei*) have an economic value as a source of fiber. Even when the long-lived fans die, they hang as a heavy mantle below the living green leaves. This habit is found among many palms, including the impressive desert fan palm (*Washingtonia filifera*), the species that has given Palm Springs in California its name. The Chusan palm, unlike most of its kind, is remarkably tolerant of cold conditions and is the most versatile large palm for temperate gardens.

Most herbaceous perennials lose their leaves annually. Leathery foliage is found mainly in those that retain it for more than one growing season. The bergenias are a classic case, and these tough plants have a special value in winter, when the foliage of many takes on liverish tones and the odd leaf colors especially strongly. Hellebores, too, hold onto their leaves through the winter, but in the case of the lenten roses (*Helleborus orientalis*), the old untidy leaves are best cut away as the flowers start to open. The New Zealand flaxes (*Phormium*) have very tough foliage, and it is not surprising that in the past great use was made of the fibers. In the garden old leaves need to be cut out to keep clumps looking spruce. It comes perhaps as a surprise that so many ferns should have leathery fronds. In fact, the thickness and leatheriness of the foliage depends very much on the growing conditions. The hart's-tongue fern (*Asplenium scolopendrium*) is particularly versatile, and its leathery straps make a strong contrast with finely cut and delicate fronds.

Left: The rosettes of the ice plant (*Sedum spectabile*) have the quality of fleshy flowers long before late summer, when this perennial's true flowers, starry and gathered in flat heads, become a magnet for butterflies.

waxy and succulent

SELECTION

TREES & SHRUBS *Aeonium* "Zwartkop"

PERENNIALS *Agave americana* • *A. parryi* • *A.victoriae-reginae* • *Crambe maritima* • *Euphorbia myrsinites* • *Hosta* "Halcyon" • *H. sieboldiana* var. *elegans* • *Nelumbo nucifera* • *Pelargonium*, ivy-leaved hybrids • *Sedum acre* "Aureum" • *S. sieboldii* "Mediovariegatum" • *S. spathulifolium* • *S. spectabile* • *S. telephium* subsp. *maximum* "Atropurpureum" • *S.* "Vera Jameson" • *Sempervivum arachnoideum* • *S. ciliosum* • *S. tectorum*

EDIBLE PLANTS Cabbage • Seakale

Although leaves are enormously varied in their configuration, most take the form of relatively thin, flat blades. There are, however, some highly adapted plants native to arid regions that have fleshy leaves capable of storing water. These succulents have the trick of transpiring at a low rate so they lose relatively little water vapor when they are taking in their reduced requirement of carbon dioxide.

The most sensational stem succulents are the cacti, the large species including the barrel-shaped *Ferocactus cylindraceus* of the Southwest and neighboring Mexico, and the tree-like saguaro (*Carnegiea gigantea*) of the Arizona desert. But there are numerous other succulents of fascinating appearance, including euphorbias from Africa that mimic the forms of the cacti found in the American continent. In the past the oasis has served as the model for gardens in really desert conditions, but the current trend is toward xeriscaping, that is, using plants such as cacti that are totally at home in areas of minimal rainfall.

In temperate regions the large succulents usually play only a minor role in gardens during the summer months, in winter requiring protection from cold. Nonetheless, they have great value as powerfully sculptural container plants. The most familiar is a Mexican species, *Agave americana*, usually seen in one of its variegated forms. It makes a monumental rosette of weighty leaves, their toothed margins leaving their print on the neighboring leaves. Smaller and also rather tender succulents suitable for container gardens include other agaves, aeoniums such as the purple-black *Aeonium* "Zwartkop," and exquisitely rosetted species such as *A. canariense*. In mild climates, South African aloes can be planted outdoors to make a mass of jagged rosettes, topped in spring by spikes of orange-red flowers. The two species most commonly grown are *Aloe arborescens* and *A. ferox*.

The more familiar fleshy-leaved plants of temperate gardens do not have the sculptural weight of large-scale succulents, but they are valuable in sunny dry gardens. Even ivy-leaved pelargoniums (derived from *Pelargonium peltatum*) have fleshy leaves, a fact that helps them survive the rigors of life on a balcony. The rosettes of the houseleeks (*Sempervivum*) survive with practically no soil – on a roof they are supposed to ward off lightning – and in pans, the mother plant, often with red-tinted leaves, will spawn a tribe that eventually clusters tightly over the whole surface.

In some cases, the bloom on the waxy surface of succulent leaves is conspicuous. It is, for example, striking in forms of *Sedum spathulifolium* such as "Cape Blanco" and "Purpureum," plants that make tight mats of small fleshy rosettes. In other cases, though, waxiness seems to be a way of helping plants shed water. The sacred lotus of India (*Nelumbo nucifera*), an aquatic of sublime beauty in flower and leaf, makes glorious stands in shallow water. (It can be grown outdoors in temperate gardens where the weather is mild enough, but needs to be overwintered in frost-free conditions.) The large circular leaves, depressed at the center and with gently undulating margins, often hold droplets of water that slide around like quicksilver with every slight movement of the tall stems. Minute waxy outgrowths over the surface of the leaves provide them with a kind of waterproofing. Waxiness with a similar function is found in some of the most impressive hostas, their glaucous surfaces making them distinctive plants to mix with greens and yellow-tinted foliage in partial shade.

Even some annuals have succulent leaves, notably the Livingstone daisy (*Dorotheanthus bellidiformis*) from South Africa and portulacas, mainly hybrids of the South American *Portulaca grandiflora*. In neither case is the foliage remarkably beautiful, although crystal-like structures in the leaves of Livingstone daisies cause them to sparkle. However, their fleshiness is an indication that these bright and cheerful plants do well in full sun on poor and sandy soils.

Below: The aeoniums are a diverse group of rosetted succulents, some shrubby, with rather gaunt stems terminating in flower-like leaf clusters. *A.* "Zwartkop" is in this mold but what marks it out is the polished dark chocolate of its fleshy rosettes and the minute hairs fringing the leaves. It needs protection from frost, but is a good container plant for summer displays.

hairy and bristly

SELECTION

Above: The fleshy rosettes of the cobweb houseleek (*Sempervivum arachnoideum*) seem held together by silky filaments spun by a fastidious spider. In "Rubrum" the red-tipped leaves are less encased, but the webbing still criss-crosses the central leaves.

Top right: Blue poppies, *Meconopsis betonicifolia*, are grown for their flowers, and yet the basal rosettes of hairy leaves, usually toothed and lobed, are highly ornamental.

Left: Frost-tender begonias include many dramatic foliage plants that can be moved outdoors to bright but lightly shaded positions during summer. The conspicuously hairy *Begonia scharffii* is an unusual alternative to the better-known, wonderfully varied Rex hybrids.

Although the hairiness of foliage often goes unnoticed, it can be a very conspicuous characteristic of plants. Whether the leaves are shaggy, bristly, silky, or felted, the hairs are playing a practical role, shading the leaf surface, protecting it from exposure to excessive radiation, and reducing water loss. They may also help make leaves less palatable to browsing animals and to insects. In some cases, the bristles are stiffened to sharp spines, but even apparently innocuous hairs, such as those on the leaves of buglosses (*Echium*), can cause irritation to the tender skin of the mouth and will therefore discourage heavy grazing. Nettles (*Urtica*) and other stinging plants go one step farther, injecting an irritant into the skin.

Many plants with bristly leaves are thought to be rather coarse and do not get a good press. The borage family comes under suspicion, despite the genus including so many blue flowers of great beauty and intensity. The common comfrey (*Symphytum officinale*) is the model for these coarse plants, and many gardeners would say that other comfreys, including *S. caucasicum*, are fit only as weedproof cover in the wildest parts of a large garden, where uncontrolled spread will not be troublesome. The comfreys with the most ornamental foliage, *S.* "Goldsmith" and *S.* x *uplandicum* "Variegatum," are both variegated. The deep blue of their flowers, not the hairiness of their leaves, make *Anchusa azurea* and *Cynoglossum nervosum* such appealing plants, but another member of the borage family, *Brunnera macrophylla*, owes more to its large and softly hairy leaves for a place in the garden.

There are many other perennials that are to some degree hairy, although one might not pick out this characteristic as ornamentally important. It does, however, bring a softness to the foliage of avens (*Geum*), making a lovely foil to the bright flowers. And it gives a special character to several large-leaved plants, including *Bergenia cordifolia*, unusual in its genus in having hairy leaves, and a really handsome moisture-lover with large light green leaves, *Astilboides tabularis*. In trees and shrubs one is often slow to take in the degree to which leaves are hairy, the more important question being whether they are glossy or matte. However, it is still interesting to contrast leaves that are soft, such as those of the Chinese witch hazel (*Hamamelis mollis*), and others that are distinctly bristly, such as those of *Hydangea aspera* subsp. *sargentiana*.

Although I know to expect it, animal shagginess and furriness can still take me by surprise when I come across it in plants. It seems comic in the old man cactus (*Cephalocereus senilis*), with the column swathed in white hairs. This is a plant that most of us would need to grow under glass. On quite a different scale, there is a little houseleek, *Sempervivum ciliosum* var. *borisii*, also almost white with its hairy covering. In a garden setting you are most likely to come across animal hairiness in ferns. On a tamed scale you see it on the unfolding fronds of the golden male fern (*Dryopteris affinis*). More disconcerting are the hairy base and rib of the fronds of *Dicksonia antarctica*, an Australian tree fern. An extreme of fuzziness is found in the kiwi fruit (*Actinidia deliciosa*). Although this climber may not fruit reliably in cool temperate regions (in any case, a female plant needs a male nearby), it can grow luxuriantly, and the young growths and margins of the leaves are bristly, as might be expected from a climber that presents its fruit so liberally covered with short brown hairs.

silk, satin, and velvet

Above: Few plants combine robustness and refinement more successfully than lady's mantle (*Alchemilla mollis*). The rounded leaves of this perennial, scalloped into a fan, are soft green, and their velvety hairiness traps water as glistening beads. A froth of lime-green flowers lasts for weeks.

Opposite: Fingered leaves of silky hairiness are typical of the lupines, including the annual Texas bluebonnet (*L. texensis*), subshrubby California species such as *L. albifrons*, and the coarser, yellow-flowered shrubby *Lupinus arboreus*.

Below: The short pile of dense silvery hairs gives the lobed leaves of *Pelargonium tomentosum* a luxurious velvety texture. When lightly bruised, the foliage releases a powerful peppermint scent.

The tactile qualities of several plants with hairy leaves, sometimes evident to the eye but in other cases appreciated only when the foliage is handled, strongly suggest luxurious fabrics.

Silky foliage is a delightful feature of some alpine plants. One of the silkiest of the pasque flowers is *Pulsatilla halleri*, the newly emerging growths shimmering with their fine-spun hairs. But even the common pasque flower (*P. vulgaris*) is a remarkable sight, best when backlit to show off the fine hairiness of the young leaves and stems, the flowers, and later the seedheads. The plantains include some weed plants, but *Plantago nivalis*, from mountainous areas of southern Spain, makes an astonishing silky rosette of narrow leaves. Silky threads – they appear to have been woven by a neurotic spider – make a dense web over the small rosettes of *Sempervivum arachnoideum*.

It is sometimes difficult to believe that tiresome weeds can have beautiful and well-behaved relatives. Related to bindweed, *Convolvulus cneorum* is a small silver-leaved shrub of irresistible silkiness and the happiest combination of foliage and flowers. The beautifully shaped white trumpets, tinted pink on the outside and yellow in the throat, are produced over a long period when plants are grown in sun and well-drained soil. The hairy canary clover (*Lotus hirsutus*) requires similar conditions and is a delightfully silky small bush carrying numerous white pea flowers that are tinged pink. It is short-lived, but self-seeds freely. A more substantial shrub, the pineapple broom (*Cytisus battandieri*), has silky leaves divided into three leaflets. In temperate gardens this Moroccan species is often grown against a wall, but it does well in a sheltered open position where the combination of foliage and flowers is much more pleasing.

The lupines in general, including the popular hybrids grown for their flowers, have very lovely foliage. Even the tree lupine (*Lupinus arboreus*), which is naturalized as a coastal plant in many parts of the world, has beautiful fingered and silky leaves that look ravishing covered with droplets of water. Another shrubby California species, *L. albifrons*, is even more refined in its silver silkiness, but it needs a mild climate and excellent drainage to do well.

Velvety and satiny textures are found on leaves where numerous short hairs make a soft pile. After feeling the very bristly leaves of *Hydrangea aspera* subsp. *sargentiana*, the velvety dark green of the closely related *H. a.* Villosa Group comes as a real surprise. The best known of the velvety perennials is lady's mantle (*Alchemilla mollis*), a plant that is hard to fault even when it seems to be used to excess. The horehounds (*Marrubium*) are less adaptable, but several species are remarkable for the fineness of their texture. One of the loveliest of these small plants is *M. cylleneum* "Velvetissimum."

Few plants so call out to be touched as the scented-leaved pelargoniums. Their aromatic range never ceases to surprise, and their textures are a source of tactile delight. One of the most remarkable of these is the peppermint-scented pelargonium (*Pelargonium tomentosum*). This species, unlike most of the hybrids in cultivation preferring part shade, can easily be trained up to a height of 3ft/90cm and makes a superb container plant for a small courtyard. The sprays of small white flowers are of secondary importance to the leaves. Although I find their minty scent almost too much, I am repeatedly drawn back by their velvety pile. Less dramatic are the bushy little plants of *P.* Fragrans Group whose small, prettily scalloped leaves are so fine between the fingers that one hesitates to bruise them for their pine scent.

Left: Common names such as lambs' ears refer to the silver woolliness of the perennial *Stachys byzantina*. It forms a mat but is easily controlled, fitting in well among other plants at the front of a sunny bed.

SELECTION woolly and felted

TREES & SHRUBS *Ballota acetabulosa • B. pseudodictamnus • Brachyglottis "Sunshine" • Buddleja crispa • B. fallowiana • B. "Lochinch" • Calluna vulgaris "Silver Knight" • Helichrysum petiolare • H. petiolare "Limelight" • H. splendidum • Lavandula lanata • Leucophyta brownii • Rhododendron yakushimanum • Salix lanata • Senecio cineraria "White Diamond"*

CLIMBERS *Vitis vinifera "Incana"*

PERENNIALS *Achillea tomentosa • Artemisia stelleriana "Boughton Silver" • Lobelia tupa • Lychnis coronaria • Origanum dictamnus • Stachys byzantina "Silver Carpet"*

ANNUALS & BIENNIALS *Salvia argentea • Verbascum olympicum*

EDIBLE PLANTS Sage • Thyme (*Thymus serpyllum* "Minimus")

The thick hairiness of some leaves strongly resembles wool and, more frequently, when short and densely packed, the matted fibers of felt. The woolly extreme is shown by the rosette-forming *Salvia argentea*, which makes an impressive base of white softly hairy leaves, from which erupts a candelabra bearing hooded white flowers. By comparison, the huge rosette formed by one of the short-lived mulleins, *Verbascum olympicum*, also nearly white, is densely felted, but forms the base for a massive stem, covered in white wool, that carries numerous yellow flowers.

Woolly and felted leaves are a typical adaptation of plants living in hot dry regions, and many of the ornamentals showing these characteristics that are grown in temperate gardens are plants from the Mediterranean region. Woolliness is also an insulating feature of giant lobelias found in the mountains of Equatorial Africa and plants such as the Andean espeletias – these plants live under intense daytime radiation, but plunging temperatures bring winter every night. Most of the woolly and felted plants in general cultivation need full sun and well-drained conditions, many looking their near-white best on poor soils. The woolly willow (*Salix lanata*) makes an interesting exception, for this small shrub, with a generous covering of gray wool on its dark green leaves, is a plant from northern Europe that enjoys reasonably moist conditions. Among perennials its match is *Anaphalis triplinervis*, which likes moisture and tolerates partial shade. Another curious shrub is *Rhododendron yakushimanum*. This compact Japanese species, like many other rhododendrons, has a thick felt or indumentum on the underside of the leaves, but when they are young, the cinnamon-brown fuzz covers the upper surface as well.

One of the choicest of Mediterranean felted plants, the Cretan dittany (*Origanum dictamnus*) shows the demanding side of these plants. In Crete, where it is now considered an endangered species, this subshrub clings to the calcareous cliffs of mountains and gorges. In cultivation it insists on sharp drainage, and its aromatic felted leaves so resent winter wet that it is difficult to grow without the protection of an alpine house.

Fortunately many other plants are much easier to please. In sunny gardens with free-draining soil, dusty miller (*Lychnis coronaria*) seeds itself freely and is generally best treated as a biennial. The shocking magenta-purple of the flowers is perfectly calmed by silver-gray foliage, but if you want subtlety, there is a white-flowered form and even white with a pink eye (*L. c.* Oculata Group). Flowers make these plants, as they do *Helichrysum* "Schweffellicht," a perennial in which the felted leaves are topped by small, tightly clustered sulfur-yellow daisies. In a little yarrow, *Achillea tomentosa*, I also like the contrast between yellow flowers and ferny, yet woolly, leaves.

There are, however, many other plants with felted leaves that are grown for their foliage alone. This is so with the popular edging plant *Stachys byzantina*, which goes by such fanciful common names as lambs' ears, lambs' tails, and lambs' tongue. A non-flowering form, *S. b.* "Silver Carpet," gets on with the business of covering the ground without wasting energy producing flowers. Another good edging plant, and you hardly notice its flowers, is *Artemisia stelleriana* "Boughton Silver." Well placed, it will push out over a path almost prostrate sprays of artfully cut, nearly white felt. Although they are so commonly used in bedding schemes, the various forms of the shrubby *Senecio cinereria* are worth looking at with fresh eyes. Plants are often discarded at the end of the season, but "White Diamond" may prove hardy enough to treat as a perennial, coming away with new oak-like leaves after drastic clearing in spring. For a few weeks they may be rather green, but in hot dry weather their felted white is startling. The lax and shrubby *Helichrysum petiolare*, much used in container gardening, is another felted foliage plant that is usually replaced annually. It is a predictable choice, but it has a wonderful way of wreathing and writhing (often needing judicious pinching back), and its several forms allow variations on the gray theme.

Above: The crinkled basal leaves of *Salvia argentea*, a biennial or short-lived perennial, are thickly covered with white down, which is gradually shed as the branched flowering stems develop.

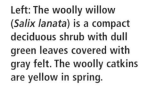

Left: The woolly willow (*Salix lanata*) is a compact deciduous shrub with dull green leaves covered with gray felt. The woolly catkins are yellow in spring.

veined, quilted, and pleated

Turn over any leaf and you realize that it is not simply a bland cutout from a swatch of vegetable material. There is, of course, green soft tissue, perhaps with the color bleached by variegation or overlaid with other pigments. But every leaf also has a framework of veins, usually more conspicuous on the underside than on the upper surface. They give the leaf strength and a certain degree of rigidity, spreading out the soft tissue so it catches the light. In effect, the veins are a structural extension of the plant's stems and, like them, act as conduits for food and water.

Far from being random, a leaf's pattern of veins is a bit like a fingerprint and helps to give plants with the same genetic makeup their characteristic appearance. Two broad patterns emerge. Plants such as grasses, lilies, orchids, and palms that begin life with a single seedling leaf (monocots) have parallel veins running the length of their leaves. Other plants, that is those that start off with two seedling leaves (dicots) – and this includes most ornamental trees, shrubs, and perennials – have mature leaves with net-like veins.

The way leaves are veined is a less important ornamental feature of garden plants than qualities such as foliage color. And yet I am surprised at the way the structure of leaves brings me up short when I am coasting through a garden thinking that I know what is going to please me. It is often backlighting that does the trick. In the spring, for example, light shining through the fresh leaves of hornbeam (*Carpinus betulus*) catches their ribbing; in the fall, it picks out the fan sticks of coloring maples such as *Acer saccharum*. Backlighting effects are more likely to

Top left: The Japanese painted fern (*Athyrium niponicum* var. *pictum*) gets its name from the subtle contrast of the maroon ribs against the silver frond segments.

Far left: *Veratrum nigrum* is a perennial with deeply veined and pleated leaves forming a heavily textured base for a funereal candelabra of starry maroon flowers.

Right: In tropical bedding, the large paddle-like blades of cannas are as important ornamentally as the gaudy flowers. The leaves of *Canna "Striata"* have sinuous cream veins.

Left: In the wild, the distribution of the dwarf fan palm (*Chamaerops humilis*) extends from North Africa into south-western Europe. Although this species will tolerate short spells of light frost, its pleated fans are seen at their best when the plant is grown in a warm, sheltered garden.

Right: Hostas are among the most commonly used perennials for ground cover in full shade. But most flourish in dappled shade, and many do well in full sun, where the play of light shows up the prominent veining of the leaves.

he accidental than successfully contrived by the gardener, especially in the case of plants near the ground. What gardeners can create are plantings where the shadowed texture of strongly veined leaves makes a contrast to blander leaf surfaces or to massed flowers. Hostas with deep-set veins are ideal material, and a delicate companion for these is the deciduous fern *Adiantum pedatum*, with the framework of fresh green fronds apparently consisting of black wire. Equally good for their dramatic shadows are plants with pleated foliage. The handsomely funereal plume of *Veratrum nigrum*, a perennial, rises above an impressive mound of fastidiously folded leaves.

For really bold effects use foliage in which the color of the veining makes a contrast with the base color of the leaf. In many cases, the contrasts develop or intensify as the leaves change color in autumn. Even before coloring vividly, the leaf veins of *Parthenocissus henryana* make this a distinguished climber – they stand out silvery gray against dark green. *Arum italicum* subsp. *italicum* "Marmoratum" is a perennial that makes a point in the winter garden, its glossy arrow-shaped leaves dark green and heavily mottled with ivory along the veins. Blessed Mary's thistle (*Silybum marianum*), an annual or biennial, elaborates a similar theme, but the veining on the jagged leaves is finer. A pretty clover, *Trifolium pratense* "Susan Smith," is even subtler in effect, the three leaflets netted with gold.

In the vegetable garden there are several strongly veined plants. The Savoy cabbages, such as "Tarvoy," take the prize for a combination of heavy veining and wrinkling, which is dramatically shadowed by low lighting. The most colorful leaf vegetables are the Swiss chards, and you can cheat by putting them among the ornamentals.

Right: A detail of veins cutting their way through a frosted leaf of the giant moisture-loving perennial *Gunnera manicata* suggests an aerial view of a complex drainage system.

waved, twisted, and curled

Numerous plants have leaves with twisted or wavy margins. In many cases we hardly take note of these characteristics, although their general effect adds textured contrasts of light and shade to the garden. The common beech (*Fagus sylvatica*) has leaves with an undramatic but distinctively wavy margin, and the needles of the Scots pine (*Pinus sylvestris*) are unmistakably twisted.

More pronounced waviness is found in the foliage of plants that are otherwise very different in character. *Disporum smithii*, a lovely woodland perennial from western North America, has fresh green leaves with a prettily undulating margin. In the spring they almost hide small ivory bells, followed later by orange berries. Evergreen shrubs with wavy leaves include *Mahonia* x *wagneri* "Undulata," which eventually makes a large bush as wide as it is high. The undulations of the leaves enhance the effect of their sheen, which in winter is burnished.

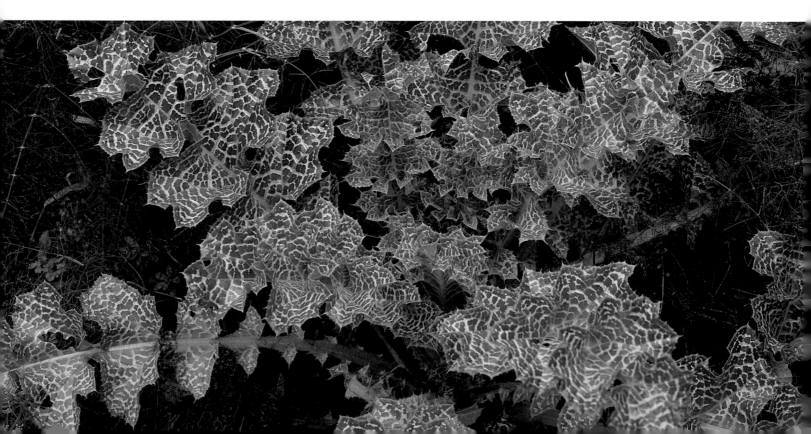

Opposite: *Pittosporum tenuifolium* is an evergreen shrub or small tree whose light green leaves with wavy margins contrast strongly with the near-black stems; the maroon flowers are sweetly scented.

Right: The yellow horned poppy (*Glaucium flavum*), sometimes a short-lived perennial but usually a biennial, makes a blue-green rosette of lightly hairy leaves with twisted and curled divisions. The papery flowers come and go through summer.

Left: The Blessed Mary's thistle (*Silybum marianum*) is a biennial that flowers in its second year. Its real splendor is a rosette of heavily veined leaves, which have stiffly waved and spiny lobes.

A favorite with flower arrangers is the New Zealand kohuhu (*Pittosporum tenuifolium*). The leaves are glossy light green, and the undulating margins make their effect very lively, although they do not move about loosely in a breeze. What makes the foliage a winner is the way the leaves are presented on black twigs. The forms with variegated and colored leaves are those most often grown as individual specimens, but where the climate is mild enough the plain-leaved form makes a bright and effective hedging plant. Many of the hollies are excellent hedging plants, and the twisting of their shiny leaves helps give their massed effect a special glitter.

Plants with tight crisping of the leaf margins or extreme twisting of the leaf tend to come across as mere curiosities. It is difficult to view the corkscrew rush (*Juncus effusus* "Spiralis") as anything but a hopeless case of indecision. There are, however, some that I like, and planted sparingly, they add usefully to the pattern of textures in the garden. *Brachyglottis monroi* is an evergreen shrub that makes a good show of yellow daisies, but I prefer it for the wrinkly edge of its leaves, which show the white felt of the underside. *Hedera helix* "Parsley Crested" is an interesting alternative to some of the blander ivies, and *Pelargonium* "Crispum Variegatum" is a pretty variegated kind to add to container plantings. Gathered margins along its strap leaves make a form of the hart's-tongue fern, *Asplenium scolopendrium* Crispum Group, one of the loveliest plants with crimped edges on the foliage.

Waved and crisped leaves go a long way to make the vegetable garden ornamental. The waved leaves of cabbages are often attractive enough, but the undulations and sea-blue waxiness of seakale foliage puts it in another class. There is renewed interest in growing this vegetable, the stems of which are blanched to make them tender. But I would look out for it as *Crambe maritima* and hang onto it as an impressive ornamental for well-drained soil – in the wild, it is a plant of pebbled seashores. The kales are tough plants, and their tightly curled leaves look exceptionally beautiful when dusted with snow. The deep purple of "Redbor" makes a good contrast with green kale. Lettuces are some of the prettiest foliage plants of the vegetable garden in summer. Texture, rather than flavor, has always been the point of the classic cabbage-head variety "Webb's Wonderful." To the eye, the form and texture of the heart surrounded by a rosette of crinkled and waved leaves is very appealing, but harvesting creates an awkward gap. There is plenty of wavy texture as well as color choice in the loose-leaf kinds of lettuce, and they have the advantage that after leaves are gathered, the plants make new growth. The indispensable garnish, curled parsley, can also be picked to come again.

leaf color

Whatever our background or culture, most of us respond to a green landscape in much the same way. Our eyes rest easy on meadow, prairie, forest, and glade, while, by contrast, we are daunted, even repelled, by volcanic lunar landscapes or vast expanses of rock and ice. Perhaps there is a subliminal recognition that, but for the green pigment in plants, life as we know it would not exist. This pigment, chlorophyll, serves as the essential agent in the miraculous chemistry of photosynthesis, in which the energy of sunlight is transformed into the energy of food – food for plants and for all living things.

The green "room" or a series of rooms is one ideal of the garden, reaching its perfection in the Renaissance gardens of Italy. An alternative to its severe calm is a garden filled with the color of flowers. But foliage, too, offers a range of colors – although it is vital, chlorophyll is not the only pigment found in leaves. In temperate regions of the world, the range of pigments is most obvious in spring and fall. Before the production of chlorophyll in deciduous plants has reached full strength, young growths show colors that range from pale yellow and light bronze to vivid pink and red. When the production of chlorophyll ceases, there is a chance for brilliant red and orange, soft yellow and russet to show through, as they do in the spectacular fall colors of New England. More enduring pigments may play a masking role, protecting plants from excessive exposure to sunlight, or in some cases absorbing light from parts of the spectrum untapped by chlorophyll. Other color effects are produced in variegated leaves, where there is a lack of pigments, and by protective surfaces and hairs that make the foliage look gray.

There is an astonishing palette available in cultivated plants, drawn from every corner of the world and supplemented by countless hybrids and selected forms that have caught the eyes of discerning gardeners. When you are exploiting the color of foliage, the real challenge is to create bold and subtle effects by bringing plants together in an apparently artless way.

Right: The leaves of *Canna* "Durban" are a saturated mixture of purple and red veining.

Left: Bear's breeches (*Acanthus mollis*) has deep green leaves, glossy on the upper surface and attractively lobed, that make a weighty podium for the spikes of purple-hooded white flowers.

SELECTION rich and dark greens

TREES & SHRUBS *Buxus sempervirens • Arbutus unedo • Calluna vulgaris "Darkness" • Camellia japonica • Erica carnea • Ilex x altaclarensis "Camelliifolia" • Ligustrum lucidum • Olearia macrodonta • Pachysandra terminalis • Phillyrea angustifolia • Prunus lusitanica • Quercus coccifera • Q. ilex*

CONIFERS *Cupressus sempervirens • Taxus baccata • Tsuga heterophylla*

CLIMBERS *Hedera colchica • H. helix "Ivalace" • H. hibernica*

PERENNIALS *Acanthus spinosus • Agapanthus praecox subsp. orientalis • Anemone x hybrida • Asarum europaeum • Geranium x magnificum • Helleborus foetidus • Hosta lancifolia • Waldsteinia ternata*

GRASSES *Phyllostachys bambusoides • Shibataea kumasasa*

FERNS, PALMS, & CYCADS *Blechnum penna-marina • Cycas revoluta • Cyrtomium falcatum • Trachycarpus fortunei*

EDIBLE PLANTS Chard • Parsley, moss • Thyme (*Thymus vulgaris*)

Although plants take their green from the nearly ubiquitous presence of chlorophyll, the result is not a verdant monochrome. There is, in fact, no color in the vegetable world that is so richly varied and presented with such infinite gradations of shade and tone as green. Numerous factors account for this. Tints from other pigments cause color biases, in particular to yellow or blue. The thickness of leaves and the amount of light they let through is also significant, as are the effects of light reflection from matte, hairy, or smooth surfaces.

Right: The evergreen leaves of *Olearia macrodonta* vary from sage green to a much richer coloring, but the undersides are always felted and silver to gray. There are white daisy flowerheads in summer.

Below: *Camellia japonica* and its close relatives are flowering evergreens of the first rank. The neatly formed leaves, dark and glossy, are beautiful on their own account and a superb foil for the flowers.

It is a cliché to describe the vast coniferous forests that eventually peter out in the limitless tundra of the far north as gloomy. The cliché has attached itself to almost any dark-leaved evergreen, and yet, whether broad-leaved or coniferous, these evergreens are among the most valuable trees and shrubs for creating a garden of architectural solidity. It is not by chance that the finest use made of their year-round presence is in the sunny gardens of Italy. The spaces of the Renaissance garden are dramatically arranged, but their cabinets of cool green have an underlying calm. These magical gardens use a surprisingly small repertoire of plants, a standard mix consisting of clipped box (*Buxus sempervirens*) and yew (*Taxus baccata*), with free-growing cypress (*Cupressus sempervirens*) and holm oak (*Quercus ilex*).

My own preference even in a danker, cooler climate is for a structure based on dense, dark surfaces and shapes, with hedges of box, yew, hollies (*Ilex*), which have glittering leaves, or less familiar plants such as the richly colored and glossy western hemlock (*Tsuga heterophylla*). Spring growth, and with it changing textures and colors, adds to the appeal of these hedges, the contrast between dark old growth and fresh new green being especially attractive in box and yew.

Dark-leaved wall-trained climbers such as *Hedera colchica* can make equally effective backdrops to other shades of green and a wide range of flower and foliage colors. Red, the complementary color, goes particularly well with the darkest greens, but so, too, do white, cream, and almost all pale shades. Separated blocks of dark foliage make powerful accents, for example, in a row of clipped or free-growing Portugal laurel (*Prunus lusitanica*) or topiary of Irish yew (*Taxus baccata* "Fastigiata").

In informal planting dark green shrubs and trees, or even a bamboo such as *Pleioblastus simonii*, can be used as a screen with clumps, mounds, and mats of dark foliage being planted to set off other leaves and flowers. In the case of numerous valuable perennials, both the foliage and the flowers are well above average in quality. This is the case, for example, with many of the geraniums, including *Geranium* x *magnificum*, with violet-blue flowers over deeply cut dark leaves that often color well in the fall. One of my favorites among perennials is *Acanthus spinosus*, which makes a substantial clump of arching dark green and spiny leaves topped by spires of white-lipped flowers that are purple-hooded.

bright and soft greens

Left: The tenderness and vulnerability of new growth is an unfailingly appealing feature of the spring garden. Here bronze fennel (*Foeniculum vulgare* "Purpureum") adds a deeper tone to the lively greens of an ice plant (*Sedum*) and a hosta.

No plant is absolutely constant in its foliage color. Vast numbers of perennials and deciduous trees and shrubs settle down to a pleasant if unremarkable summer mid-green. But the prelude to this is in many cases a flush of the tenderest green, and the sequel may be russet or more colorful autumn tints. The delicate freshness of spring foliage is seen in two outstanding deciduous trees that, as specimens, are too large for the majority of gardens, but can be used effectively as hedging plants. In spring the leaves of beech (*Fagus sylvatica*) and the more prominently ribbed leaves of hornbeam (*Carpinus betulus*) are a delicious salad green. They become more sober in summer and on clipped hedges hold onto their tawny leaves through fall and winter. The freshness of spring green also makes many perennials appealing foliage plants well before their flowering season. The grassy leaves of day lilies (*Hemerocallis*) push through the ground early, and the bright green arching clumps set off spring flowers that may themselves have indifferent foliage.

Plants that retain something of their spring brightness help give the impression that the garden is up to scratch even in periods of summer heat. To create a canopy of bright green, for example of the oriental plane (*Platanus orientalis*) or the pin oak (*Quercus palustris*), takes time, and in many gardens these trees will ultimately prove too large. The same is also true of several conifers, but it comes perhaps as a surprise to find any at all that have bright green foliage. Two remarkable examples, both deciduous, are the swamp cypress (*Taxodium distichum*) of the southern United States and the dawn redwood (*Metasequoia glyptostroboides*), a relic of a fossil genus that caused a stir when populations of the plant were found in China in the mid-twentieth century. The foliage of the dawn redwood turns tawny and gold in the fall, that of the swamp cypress rust-red and yellow. More realistic in the average garden are the slow-growing and dwarf conifers such as *Juniperus sabina* "Tamariscifolia" that may be used to introduce evergreen brightness.

One way to keep a highly managed garden looking fresh is to lay a quality lawn, in reality a community of fine-leaved grasses. There is a lot of work involved in maintaining fine sod in peak condition, but it makes a beautifully placid emerald surface on which the eye can rest and is luxurious underfoot. Careful mowing in parallel strips creates a pleasing contrasting pattern of light and dark.

For the small or medium-sized garden the most valuable plants with bright or soft green foliage are those that can be easily mixed with other foliage and flowering plants in relatively small-scale situations. Those that are shade-tolerant such as the moisture-loving sensitive fern (*Onoclea sensibilis*) or the Japanese woodlander *Kirengeshoma palmata* help bring life to darker corners of the garden. But just as important are the vivid greens, say of *Santolina rosmarinifolia* subsp. *rosmarinifolia*, that give zest to a dry garden dominated by gray-leaved shrubs.

Below: "Simba," a relatively short-growing cultivar of the bamboo *Fargesia murieliae*, rarely exceeds 6½ft/2m, and its apple-green foliage makes it an attractive plant for the open garden or container.

Above: The moisture-loving ostrich plume fern (*Matteuccia struthiopteris*) unfurls its salad-green fronds in spring to form a shuttlecock of fresh lacy symmetry.

lemon to gold

TREES & SHRUBS *Acer cappadocicum • A. palmatum "Sango-kaku" • A. shirasawanum "Aureum" • Catalpa bignonioides "Aurea" • Corylus avellana "Aurea" • Gleditsia triacanthos "Sunburst" • Hebe ochracea "James Stirling" • Philadelphus coronarius "Aureus" • Robinia pseudoacacia "Frisia" • Sambucus racemosa "Sutherland Gold"*

CONIFERS *Chamaecyparis obtusa "Crippsii" • Ginkgo biloba • Pseudolarix amabilis • Taxus baccata "Standishii"*

CLIMBERS *Hedera helix "Buttercup" • Humulus lupulus "Aureus" • Jasminum officinale "Fiona Sunrise"*

PERENNIALS *Filipendula ulmaria "Aurea" • Geranium "Ann Folkard" • Hosta "Sum and Substance" • Lysimachia nummularia "Aurea" • Symphytum "Belsay" • Tanacetum parthenium "Aureum" • Valeriana phu "Aurea"*

GRASSES *Carex elata "Aurea" • Milium effusum "Aureum"*

EDIBLE PLANTS Balm, lemon (*Melissa officinalis* "All Gold") • Thyme (*Thymus* x *citriodorus* "Bertram Anderson")

The sharp acidity of yellow-green young foliage tones up the garden in spring, while clear yellow and deeper tints of old-gold and bronze are the mellow notes of fall. Before getting carried away with yellow foliage, remember that leaves often turn yellow as a result of mineral deficiency or disease when plants are ailing. This fact must be behind my own prejudice against several plants with lime-green and yellow foliage, most notably a form of the Mexican orange blossom, *Choisya ternata* "Sundance."

Plants that retain strong yellow foliage well into summer often do so best when grown in full sun, but the catch is that the leaves may scorch. This is the case, for example, with *Acer shirasawanum* "Aureum," a Japanese maple with pleated fan-shaped leaves opening to soft yellow-green. Plants that are less prone to scorching are more versatile. In this respect *Sambucus racemosa* "Sutherland Gold," an elder with deeply cut leaves, is preferable to the more refined but scorch-prone *S. r.* "Plumosa Aurea." Regular hard pruning in early spring combined with generous feeding (see pages 153-154) is a way of getting particularly good foliage effects with the elders and several other deciduous trees and shrubs.

Top: The comfreys are coarse plants, but those with yellow or variegated leaves like *Symphytum* "Belsay" can brighten wild parts of the garden.

Although less vigorous than the plain-leaved hop (*Humulus lupulus*), the golden-leaved cultivar "Aureus" can still be invasive. This twining herbaceous climber does best in full sun, where its cheerful radiance can mask a dull wall or fence.

Above: The lobed leaves of the Cappadocian maple (*Acer cappadocicum*) are dark green and glossy in summer, but in the fall turn rich yellow. This deciduous species is of medium size.

I like to see yellow foliage set off and preferably broken up by a generous expanse of plain greens. Evergreen conifers, which provide some of the most enduring yellows and old-golds, unfortunately present dense blocks of color that are not easy to place in a garden. Those that are most easily integrated are strongly textured, with a good range of tones and shadows, as is the case with a slow-growing form of the Hinoki cypress, *Chamaecyparis obtusa* "Crippsii."

A happy balance between yellows and true greens is most easily achieved on a small scale with herbaceous plants and grasses. When growing among other plants, the clear yellow leaves of *Valeriana phu* "Aurea" and the straps of Bowles' golden grass (*Milium effusum* "Aureum") suggest patches and flecks of spring sunshine.

Among the best foliage yellows of the year are those produced when shortening day length triggers a halt to the process of photosynthesis. Clear autumnal yellows are surprisingly found in a deciduous conifer, the golden larch (*Pseudolarix amabilis*), and in the intriguing and primitive conifer ally, the maidenhair tree (*Ginkgo biloba*). A similar yellow is found more conventionally in various deciduous broad-leaved shrubs and trees, in the case of the Japanese maple *Acer palmatum* "Sango-kaku," contrasting vividly with coral-red stems. The ornamental value of perennial foliage in the fall is often overlooked, but there can be a short and glorious transformation, as when the gray-blue leaves of *Hosta sieboldiana* var. *elegans* pass through amber-tinted yellow shades before their final collapse.

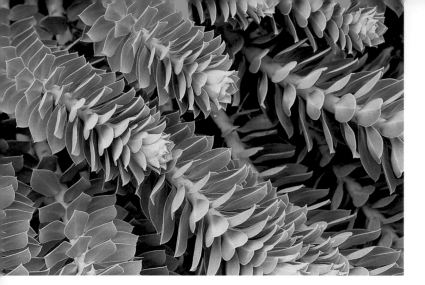

Left: The blue-green waxy leaves of *Euphorbia myrsinites*, an evergreen perennial, are arranged spirally on lax stems that radiate from a central point. The long-lasting bracts of the flowerheads are lime green.

SELECTION gray to blue

TREES & SHRUBS *Calluna vulgaris* "Silver Knight" • *Eucalyptus globulus* • *E. gunnii* • *E. pauciflora* subsp. *niphophila* • *E. perriniana* • *Hebe pimeleoides* "Quicksilver" • *H. pinguifolia* "Pagei" • *Helichrysum italicum* subsp. *serotinum* • *H. petiolare* • *Ilex* x *meserveae* • *Lavandula* x *intermedia* Dutch Group • *L. lanata* • *Melianthus major* • *Olea europaea* • *Rhododendron campanulatum* subsp. *aeruginosum* • *R. cinnabarinum* • *Rosa glauca* • *Ruta graveolens* "Jackman's Blue" • *Santolina pinnata* subsp. *neapolitana* • *Senecio cineraria* "White Diamond" • *Yucca flaccida*

CONIFERS *Abies concolor* "Compacta" • *Cedrus atlantica* Glauca Group • *Cupressus arizonica* var. *glabra* • *Juniperus squamata* "Blue Star" • *Picea pungens* "Koster"

PERENNIALS *Acaena saccaticupula* "Blue Haze" • *Agave parryi* • *Artemisia* "Powis Castle" • *Dicentra* "Langtrees" • *Euphorbia characias* subsp. *wulfenii* • *E. myrsinites* • *Hosta* "Halcyon" • *H. sieboldiana* var. *elegans* • *Thalictrum flavum* subsp. *glaucum*

GRASSES *Arundo donax* • *Festuca glauca* "Elijah Blue" • *F. punctoria* • *F. valesiaca* "Silbersee" • *Helictotrichon sempervirens* • *Leymus arenarius*

Virtually all the plants with gray or blue-tinted leaves could equally be included in a section under texture. It is rarely pigment that gives these plants their color; they take on their particular hue either because the leaf surface is more or less liberally covered with hairs or has a markedly waxy skin. The hairs shade the leaves, and they or the wax reflect at least some of the excessive sunlight and reduce water loss. It comes as no surprise that it is usually plants from hot, dry climates, typically the Mediterranean, whose leaf surface is protected this way. A convenient distinction of a kind can be made between plants that have a generally gray appearance and those that are obviously tactile because of their hairiness, or because they have a conspicuously waxy surface (see pages 48-49).

It is quite likely that 50 years on, perhaps much sooner, gardening writers will be describing disparagingly that horticultural phase in the second half of the twentieth century when gray was the indispensable color. It is true that one does occasionally see gray gardens calling out for a blade of green and not necessarily a riot but at least a little commotion of color. Still, I am happy with the fashion for gray foliage and hope that it is long lasting, for it does much to enhance flower colors, appearing to enrich some while softening others, and generally creating calm and peace in busy gardens overloaded with flowers. The grays are remarkably varied in their tones, the white extremes being strikingly metallic looking (see pages 78-79).

Pinks and carnations (*Dianthus*), bearded irises, lavenders (*Lavandula*), catnip (*Nepeta*), and Alba roses (the pick is *Rosa* "Céleste") are among the familiar and long-established flowers with gray leaves that make a real contribution to the garden. Sun-loving plants to put with them, some qualifying as silver, include yarrows (*Achillea*), artemisias, helichrysums, and santolinas. The most useful exceptions to the general rule that gray-leaved plants do best in full sun and free-draining soil are several species of *Anaphalis*, perennials with clusters of everlasting white flowers, and dwarf

Above: "Koster" is a relatively compact cultivar of the Colorado spruce (*Picea pungens*), with stiff leaves of bright silver-blue. It retains a conical shape.

Left: In frost-prone areas *Agave parryi*, an armed succulent of bland blue-gray, is best grown as a container plant.

willows (*Salix*). Tall perennials include the cardoon (*Cynara cardunculus*), a great fountain of jagged gray, and the plume poppies (*Macleaya*). The choice of large shrubs and trees is limited, but *Rosa glauca*, with purplish-gray foliage, is a shrub of exceptional quality, and the willow-leaved pear (*Pyrus salicifolia* "Pendula") is tailor-made as a focal point for a medium-sized garden.

Blue is especially conspicuous in a number of conifers. Among the largest and most handsome are the glaucous forms of the cedar (*Cedrus*). Most are far too large for the suburban gardens for which many seem destined, but a weeping and compact form of the cedar of Lebanon (*C. libani* "Sargentii") is a suitable slow-growing choice. But, like other blue conifers, it is not an easy plant to integrate. To me, the problem is that these conifers present unyielding blocks of color, and either the blue is so startling that it jumps forward or the blue-green is so cool that it casts a chilly spell.

Tufts and clumps of blue grasses such as *Helictotrichon sempervirens* are much easier to use successfully and most vivid in hot, dry weather. A low aromatic shrub that would go well with these sun-loving grasses is *Ruta graveolens* "Jackman's Blue," a form of rue. My own favorites among the blue-leaved plants are, however, several shade-tolerant and moisture-loving hostas. Even when the plantain lilies fall from the state of grace that they currently enjoy, some will remain as prized perennials, none more deservedly so than *Hosta sieboldiana* var. *elegans*, which makes a superb blue-gray clump of puckered heart-shaped leaves.

Left: The leaves of the sycamore *Acer pseudoplatanus* "Brilliantissimum" open pink and then turn yellow before changing to summer green.

Right: The red burrs of *Acaena microphylla* "Kupferteppich" contrast with a foliage carpet of bronze-purple.

pinks, reds, and purples

Many plants have new leaves that are pink, red, or purple, sometimes even flower-like. Rich colors in young growths are a marked feature in plants of tropical forests, where, for a short period before the leaves begin to produce chlorophyll, the dominance of other pigments may be a defense against leaf-eating insects. In temperate gardens, evergreen shrubs with vivid red new leaves include several *Pieris*, the best being *P.* "Forest Flame," all requiring acid soil, and *Photinia* x *fraseri* "Red Robin," an alternative for a broader range of soil conditions. More delicate are the pink new leaves of several deciduous trees and shrubs such as *Acer palmatum* "Corallinum," which makes an unforgettable shrimp-pink display in a sheltered position. Trees with a very arresting pink phase include the sycamore *Acer pseudoplatanus* "Brilliantissimum." Pinks and reds in the young foliage of herbaceous plants are particularly impressive in the peonies. Molly-the-witch (*Paeonia mlokosewitschii*) has a superb but brief moment when it carries its cool, trembling chalices of lemon gold, but there is a sustained prelude, when the purplish-pink foliage emerges and unfurls.

In some tropical plants, brightly colored foliage may help attract pollinators to relatively insignificant flowers, a trick that also seems to be at work in the curious variegation of a climber for temperate gardens, *Actinidia kolomikta*. During early

Below: The purple leaves of *Euphorbia dulcis* "Chameleon" color richly in the fall.

Right: The self-clinging climber Virginia creeper (*Parthenocissus quinquefolia*) is best on a high wall or climbing into a substantial tree. When covering a large area or appearing to trail from a height, its autumnal brilliance makes a sensational effect.

Below: The intense purple-red of *Berberis thunbergii* f. *atropurpurea* in the fall follows summer's copper-purple. This compact deciduous shrub has yellow flowers in spring.

summer, leaves in full sun may be partly or wholly white, but tinged or strongly stained pink. Pink tints are in fact common in variegated plants, usually developing under the stress of dry conditions or cold. It can be an attractive feature, as in the ivy-leaved *Pelargonium* "L"Elégante." A more durable red or pink is found in the zonal markings of several fancy-leaved pelargoniums such as *P.* "Mr Henry Cox."

The lasting pigments that mask the green of chlorophyll are most commonly purplish-red, chocolate, or maroon. In large trees, such as the various purple-leaved forms of the common beech, for example *Fagus sylvatica* "Riversii," the effect can be an overwhelming monumental presence or simply a dark hole in the landscape; the fern-leaved *F. s.* "Rohanii" is less oppressive. Perhaps the best use of a purple-leaved beech is in a tapestry hedge, mixed with plain beech. Excessive visual weight can be a problem even with smaller trees and shrubs in the maroon and purple range, as well as climbers like the handsomely dark vine *Vitis vinifera* "Purpurea." Deep colors in herbaceous plants are on a more manageable scale. They are most pleasing when there is a variation in tone, as in the spurge *Euphorbia dulcis* "Chameleon." The ultimate near-black density of *Ophiopogon planiscapus* "Nigrescens," just hinting at green near the base of its grass-like leaves, is an easily accommodated curiosity, but all the better for being set against light foliage and flowers.

The assertion of other pigments over disintegrating chlorophyll produces the rich and brilliant colors of autumn. The strong late sunlight in a continental climate boosts the conversion of sugars to anthrocyanins, the pigments that give rich scarlets and purples, the reds being most intense when plants are growing on acid soils. But there is a genetic component to fall color, too, which

Above: *Pieris* "Forest Flame" is an attention-seeking evergreen shrub for lime-free soils. The brilliant red young foliage passes through shades of pink and cream before turning green.

explains the value of selections such as the maple *Acer* "Scanlon" and *Cotinus* "Flame." Even in murky temperate climates, these will often perform well. Several climbers are a match for them, the Virginia creeper (*Parthenocissus quinquefolia*) and the large-leaved *Vitis coignetiae*, for example, flaming with an intense radiance for a few weeks in the fall. More surprising is the show of autumn brilliance in the burning bush (*Bassia scoparia* f. *trichophylla*), an annual that at the end of summer looks like a small and incandescent cypress.

Right: Cultivars of *Photinia* x *fraseri* such as "Red Robin" produce young leaves that are nearly as colorful as those of *Pieris*, but these evergreen shrubs are tolerant of lime.

Left: The rich yellow celandine flowers of *Ranunculus ficaria* "Brazen Hussy" stand out against the polished purple-bronze of heart-shaped leaves.

metallic lusters
SELECTION and tones

TREES & SHRUBS *Elaeagnus* "Quicksilver" • *Leucothoe* "Zeblid" • *Pittosporum tenuifolium* "Tom Thumb" • *Pyrus salicifolia* "Pendula" • *Ricinus communis* "Impala" • *Salix alba* var. *sericea* • *S. exigua*

CONIFERS *Cryptomeria japonica* "Elegans"

CLIMBERS *Parthenocissus henryana* • *Trachelospermum jasminoides*

PERENNIALS *Acaena saccaticupula* "Blue Haze" • *Ajuga reptans* "Atropurpurea" • *Artemisia ludoviciana* "Valerie Finnis" • *Astelia chathamica* • *Astilbe* "Bronce Elegans" • *Bergenia* "Ballawley" • *Cyclamen coum* Pewter Group • *Epimedium* x *perralchicum* "Frohnleiten" • *Heuchera* "Pewter Moon" • *Lamium maculatum* "White Nancy" • *Phormium* "Bronze Baby" • *Pulmonaria saccharata* Argentea Group • *Saxifraga fortunei* "Rubrifolia"

GRASSES *Elymus magellanicus*

FERNS, PALMS & CYCADS *Athyrium niponicum* var. *pictum* • *Dryopteris erythrosora* • *Osmunda regalis*

EDIBLE PLANTS Fennel, bronze • Lettuce, "Oakleaf Red"

It is astonishing on the face of it that comparisons should be made between the living tissue of plants and the inanimate surfaces of metal. However, the description of foliage color as silver, pewter, copper, bronze, and even aluminum is not merely a fantasy of gardening writers.

The term silver is appropriately applied to the brightest shades of gray, some startlingly white or with just a hint of ash. An exceptional large shrub or tree with silver foliage is the deciduous *Elaeagnus* "Quicksilver," a form or hybrid of *E. angustifolia*. It is drought-tolerant and its inconspicuous but silvery flowers have a wonderfully fruity scent. Smaller shrubs and perennials, including artemisias, helichrysums, and santolinas, are among the most useful plants in dry gardens, which weeks of hot sun bleach to silvery perfection. They are least satisfactory in sustained wet weather and look dejected in winter, when they may give up the ghost if the drainage is in any way inadequate. It is always worth taking a few cuttings in late summer.

Requiring moister soil, but also deserving to be described as silver, are several forms of deadnettle (*Lamium*). Some of these are aggressive spreaders, but *L. maculatum* "White Nancy" is one that makes bright and manageable ground cover in shade. Pewter accurately describes a more clouded gray, which is seen in several forms of the winter-flowering *Cyclamen coum*, especially in those known as the Pewter Group.

Above Silvery and pewter patterns are common in forms of *Cyclamen coum* and *C. hederifolium*, both of which have leaves that are red-purple on the underside. The magenta, pink, or white flowers have a poised charm.

Left *Saxifraga fortunei* and its cultivars are remarkable for the coppery luster of their new leaves, with red-purple undersides, and their airy sprays of white flowers in the fall.

Among the most beautifully silvered leaves are those of several Rex begonias. These magnificent foliage plants are usually reserved for the conservatory, but also make lovely container plants for lightly shaded and sheltered positions outdoors during the summer.

The reddish-brown to purple tones of copper and bronze are often found in young foliage, for example, in epimediums. These are plants where the old leaves are best trimmed away in early spring so the small flowers can be seen above the newly emerged foliage, in the case of *E. x perralchicum* "Frohnleiten" and others beautifully tinted. By contrast, it is generally in the fall and winter that several conifers become bronzed, the most beautiful in this respect being *Cryptomeria japonica* "Elegans," a form of the Japanese cedar that never gives up its feathery juvenile foliage.

More pronounced and enduring bronze is often combined with a metallic luster. This is so in the evergreen shrub *Pittosporum tenuifolium* "Tom Thumb" and in several forms of the castor oil plant (*Ricinus communis*). In temperate gardens the compact and very dark *R. c.* "Impala," like other forms of this half-hardy shrub, is used in summer bedding schemes or as a conservatory plant. The enormous popularity of the lustrous purple-bronze perennial *Heuchera micrantha* var. *diversifolia* "Palace Purple" has reduced its impact somewhat, but there are other interesting heucheras, such as *H.* "Huntsman" and *H.* "Pewter Moon," with foliage that combines bronze and pewter tones. A surprising number of lettuces with bronze- or copper-tinted foliage are quite the equal of many purely ornamental plants.

Of all the plants with metallic lusters, one of the most surprising is the Japanese painted fern (*Athyrium niponicum* var. *pictum*). The fronds, laid out almost horizontally, have a maroon stalk and pewter-gray divisions with a purplish bronze flush from the center.

cool variegation

Among the new plants introduced each year, a high proportion are variegated, that is to say the green of the leaves, instead of being uniform, is broken by a color pattern. This variegation is usually white, cream, or yellow, but other colors can be present and are what make the foliage of many tropical plants so eye-catching. The less colorful variegations in temperate garden plants can themselves be very striking. The Japanese angelica tree (*Aralia elata*), with very large leaves composed of numerous leaflets, has two spectacular variegated forms, one in which the leaflets have irregular creamy white margins ("Variegata"), the other in which the margins are more yellow early in the season ("Aureovariegata"). Many other trees and shrubs as well as almost every other kind of plant have variegated forms that can be dazzling, shimmering, and subtly shadowed in ways that make them a valuable complement to plain foliage and flowers.

Variegation is, however, no guarantee of beauty – not surprisingly, given some of its causes. It can be produced by a virus, as in the case of the agitated yellow-green pattern in the leaves of *Abutilon pictum* "Thompsonii," a half-hardy shrub sometimes used in summer bedding. Mineral deficiencies can also cause streaking. Many of the variegations that are interesting to gardeners are due to differences between plant cells, frequently genetic and the result of mutation. A few of these plants, including the variegated money plant (*Lunaria annua* "Variegata") and a nasturtium (*Tropaeolum majus* "Alaska"), may breed true from seed, but most must be propagated vegetatively, usually from cuttings.

As a result of their chlorophyll deficiency, variegated plants are underpowered and grow less vigorously than their plain-leaved counterparts (a variegated form may be the best choice when looking for a plant to fill a small gap). In evolutionary terms this lack of vigor makes variegated plants losers, and to prosper, they often need the help of the gardener. Many variegated plants "revert," that is, they produce hearty plain-leaved shoots that can eclipse the variegated core of the plant unless removed. A strong tendency to revert counts against the garden value of several plants, especially trees and large shrubs such as the variegated box elder (*Acer negundo* "Variegatum").

There are many poor variegated plants with a feeble invalid air or, perhaps worse, an hysterical liveliness. But the best of the variegations in white and cream have a way of sharpening up the

Top: The pineapple mint (*Mentha suaveolens* "Variegata"), a brilliantly variegated perennial for moist shade, will run unless restricted.

Below: The variability in the shape of the creamy white central stripe adds to the twisting animation of *Hosta undulata* var. *univittata*.

Above: Although they have supernumerary digits, the leaves of *Fatsia japonica* immediately suggest open hands. "Variegata" is randomly marked with touches of near white.

garden, introducing a crisp note and brightness in shady corners. In some cases the precision of the variegation is lost when plants are growing in full shade, but white variegations, particularly those in the center of the leaf, are likely to scorch if they are not shaded for at least part of the day. The cool tones go particularly well with flower colors in the blue, purple, pink, and magenta family. Among my own preferences are plants in which the variegation dissolves to create a shimmering effect, as in a form of the common thyme (*Thymus vulgaris* "Silver Posie") and on a larger scale in the silvery tiers of the variegated pagoda dogwood (*Cornus alternifolia* "Argentea").

Unfussy vertical stripes are pleasing in a number of irises and grasses, for example, for dry conditions *Iris pallida* "Argentea Variegata" and for the waterside *I. laevigata* "Variegata." Irregular margins and central splashes, often only distantly echoing the outline of the leaf, are among the most appealing variegations when seen close up, but frequently make a disappointing general effect. Nonetheless, the boldest include plants of real distinction, among them hostas such as the mysteriously writhing *Hosta undulata* var. *univittata*.

Left: The masterworts (*Astrantia*) are mainly grown for their unusual flowers, but all have attractive fingered leaves. Those of *A. major* "Sunningdale Variegated" are elegantly marked with creamy yellow.

SELECTION warm variegation

TREES & SHRUBS *Aralia elata* "Aureovariegata" • *Buddleja davidii* "Harlequin" • *Cornus alba* "Spaethii" • *Daphne odora* "Aureomarginata" • *Elaeagnus* x *ebbingei* "Gilt Edge" • *E.* x *ebbingei* "Limelight" • *E. pungens* "Maculata" • *Euonymus fortunei* "Emerald 'n' Gold" • *Griselinia littoralis* "Dixon's Cream" • *Ilex* x *altaclarensis* "Golden King" • *I. aquifolium* "Golden Milkboy" • *Ligustrum lucidum* "Excelsum Superbum" • *Yucca flaccida* "Golden Sword"

CLIMBERS *Hedera colchica* "Dentata Variegata" • *H. colchica* "Sulfur Heart" • *H. helix* "Oro di Bogliasco" • *Jasminum officinale* "Aureum"

PERENNIALS *Astrantia major* "Sunningdale Variegated" • *Hosta* "Frances Williams" • *H.* "Gold Standard" • *Phormium* "Yellow Wave" • *Sisyrinchium striatum* "Aunt May" • *Symphytum* "Goldsmith"

GRASSES *Carex elata* "Aurea" • *C. oshimensis* "Evergold" • *Hakonechloa macra* "Alboaurea" • *Miscanthus sinensis* "Zebrinus" • *Pleioblastus auricomus*

EDIBLE PLANTS Lemon balm (*Melissa officinalis* "Aurea") • Mint (*Mentha* x *gracilis* "Variegata")

Variegations ranging from creamy yellow to gold are very common, in fact far more so than those of startling white. The yellow can be a splash, a margin, usually irregular but sometimes scrupulously neat (see also Margins and Undersides, pages 86–87), lengthwise stripes, as is usually the case with grasses, or speckling and spotting (see Spotted, Mottled, and Splashed, pages 84–85). The great strength of plants with yellow variegation, like those with foliage in the lime-green to gold range, is that they help to create a pleasing sunny effect. True, it is an effect that is easily overdone. Too many plants radiating bonhomie and you feel that the jaunty sunniness of the garden is bogus.

Evergreens are particularly useful for creating the impression of a ray of light falling across part of the garden or penetrating shaded areas under trees. The year-round radiance of variegated hollies such as *Ilex* x *altaclarensis* "Golden King" owes something to the glitter of their polished foliage. This is a large shrub rather than a tree and lends itself to light shaping, making it a good choice for the smaller garden. Other bright shrubs are *Elaeagnus* x *ebbingei* "Limelight" and *E. pungens* "Maculata," both with sun-splashed leaves but in common with many other yellow-variegated shrubs showing a tendency to revert. The ivies (*Hedera*) are another valuable group of evergreens that include numerous variegated forms. The relatively small-leaved *H. helix* "Oro di Bogliasco" makes a superb sunny patch on a wall but does not hold its gold well when grown as ground cover. Two variegated large-leaved ivies that are dependably sunny whether climbing or trailing are *H. colchica* "Sulfur Heart," the yellow with a pale green halo on green, and *H. c.* "Dentata Variegata," dark green, sometimes mottled gray-green with yellow margins that turn paler as they age. If your intention is to create an impression of sunniness, do not spoil it by placing cool and warm variegations in close proximity.

It is as true of variegated plants as it is of fabrics and wallpapers that what looks an attractive pattern when seen in isolation may prove difficult to integrate in an overall scheme. As a general rule it seems to me better to use variegated plants sparingly in beds and borders, surrounding them generously with plain-leaved plants. By all means put some vim in the garden with the dashing variegations of bold hostas or the splashed zigzag pattern of *Miscanthus sinensis* "Zebrinus." But avoid an overload of patterns – unless, of course, that is precisely what you are setting out to create.

Right: Irregular banding on the narrow leaves of the grass *Miscanthus sinensis* "Zebrinus" gives a garden a sun-flecked liveliness.

Below: The variegation of the neatly notched foliage of *Melissa officinalis* "Aurea," a form of aromatic lemon balm, has the quality of light gilding.

speckled, spotted, and mottled

Do other gardeners find it difficult to hold a consistent line on spotted and speckled foliage? Received opinion is weighted against plants with these random or loosely patterned markings, generally the result of variegation. (In some cases, though, the marks are caused by air pockets beneath the surface tissues of the leaf.) The jittery energy of speckled markings can be disconcerting, and it is difficult to place the foliage of a spotted laurel such as *Aucuba japonica* "Crotonifolia" with flowers and all but the plainest leaves. My solution is to enjoy what I can of speckled foliage at close quarters and not to worry too much about integrating the plants in broader schemes. *Solenostemon* "Paisley Shawl" and *Tropaeolum majus* "Alaska" are good examples of speckled plants that come off best when they are grown in containers where the mixture is made with a flower-arranger's deliberation. I would use the perennial *Heuchera sanguinea* "Snow Storm" in this way, too, since in the garden it comes across as artificial. In a container planting its near-white leaves, variably edged and finely peppered with green, have a wonderfully bright and intriguing effect.

Heavier spotting is probably also best enjoyed as detail. This approach is certainly appropriate for the random spotting of lungworts (*Pulmonaria*) and the curious aluminum dots on *Brunnera macrophylla* "Langtrees." How else can one look at the outrageous spotting on the large kidney-shaped leaves of *Farfugium japonicum* "Aureomaculatum?"

It is easier to feel confidently enthusiastic about most kinds of mottling and marbling, and indeed some mottled plants have a mysterious beauty. Such is the case with *Podophyllum hexandrum*, a woodland perennial that produces a red, egg-shaped fruit (reputedly edible although the other parts of the plant are poisonous) whose lobed leaves are mottled reddish-brown. Trilliums thrive in similar conditions. Their leaves, like the sepals and petals, are gnostically arranged in threes, and in *T. sessile* they are shadowed with gray marbling.

Relatively few bulbs have leaves of ornamental value, so it is pleasing to find some with mottled foliage. In spring the single but widely distributed European and Asian species of the dog's-tooth violet (*Erythronium dens-canis*) carries its beautifully poised flowers over mid-green leaves that are heavily blotched with purplish brown. Several of the North American species and their hybrids also have attractively mottled foliage, the common name of the trout lily (*E. revolutum*) alluding to the markings on its leaves. These woodland plants look especially beautiful naturalized among colonies of the fall-flowering *Cyclamen hederifolium*, the foliage of which is still present in spring and

Top: The arresting white-and-pink splashed variegation of *Actinidia kolomikta* breaks up in chalky marking.

Below: Green speckling on the moonlit leaves makes *Heuchera sanguinea* "Snow Storm" a beautiful detail in cool moist shade.

Above The toad lily (*Trillium sessile*) is a somber study in threes, the maroon tuft-like flowers rising at the junction of a trio of heavily mottled leaves.

marbled with an infinite variety of silvery markings. Several short-growing and early tulips have conspicuously mottled foliage, the purple usually with a mauve tint. These easily grown bulbs are forms or hybrids of the magnificent scarlet Central Asian species *Tulipa greigii*.

The pads of water lilies (*Nymphaea*) may be too distant to make more than a general impression of floating vegetation. However, in a small pool the mottled foliage of some cultivars can be very attractive. "Aurora," the flowers of which make chameleon-like color changes, is small enough to grow in a large pot, and its olive-green leaves are mottled purple.

TREES & SHRUBS *Acer palmatum* "Butterfly" • *Berberis thunbergii* "Golden Ring" • *Hebe* "Red Edge" • *Magnolia grandiflora* "Exmouth" • *Populus alba* • *Rhododendron macabeanum* • *R. sinogrande* • *Tilia* "Petiolaris" • *Sorbus aria*

CONIFERS *Abies koreana* "Silberlocke"

PERENNIALS *Alchemilla conjuncta* • *Bergenia purpurascens* • *Cyclamen hederifolium* • *Ligularia dentata* "Desdemona" • *Rheum* "Ace of Hearts" • *Sedum sieboldii* "Mediovariegatum" • *Trifolium repens* "Purpurascens Quadrifolium"

GRASSES *Phyllostachys viridiglaucescens* • *Sasa veitchii*

ANNUALS & BIENNIALS *Solenostemon*

Right: The large, leathery glossy green leaves of *Magnolia grandiflora* are usually covered with rust-colored fuzz underneath. This evergreen tree bears creamy flowers that open to a large shallow cup.

Left: Coleus (*Solenostemon*) has many brightly colored and richly patterned cultivars; they are frost-tender perennials widely grown as annuals. A narrow, yellow-green irregular outline defines the vibrant hues of *S.* "Royal Scot."

Below: The gray-green leaves of the dwarf evergreen shrub *Hebe* "Red Edge" are suffused red when young and retain a narrow red margin.

It is the upper surface of leaves, catching light and therefore harnessing energy, that usually commands our attention, while the duller underside is left for the botanically inquisitive. But for the observant gardener, the backs of leaves and their margins are pleasing details.

The underside of a leaf can help in the identification of a plant and, examined closely, can give clues to the way it is adapted to a particular environment. In most plants the breathing pores, the stomata, are concentrated on the lower surface, their numbers sometimes exceeding 10 million per leaf. Recessing of the stomata can help reduce excessive water loss in the process of transpiration. You need a magnifying glass to see this, but much more conspicuous are different degrees of hairiness or felting, which also help to prevent the loss of water, and marked differences in pigmentation.

Although they may be dramatic, the color contrasts between the upper and lower surfaces of leaves are sometimes of little ornamental value to gardeners. Several cyclamen have leaves that are prettily marked on the upper surface and purplish red on the underside, but the plants are so low to the ground that it is difficult to make anything of this contrast. The case is different, however, with some taller perennials. Many bergenias, sometimes called elephants' ears because of their large leathery leaves, show a marked contrast between a dark green upper surface and a purplish underside. Even if the upper surface takes on a liverish color in winter, there is a difference in texture and tone. The contrast is clear to see in bergenias with a stiff upright posture and also in others that are more lax and flop in the wind.

In fact, many dramatic revelations of colorful and contrasting undersides depend on wind stirring the foliage. A breeze might just tip the large leaves of *Rheum* "Ace of Hearts" to show that its purplish-red veins and underside are color-coordinated or flip the foliage of *Ligularia dentata* "Desdemona" to reveal an underside of astonishingly rich maroon. Striking effects are produced when wind exposes the white-backed leaves of large trees such as those of the white poplar (*Populus alba*), but these are for landscaping rather than gardening. The large leaves of several rhododendrons are downy, even heavily felted, on the underside, but are usually held stiffly. However, in cold weather they tend to droop and then the creamy or rusty indumentum, as the covering is called, can be conspicuous.

In a number of plants, the color of the underside extends to the margins, and can be seen from above. This is appealingly demonstrated on a small scale by a miniature lady's mantle, *Alchemilla conjuncta*. The silky underside extends to the edge, giving each leaf a silvery rim. The precise definition of a leaf in a contrasting color can be produced in a variety of ways. Most of the leaf might be covered by a dark pigment with the chlorophyll showing only at the margin. A zinging green edge outlines the maroon leaflets of a four-leaved clover, *Trifolium repens* "Purpurascens Quadrifolium." In most cases of variegation, the outline is irregular and often broad, but in some instances, the margin is picked out in a fine line of color. In the shrub *Berberis thunbergii* "Golden Ring" the purplish leaves are outlined in gold.

the plant

A close look at leaf size, shape, color, and texture tells us a lot about the character of plants and their ornamental value. But plants are more than the sum of their leaves and flowers. They all have distinctive forms, their manner of growth determining the way they hold their foliage to the light, expose their flowers to pollinators, and distribute their seeds. The way foliage is presented is part of the genetically determined consistency of the natural world. There may be variations in individual plants, different rates of growth, and outlines that reflect exposure to light and wind, the nature of the soil, moisture levels, and the effects of grazing or human interference. But the success of a species in the wild hangs on the disciplined unfolding and ordering of leaves that form a particular shape and, in some plants, a well-defined sequence of shapes. At one extreme the form might be a ground-hugging mat or a tight hummock. At the other it can be a billowing crown or dense column of foliage over 80ft/25m high.

The underlying structure of trees, shrubs, and many climbers is a woody skeleton of trunks, branches, and twigs. The outline of deciduous trees in winter shows how beautiful this framework itself can be. The non-woody stems of perennials, annuals, and biennials are in their way just as remarkable and in some species, such as the waterside plant *Gunnera manicata*, achieve phenomenal growth in a single season. Whatever their structure, it is the clothed frame, defined by its foliage, that makes plants of markedly different forms so valuable ornamentally. In some cases, they are most effective planted in colonies to form an integrated whole. This is usually so with low-growing heaths and heathers (*Erica* species and *Calluna vulgaris*). Often a collection of clumps, say of perennials such as the Japanese anemones (*Anemone* x *hybrida*), makes far more impact than the same number of plants dotted about. There are, however, countless plants so individual in the way they bear their foliage that they can easily stand alone or form the key element in a mixed group.

Right: Stiff gray-blue tufts of the perennial grass *Festuca glauca* "Elijah Blue" appear to be trapped beneath a crisscrossed pattern of dead flower stalks.

Left: The stone or umbrella pine (*Pinus pinea*) is one of the most picturesque trees of Mediterranean landscapes. Although it is conical when young, in maturity it develops its characteristic spreading flat top.

SELECTION canopies

TREES & SHRUBS *Acer cappadocicum • A. japonicum • A. saccharum • Arbutus* x *andrachnoides • Catalpa bignonioides • Cercis siliquastrum • Cornus "Eddie's White Wonder" • Crataegus persimilis "Prunifolia" • Enkianthus campanulatus • Eriobotrya japonica • Koelreuteria paniculata • Ligustrum lucidum • Magnolia macrophylla • Malus "Royalty" • Meliosma veitchorum • Olea europaea • Parrotia persica • Phillyrea latifolia • Platanus* x *hispanica • P. orientalis • Prunus sargentii • Quercus ilex • Q. robur • Q. rubra • Zelkova serrata*

CONIFERS *Cupressus macrocarpa • Pinus pinea*

PERENNIALS *Darmera peltata • Gunnera manicata • Rheum palmatum • Rodgersia podophylla*

The astonishing variety in the forms of plants is conspicuously represented by the highly distinctive canopies of different trees and shrubs. Their shape is in large measure determined genetically, although climate factors such as wind can in certain conditions cause considerable distortions. What is remarkable is that there should be such variety when all plants are balancing out the same requirements. They all need to display their leaves in such a way that they get exposure to light; they all (or nearly all) need to present their flowers for pollination; and eventually they have to disperse their seed to fulfill their role in the succession of generations. Of course, there are environmental factors, with plants adapted to a remarkable range of different conditions, slotting in with one another even in the same broad habitat.

A complex play of forces is involved in the formation of a canopy that meets all the plant's requirements. In shrubs and trees there is a woody framework of branches and twigs to support the complex mosaic of leaves arranged in such a way that there is little self-shading. A frequently recurring formation on more or less vertical stems is the spiral and the position of the leaves along it can be calculated by a mathematical progression, the Fibonacci series, that predicts the angle between one leaf and the next. But there are various devices – mechanical twisting of the leaves, differences in the length of leaf stalks, and differences in leaf size – that all help to make a pattern of interlocking forms. Some trees and shrubs – the sugar maple (*Acer saccharum*) is an example – produce what is in effect a single layer of leaves. Others, such as the poplars (*Populus*) have one layer stacked above the other. The latter are almost all plants that thrive in open positions, while the former are often remarkably shade tolerant.

It goes without saying that the ornamental quality of a tree or shrub depends heavily on the character of its canopy. Many of those that are rounded and spreading make a strong visual appeal. The golden form of the Indian bean tree (*Catalpa bignonioides* "Aurea") provides a dramatic example, with the framework of branches forming a broad head decked with large, nearly heart-shaped leaves. In many cases, the spreading head is approximately symmetrical, sometimes to a striking degree. For example, the stone pine (*Pinus pinea*) has a profile that is just as evocative of southern Europe as the narrow outlines of the Italian cypress. The flat-topped parasol or umbrella shape is, in fact, well suited to a climate with hot desiccating winds, encouraging a good updraft through the canopy to help lose heat, while within the canopy the needles escape the wind by sheltering behind one another.

There are some trees and shrubs that in their early lives are approximately symmetrical, but with age develop their own quirky shapes. A good example of this is the black mulberry (*Morus nigra*), a tree of moderate size that is often very long lived. The toothed heart-shaped leaves are attractive, but it does not make a remarkable tree as a young rounded specimen. When with age the tree becomes gnarled, with a tendency to lean one way or another, even requiring supports to compensate for imbalances in its shape, it becomes a distinguished elderly citizen of great character. The strawberry trees (*Arbutus*) are quicker to show their idiosyncracies, the unusually broken crowns of leathery leaves allowing views in to the highly ornamental red-brown and shaggy trunks.

In the smaller garden, the ornamental value of a spreading canopy often has to be set against the disadvantage of heavy shade over a wide area. It is not surprising that there is keen interest in trees and shrubs of narrow habit. It is difficult as a gardener to resist the temptation to collect, but when I see a garden dominated by verticals, I sometimes think it might be better to reconcile oneself to a limited selection of plants, including a first-rate tree or shrub that spreads generously. A good choice for a medium-sized garden would be *Crataegus persimilis* "Prunifolia." It has glossy, deep green leaves that color well in autumn and attractive flowers in spring that are followed by bright red fruit. But you might prefer an almost leafless tree, although one that is green in appearance. The Mt. Etna broom (*Genista aetnensis*) makes a lovely light canopy, the green twigs, smothered in yellow flowers in summer, creating the effect of leaves. Not as light but perhaps the most beautiful of all the canopies are those formed by the radiating fronds of tree ferns such as cyatheas and dicksonias. They need a mild climate to achieve their full perfection, but then their lace patterns make superb silhouettes.

Trees and shrubs are the obvious upper layers of the garden, but it is as well to remember that even perennials create canopies, casting shade on smaller perennials, bulbs, ferns, and grasses beneath them. In fact, the canopies formed by large-leaved perennials such as gunneras and rheums cut out so much light that many smaller plants are unable to thrive in their shade.

Below: Large-leaved perennials such as the Chinese rhubarb (*Rheum palmatum*) create a low canopy, casting deep shade that inhibits growth near their base. The form "Bowles' Crimson" has deep red-purple undersides to the leaves.

Left: The Colorado spruce (*Picea pungens*) develops into a large, dense conical tree, but this evergreen conifer has several forms that are more compact, including the vividly blue-gray "Koster."

SELECTION cones and pyramids

TREES & SHRUBS *Alnus glutinosa "Imperialis" • Corylus colurna • Davidia involucrata • Ilex x altaclarensis "Camelliifolia" • I. aquifolium • Liquidambar styraciflua • Malus tschonoskii • Nyssa sinensis • Populus lasiocarpa • Quercus palustris*

CONIFERS *Abies concolor "Compacta" • A. koreana "Silberlocke" • A. lasiocarpa "Arizonica Compacta" • Araucaria heterophylla • Cedrus deodara • C. deodara "Aurea" • Cryptomeria japonica "Elegans Compacta" • Cupressus arizonica var. glabra • Metasequoia glyptostroboides • Picea glauca var. albertiana "Conica" • P. orientalis "Skylands" • P. pungens "Hoopsii" • P. pungens "Koster" • P. omorika • Pinus montezumae • P. wallichianum • Taxodium distichum • Thuja occidentalis "Holmstrup" • T. occidentalis "Rheingold" • T. occidentalis "Smaragd" • T. plicata "Stoneham Gold" • T. plicata "Zebrina" • Tsuga heterophylla*

EDIBLE PLANTS Bay laurel

For impressive symmetry in the plant world, there is little to match the cones or pyramids of the majority of conifers. In these trees, the cone shape is built up by the development of a leader that tyranically controls the growth of branches below it. These develop at regular intervals in whorls, and in a reasonably open tree, such as many of the pines, you can see gaps between the layers of foliage formed by each whorl of branches. The conical outline develops and is usually maintained into old age because the younger branches are shorter than the older lower branches. Conifers are found in such varied habitats that it is risky to make generalizations about the advantage to the tree of the conical form, but it is easy to see that at high altitudes and latitudes a tapered arrangement of steeply sloping branches can help shed excessive snow. At their far northen extremes and in the subalpine zone, the cone shape is often eroded by wind, the only surviving branches, in the lee of the prevailing wind, creating a flagged outline.

The toy conical form of a young conifer is so winning that it is often seized on as a way of making an attractive contrast to more rounded and billowing outlines. The reality is that the large conifers make imposing conical landscape trees, but they are overpowering in size and presence for most gardens. Even the widely planted deodar cedar (*Cedrus deodara*), which has a distinctive outline because of its nodding leader, can in ideal conditions reach a height of 40ft/12m in its first 25 years. For manageable symmetry you have to think in terms of slow-growing and dwarf conifers.

The term "dwarf" summons up an image of gnarled and misshapen trees of the kind you might find in a "crooked wood" of stunted conifers at high altitudes or latitudes. But there are many selections of remarkably regular outline in a broad range of foliage colors. Blue-gray is well represented by forms of the Colorado spruce such as *Picea pungens* "Hoopsii." A popular yellow with dense foliage, tinged pink when young, is a form of the white cedar, *Thuja occidentalis* "Rheingold." A Japanese cedar with soft juvenile foliage, *Cryptomeria japonica* "Elegans

Compacta," deepens from dark green to bronze in winter. It is very easy, however, to overdo contrasts of foliage color in a small garden, and it may be better to rely on contrasts of form using good greens. A small white spruce, *Picea glauca* var. *albertiana* "Conica," makes a neat cone of vivid green that even after 25 years is unlikely to be more than 6¹/₂ft/2m high. Other useful greens include forms of the white cedar such as *Thuja occidentalis* "Holmstrup."

Size counts against some of the impressive deciduous trees of conical shape, but where there is room for them, the pin oak (*Quercus palustris*) and the sweet gum (*Liquidambar styraciflua*) make impressive cones of foliage that are attractive all summer and spectacular in their autumn colors. Smaller deciduous trees that are conical to columnar and especially eye-catching in the fall include a crab apple, *Malus tschonoskii*, and *Sorbus commixta* "Embley." But it is among the hollies (*Ilex*) that you find evergreen cones of architectural solidity that are a match for the slow-growing conifers.

Right: The swamp cypress (*Taxodium distichum*) was one of the first unusual trees encountered by settlers who in the 1580s unsucessfully attempted to establish the Roanoke Colony in North Carolina. It is a conical tree, becoming less regular in old age, and, unusually for a conifer, is deciduous.

tiers and cascades

Left: The arching stems of Solomon's seal (*Polygonatum* x *hybridum*) bear alternate leaves set in a horizontal position, the tiered structure of the plant being emphasized when it is carrying little green-white bells.

SELECTION

TREES & SHRUBS *Acer palmatum* var. *dissectum* Dissectum Atropurpureum Group • *A. palmatum* var. *dissectum* Dissectum Viride Group • *Betula pendula* "Laciniata" • *B. pendula* "Tristis" • *B. pendula* "Youngii" • *Buddleja alternifolia* • *Cornus alternifolia* "Argentea" • *C. controversa* "Variegata" • *Cotoneaster atropurpureus* "Variegatus" • *C. horizontalis* • *Fagus sylvatica* "Pendula" • *Fraxinus excelsior* "Pendula" • *Parrotia persica* "Pendula" • *Prunus laurocerasus* "Zabeliana" • *Pyrus salicifolia* "Pendula" • *Salix* x *sepulchralis* "Chrysocoma" • *Tilia* "Petiolaris" • *Viburnum plicatum* "Mariesii"

CONIFERS *Cedrus atlantica* "Glauca Pendula" • *C. deodora* • *C. libani* • *Chamaecyparis nootkatensis* "Pendula" • *Juniperus* x *pfitzeriana* • *J. sabina* "Tamariscifolia" • *Larix kaempferi* "Pendula" • *Picea breweriana* • *P. smithiana* • *Taxus baccata* "Dovastonii Aurea"

CLIMBERS *Wisteria sinensis*

PERENNIALS *Polygonatum* x *hybridum*

FERNS, PALMS, & CYCADS *Adiantum venustum*

It is largely the framework of branches in trees and shrubs that produces tiered and pendulous arrangements of leaves. Some species found in the wild are of tiered or weeping form, but many of the plants in cultivation are sports that have been spotted by eagle-eyed gardeners and perpetuated by vegetative propagation and grafting. The shape of some perennials, especially arching grasses, also summons up an image of water, but in this case it is of a jet, with streams falling away as gravity defeats water pressure.

In the cedars the tiered structure of branches results in majestic landscape trees that deserve and almost require a wide open setting. Both the Atlas cedar (*Cedrus atlantica*) and the cedar of Lebanon (*C. libani*) are cone-shaped when young, and the branches are angled upward. But the mature trees are flat-topped, the branches extending more or less horizontally and supporting shelves of foliage that slope away slightly from the tree. The blue cedars, the Glauca Group of the cedar of Lebanon, get most of the attention, but trees of such handsome outline are just as impressive in sober gray-green. A much smaller tiered conifer is *Juniperus sabina* "Tamariscifolia," but in this case the layers of bright green foliage are low enough to make effective ground cover.

Like the juniper, a form of the evergreen cherry laurel, *Prunus laurocerasus* "Zabeliana," also has low tiers that make it useful as ground cover. But of far greater ornamental value among broad-leaved trees and shrubs, and suitable even for medium-sized gardens, are several deciduous dogwoods. The pick of them is the variegated form of the pagoda dogwood (*Cornus alternifolia* "Argentea"), which makes a large shrub or small tree with silvery foliage stacked one bright and weightless layer above another. More tree-like and with tabulated branches carrying foliage of cool variegation is *C. controversa* "Variegata." The herringbone pattern of branches in the deciduous shrub *Cotoneaster horizontalis* is yet another kind of tiered structure. Small leaves set off the bright red berries while they are still green and in the fall color brightly themselves.

Above: Because of the tiered arrangement of its horizontal spreading branches, *Cornus controversa* is sometimes known as the wedding-cake tree. In the slow-growing "Variegata," white edges to the leaves gives it a silvery festive appearance.

Left: "Pendula" is a graceful cultivar of the evergreen Nootka cypress (*Chamaecyparis nootkatensis*), a medium to large tree with branchlets that hang vertically.

Some of the most beautiful naturally occurring trees of weeping form are conifers. As a young plant, the Brewer's spruce (*Picea breweriana*) is wraith-like, but even when mature the little branchlets carrying the narrow leaves hang lightly to give it an ethereal grace. Almost as beautiful is the taller morinda spruce (*P. smithiana*). By comparison conifers such as *Juniperus* x *pfitzeriana* and *Taxus baccata* "Dovastonii Aurea" are stodgy, but they are useful broad evergreens for gardens of medium size, and the foliage spilling from a tiered framework softens their outline.

Even adults get a child-like pleasure entering the curtained chambers formed by the dangling leafy branches of deciduous trees such as the weeping beech (*Fagus sylvatica* "Pendula") and the weeping elm (*Fraxinus excelsior* "Pendula"). But of the large gracefully pendulous trees my favorite remains the weeping silver linden (*Tilia* "Petiolaris"). The heart-shaped leaves seem hinged to move in the slightest breeze, showing now their dark upper surface, now their white underside, at least until they turn clear yellow in the fall. It is out of the question for small and medium-sized gardens, but there are good options to consider here. The weeping silver-leaved pear (*Pyrus salicifolia* "Pendula") gets points for its silvery or gray-green narrow leaves, but its branches hang rather stiffly. *Buddleja alternifolia* is grown mainly for its long streamers of soft purple flowers, but it also has willow-like leaves, sometimes showing silver but more often dark green. To enjoy it as a very graceful small tree, train it up as a standard on a stem about 6ft/1.8m high. If these trees are too large, think of the numerous cultivars of the Japanese maple (*Acer palmatum*), many of which have foliage hanging with the elegance of finely groomed hair.

domes and mounds

SELECTION

TREES & SHRUBS *Acer palmatum "Dissectum Atropurpureum" • Aucuba japonica • Ballota "All Hallows Green" • B. pseudodictamnus • Berberis thunbergii f. atropurpurea • B. thunbergii "Bagatelle" • Buxus microphylla "Green Pillow" • Calluna vulgaris "Foxii Nana" • Choisya ternata • Cotoneaster congestus • Daphne laureola • D. odora "Aureomarginata" • Elaeagnus pungens "Frederici" •Euonymus fortunei "Emerald Gaiety" • Euryops acraeus • Fothergilla gardenii • Hebe cupressoides "Boughton Dome" • H. "Pewter Dome" • Ilex crenata "Convexa" • Lavandula angustifolia • L. lanata • Lotus hirsutus • Myrtus communis subsp. tarentina • Nandina domestica "Firepower" • Pittosporum tenuifolium "Silver Queen" • P. tenuifolium "Tom Thumb" • P. tobira "Variegatum" • Prunus laurocerasus "Otto Luyken" • Quercus coccifera • Rhododendron yakushimanum • Ruta graveolens "Jackman's Blue" • Santolina chamaecyparis var. nana • Skimmia japonica "Rubella" • Spiraea japonica "Goldflame" • Viburnum davidii*

CONIFERS *Abies balsamea* Hudsonia Group *• Chamaecyparis lawsoniana "Minima Glauca" • Juniperus squamata "Blue Star" • Picea mariana "Nana" • Pinus mugo "Mops"*

PERENNIALS *Alchemilla mollis • Artemisia schmidtiana • Dianthus erinaceus • Euphorbia polychroma • Geranium renardii • Heuchera americana •* Impatiens New Guinea Group *• Saxifraga* x *irvingii "Jenkinsiae"*

ANNUALS & BIENNIALS *Bassia scoparia* f. *trichophylla*

EDIBLE PLANTS Sage • Thyme (*Thymus vulgaris*)

Numerous compact shrubs and several perennials make neatly symmetrical rounded shapes in a range that extends down from domes to mere cushions and hummocks of tight foliage. The smaller forms are in some cases adaptations to harsh environments, the tight rounded growth, often combined with other drought-resistant characteristics such as hairy gray foliage, offering little resistance to wind and discouraging grazing. There are, however, numerous larger plants, some of them existing only as cultivated forms, where no useful generalization can be made about the advantage of the shape to the plant.

To gardeners, however, the range is very useful. Medium-sized domes of dense foliage make a good contrast to looser forms in mixed beds and shrubby ones, and can be effective when isolated as container-grown specimens. To many gardeners the spotted laurel (*Aucuba japonica*) has had its day. Perhaps the variegated forms draw too much attention to themselves, but the plain-leaved *A. j.* "Rozannie" (unlike most, it bears male and female flowers and is free-fruiting) is just the sort of plant that fills a difficult gap in sun or shade with its compact mass of dark green leaves. The cherry laurels (*Prunus laurocerasus*) are also plants tainted by their indiscriminate use in the past, but "Otto Luyken" is a really versatile glossy green bush. Perhaps we will soon tire of the deciduous barberry, *Berberis thunbergii*, but f. *atropurpurea* makes an easy-going rounded mass of purple leaves, and there are several compact options in the same color range, including "Bagatelle."

The Mexican orange blossom (*Choisya ternata*) is more distinguished than any of these, but it is also a more tender evergreen. The glossy aromatic leaves (they are made up of three leaflets) are stacked to make an impressive mound, usually not much more than 6ft/1.8m in height and spread.

Opposite: The dense rounded growth of *Hebe cupressoides* "Boughton Dome" makes it a good evergreen shrub for the front of a bed or to mix with rock-garden plants. It seldom flowers.

Right: The numerous named cultivars of the Japanese maple (*Acer palmatum*) fall into two main types, one with relatively large-lobed leaves, the other with finely dissected foliage. This second group, typified by var. *dissectum*, makes compact twiggy mounds decked with a lacy drapery that often colors brilliantly in the fall.

Below: The parent of an important group of compact, dome-shaped cultivars, *Rhododendron yakushimanum* is itself a neat evergreen shrub with young silvery growths of flower-like quality and trusses of delicate pink true flowers.

In spring, and often later, the dome is spangled with fragrant white flowers. The Japanese mock orange (*Pittosporum tobira*) also combines evergreen foliage with richly scented flowers, but unless the climate is mild it is best grown in a container and overwintered under glass. The variegated forms of *Pittosporum tenuifolium* such as "Irene Paterson" are hardier and make light-colored domes of crinkly leaves. Somewhat smaller than the pittosporum is *Rhododendron yakushimanum*, itself one of the finest compact rhododendrons for its flowers and foliage and much used in breeding. It makes a tight dome, usually no more than 3ft/90cm high. The new growths are attractively covered with fine silvery wool, and the underside of the leaves are felted and fawn colored.

My own favorites among the small rounded plants are those that thrive in open, sun-drenched, and often rather dry gardens. Many are improved by an annual clip to keep the shape neat. They include aromatic plants such as the compact lavender *Lavandula angustifolia* "Hidcote," santolinas, and the blue rue *Ruta graveolens* "Jackman's Blue." *Artemisia schmidtiana*, a silvery cushion of finely cut leaves, and the wooly lime-green *Ballota pseudodictamnus* go well with them, as do many smaller plants, such as some of the gray-leaved pinks (*Dianthus*). Another range of plants for open positions are the small, even midget, domed and bun-shaped conifers that are often mixed with dwarf bulbs and alpines in raised beds and rockeries. They do furnish the garden for twelve months of the year, but it is also true that their effect can be comic rather than beautiful whenever they are used to excess, as they often are.

tufts and clumps

SELECTION

PERENNIALS *Acanthus mollis • A. spinosus • Achillea "Moonshine" • Agapanthus campanulatus • Armeria juniperifolia "Bevan's Variety" • A. maritima • Artemisia ludoviciana "Valerie Finnis" • A. "Powis Castle" • Aruncus dioicus • Astilbe "Bronce Elegans" • Astrantia major "Sunningdale Variegated" • Bergenia purpurascens • B. "Sunningdale" • Cimicifuga simplex "Brunette" • Crambe maritima • Crocosmia "Lucifer" • Dicentra eximia • Echinops ritro • Euphorbia characias subsp. wulfenii • E. x martinii • Filipendula ulmaria "Aurea" • Geranium x magnificum • Geranium phaeum "Samobor" • Hemerocallis hybrids • Heuchera micrantha var. diversifolia "Palace Purple" • Hosta "Frances Williams" • H. "Halcyon" • H. "Krossa Regal" • Iris pallida "Argentea Variegata" • Kirengeshoma palmata • Ligularia przewalskii • Liriope muscari • Ophiopogon planiscapus "Nigrescens" • Paeonia mlokosewitschii • Pulsatilla vulgaris • Rheum "Ace of Hearts" • Rodgersia aesculifolia • R. pinnata • Saxifraga fortunei "Rubrifolia" • Sedum spectabile • Sisyrinchium "Aunt May" • Tiarella wherryi "Bronze Beauty" • Tolmiea menziesii "Taff's Gold" • Valeriana phu "Aurea" • Veratrum nigrum • Zantedeschia aethiopica*

GRASSES *Alopecurus pratensis "Aureovariegatus" • Calamagrostis x acutiflora "Overdam" • Carex oshimensis "Evergold" • C. morrowii "Fisher's Form" • Cortaderia selloana "Aurelineata" • Deschampsia flexuosa "Tatra Gold" • Elymus magellanicus • Festuca glauca "Elijah Blue" • F. valesciaca "Silbersee" • Hakonechloa macra "Alboaurea" • Holcus mollis "Albovariegatus" • Miscanthus sinensis var. purpurascens • M. sinensis "Zebrinus" • Molinia caerulea subsp. caerulea "Variegata" • Pleioblastus auricomus • Shibatea kumasasa • Uncinia uncinata*

FERNS, PALMS, & CYCADS *Blechnum penna-marina • Dryopteris erythrosora • Osmunda regalis*

EDIBLE PLANTS Chard • Parsley

A high proportion of the plants that make a strong foliage effect below chest height in the garden are clump-forming or tufted. Many herbaceous perennials are fibrous-rooted and each year produce a mass of leaf stalks and flower stems from ground level, which then die down before winter. The growth makes an inverted cone, with the leaves presented so they catch light without shading each other excessively, and the flowers are positioned to attract suitable pollinators. Many perennials that develop from underground rhizomes, in fact swollen and specialized stems, grow in the same way. Some, though, like perennials with running roots, have strong territorial ambitions and form mats or thickets rather than well-defined clumps. Tufted grasses also usually develop from a fibrous root system. More aggressive grasses, most of them spreading by rhizomes, stolons, or runners, may develop a series of interconnected tufts or form large stands that expand indefinitely.

It is the coherent massing of the foliage that makes the best of the clump-forming perennials so impressive. You see this instantly in plants like bear's breeches (*Acanthus*), which are frequently described as "architectural" or "sculptural" because the leaves form such an imposing podium for the stately stems of hooded flowers. The ornamental value of some of the clump-formers rests almost entirely on their foliage. This is true, for example, with several artemisias and two plants with golden foliage, *Filipendula ulmaria* "Aurea" and *Valeriana phu* "Aurea." And it also applies to dense clump-forming ferns, one of the most spectacular of which for temperate gardens is the royal fern (*Osmunda regalis*). Many bergenias and hostas have reasonably interesting flowers, but there is no doubt that their status as good garden plants rests on the quality of their foliage. But many of the

Opposite: The clump of variegated *Sisyrinchium striatum* "Aunt May" is iris-like, the flower spires rising above the fans of gray-green and cream leaves.

Right: Sun and good drainage are needed for the compact tufts of *Festuca valesiaca* "Silbersee" to take on their silvery-blue tone. The flowers of this perennial grass can often be more purple than shown here.

Left: Plantain lilies vary greatly in size, some of the large-leaved hostas building up clumps to 6ft/ 1.8m across. Rather than lifting large specimens to divide them, it is better to propagate from a plug or slice cut out with a spade.

perennials that are valued for their flowers are also plants with foliage that makes a real impact in the garden. A good example is *Achillea* "Moonshine," the stems bearing light yellow flowerheads rising from a clump of beautifully feathered silver-gray leaves. This example could be multiplied many times in astilbes, masterworts (*Astrantia*), globe thistles (*Echinops*), geraniums, peonies (*Paeonia*), sedums, and globeflowers (*Trollius*) – in fact, in a vast number of justly popular perennials.

The scale and density of tufted grasses vary enormously. At one extreme there are the tussocks of large pampas grasses (*Cortaderia*), although the largest do not necessarily have the most ornamental foliage. At the other there are little plants like the woolly foxtail grass (*Alopecurus lanatus*), scarcely 4in/10cm high. Their versatility as garden plants can be exploited in broad landscaping designs or in a more intimate way, with large or small tufts making textured contrasts with the clumps and rounded shapes of other perennials and shrubs. There are tufted perennials, too, that can be used as supplements to the grasses. Some of these, like the lilyturf (*Liriope muscari*), have conspicuous flowers as well as grassy leaves. But it is the concentrated blackness of *Ophiopogon planiscapus* "Nigrescens" that makes its tufts so arresting.

Left: Many alpine saxifrages form small rosettes, but those of the Pyrenean saxifrage (*Saxifraga longifolia*), composed of linear lime-encrusted leaves, can be up to 12in/30cm across. The plant builds up to produce a magnificent spray of white flowers, then the rosette usually dies.

SELECTION rosettes

TREES & SHRUBS *Aeonium "Zwartkop" • Daphne laureola*

PERENNIALS *Agave americana "Marginata" • A. americana "Variegata" • A. parryi • A. victoriae-reginae • Equisetum telmateia • Eryngium agavifolium • Eryngium variifolium • Euphorbia myrsinites • Pachysandra terminalis • Saxifraga longifolia • Sedum spathulifolium "Cape Blanco" • S. spathulifolium "Purpureum" • Sempervivum arachnoideum • S. tectorum*

ANNUALS & BIENNIALS *Silybum marianum • Verbascum bombyciferum*

FERNS, PALMS, & CYCADS *Cycas revoluta • Dicksonia antarctica*

EDIBLE PLANTS Cabbage • Lettuce

Arrangements of leaves radiating from the tip of a stem or in a condensed sequence near the tip create focused patterns that have an irresistible magnetism. On a small scale the arrangement is found in the shrubby perennial spurge *Euphorbia myrsinites*. The tight spiraling of small blue-gray leaves seems to be too much for the plant, for the stems lie prostrate, radiating from the center with casual serpentine elegance. More commonly, whorls of leaves at the end of stems create neat rosettes. The flowers of *Pachysandra terminalis*, a useful shade-tolerant evergreen for ground cover, are tiny, but this perennial seems to be a mass of dark green flowers. In *P. t.* "Variegata," these are picked out in cream.

A tight rosette formula, with leaves overlapping in a petal-like arrangement, is found in numerous plants that tolerate dry conditions, many showing other adaptations to sustained periods of drought, the foliage often fleshy and covered by a waxy bloom. In temperate gardens the aeoniums, most from the Canary Islands and North Africa, the aloes of southern Africa, and the agaves of the Americas usually need winter protection. As container plants, their mysterious flower-like quality, almost sinister in the near-black *Aeonium* "Zwartkop," make them strong focal points in a patio collection of potted plants.

The same tight rosette formula can be found in a number of perennials from mountainous and rocky habitats in temperate regions. The saxifrages are prized by alpine enthusiasts for their flowers and leaves. The rosettes of some are whitened by an encrustation of lime, and in some small species are packed into intriguing domes and mounds. A large-scale version is *Saxifraga longifolia*, with a single rosette of narrow silvery leaves almost 10in/25cm across. It is patient as well as beautiful, for the plant takes several years before producing a glorious spray of white flowers.

Easier than these alpines, but demanding sun and free drainage, are the sedums and sempervivums. Some of the smaller sedums look good at the edge of raised beds, but the fleshy-leaved sempervivums look best planted in low pans. Seen from above, the symmetry of individual rosettes, often tinted red, some dark chocolate, and the prodigally spawned family can be fully appreciated.

Numerous biennials overwinter as ground-hugging rosettes, and in some cases this foliage base is as impressive as the flowering stem that runs up in the second year. Several of the best are thistles, including the Blessed Mary's thistle (*Silybum marianum*), with bright green leaves splattered with milk. A feature of some drought-tolerant biennials is the felting of the leaves. The impressive gray-white rosette of a giant mullein, *Verbascum olympicum*, as much as 3ft/90cm across, has a magical beauty when spangled with dew.

The rosette occurs on a flamboyant cartwheel scale in a number of plants that are primitive in evolutionary terms but display designer sophistication. The leaves of the Japanese sago palm (*Cycas revoluta*), up to 5ft/1.5m long, spin above a shaggy base, their serried leaflets making a dense cross-hatch. The canopy of tree ferns such as *Dicksonia antarctica* are powerfully graphic set against blue sky and a richly textured wheel of foliage if seen from above.

Rosettes are also a common arrangement of leaves among some of the most valuable and ornamental of edible plants. In their range of textures, colors, and shapes, the culinary cabbages are foliage plants of real distinction. The ornamental cabbages and kales go farther, with leaves that are curled, fretted, marbled, flushed pink, and drenched in purple. They are of long-lasting beauty in beds or pots, especially valuable when the garden collapses in fall. Lettuces and endives are other ornamental vegetables in rosette form, and cultivars in red, bronze, and mahogany provide rich colors for the vegetable plot.

Above: The rosettes of the ornamental cabbages and kales are more decorative than those of the edible kinds, although these can be beautiful components of the vegetable garden. The kales, as in this white feathered example, have more dissected leaves than the cabbages.

Left: The succulent rosettes of the houseleeks (*Sempervivum*) can be tucked into crevices in the rock garden or encouraged to spawn in trough gardens or pans. There are many finds to make among unnamed forms with waxen, mahogany-tipped leaves, sometimes hairy, and bright green, red-brown, or purple-bronze.

SELECTION mats and carpets

TREES & SHRUBS *Arctostaphylos pumila* • *A. uva-ursi* • *Calluna vulgaris* "Darkness" • *C. vulgaris* "Sir John Charrington" • *Cotoneaster horizontalis* • *C. atropurpureus* "Variegatus" • *C. dammeri* • *Erica carnea* "Foxhollow" • *E. carnea* "Vivellii" • *Pachysandra terminalis* • *Vinca minor* "Argenteovariagata"

CONIFERS *Juniperus horizontalis* "Blue Chip" • *J. horizontalis* "Emerald Spreader" • *J. communis* "Green Carpet" • *J. communis* "Repanda" • *J. squamata* "Blue Carpet" • *Picea abies* "Reflexa" • *Taxus baccata* "Repandens"

CLIMBERS *Hedera colchica* "Dentata Variegata" • *H. helix* "Green Ripple" • *H. helix* "Ivalace" • *H. hibernica*

PERENNIALS *Acaena microphylla* "Kupferteppich" • *A. saccaticupula* "Blue Haze" • *Ajuga reptans* • *Arabis ferdinandi-coburgi* "Old Gold" • *Artemisia stelleriana* • *Asarum europaeum* • *Epimedium pinnnatum* subsp. *colchicum* • *E. perralderianum* • *E.* x *rubrum* • *Geranium macrorrhizum* • *Lamium maculatum* • *Lysimachia nummularia* "Aurea" • *Origanum vulgare* "Aureum" • *Persicaria affinis* "Superba" • *Phlomis russeliana* • *Saxifraga exarata* subsp. *moschata* "Cloth of Gold" • *Sedum acre* "Aureum" • *S. spathulifolium* • *Soleirolia soleirolii* • *Stachys byzantina* "Silver Carpet" • *Trifolium repens* "Purpurascens Quadrifolium" • *Vancouveria chrysantha* • *V. hexandra* • *Viola riviniana* Purpurea Group • *Waldsteinia ternata*

EDIBLE PLANTS Rosemary (*Rosmarinus officinalis* Prostratus Group) • Thyme (*Thymus* "Doone Valley", *T. serpyllum* "Minimus")

Moorland, mountainside, and woodland are all natural habitats of a wide range of of mat-forming and carpeting plants. These are often shrubs and perennials that have found a place in difficult but open terrain, where wind, low temperatures, poor soil, grazing, and fire restrict vertical growth. A very successful example found from mountain to tundra in the northern hemisphere is the bearberry (*Arctostaphylos uva-ursi*), a trailing evergreen shrub with long slender branches clothed in leathery evergreen leaves. It is undoubtedly a highly adaptable plant, even succeeding in pine and subarctic forest. Most of the low-spreading woodland plants, like the barrenworts (*Epimedium*), avoid standing in their own shadow, but spread out their foliage to catch angled light or flecks of sunshine filtered through a deciduous canopy.

Some low plants create a carpet simply because they are extremely sociable. Heaths (*Erica*) and heather (*Calluna vulgaris*), which are typical of moorland, make relatively small clumps, but they join

Top: Colonies of the barrenworts (*Epimedium*) spread by the extension of their rhizomes, but at a pace that means they are never troublesome. *E. pinnatum* subsp. *colchicum* is a dense grower with yellow flowers in late spring or early summer above the copper-tinted leaves.

up to form bouncy carpets that can cover vast tracts of land. Others simply have a wide-spreading framework of branches, in the case of conifers like the junipers covered with a dense mass of foliage. Many low plants extend their territory by spreading underground. The barrenworts do this and to their credit are not too pushy. The golden creeping Jenny (*Lysimachia nummularia* "Aurea") and many other plants root as they go.

In the garden many low spreading plants have great appeal, whether they are planted at the edge of a path, among stepping stones, or as a "skirt" to shrubs. Even without their floating flowers, the vancouverias are woodland charmers because of their pretty leaves, and the cut felt of *Artemisia stelleriana* catches the eye wherever it is sprawling. But what has made the mat-formers and carpeters major players in the modern garden is the promise they give of beauty without labor. The theory goes that if the ground is cleared of all perennial weeds and then planted at suitable

densities with low leafy plants that will eventually expand and knit together, there will be no room for weeds. You can see immediately that there is labor before bliss.

You must also choose your plants well: too timid and the carpet never knits; too aggressive and the carpet extends to territories you had reserved for quite different projects. The lovely snow-in-winter (*Cerastium tomentosum*), silver gray and spangled with starry white flowers, falls into the category of plants that do not know when to stop. But sturdy reliability and a certain level of aggression are advantages, especially in problem areas such as steep banks or in dry shade. It is not surprising that the standard repertoire for busy gardeners includes low conifers, trailing ivies, numerous geraniums, and, attractively rosetted and highly effective in dry shade, the perennial *Pachysandra terminalis*.

Repetition of particular plants and an emphasis on horizontals can have a dulling effect that needs to be counteracted by other planting. You could say the same of yet another kind of garden carpet, the lawn. One solution that is sometimes put forward is a combination of heaths and heathers with slow-growing conifers as rounded and vertical incidents. In practice these schemes

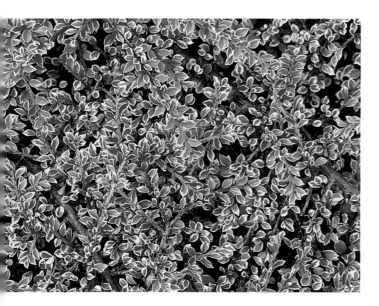

are often a numbing failure, in part due to the self-conscious overload of heaths and heathers with gold and orange foliage. But the unrelenting static character of the combination is also a difficulty. In this respect the heath and conifer gardens share something with carpet bedding, at the height of its popularity in the second half of the nineteenth century. Note that low-growing foliage plants, such as alternantheras and iresines, or succulents are able to form their own mats or carpets in this style of gardening, for individual plants are packed close together to form a geometric or representational design. The technique has enjoyed a revival in sculptural gardening.

Above: *Sedum spathulifolium* is a succulent perennial making mats of tight fleshy rosettes, above which rise stems bearing heads of starry yellow flowers. The innermost leaves of "Cape Blanco," shown here, are covered with a white bloom.

Left: Many prostate shrubs can be used to carpet the ground in a way that excludes weeds. ***Cotoneaster atropurpureus* "Variegatus"** grows like the better-known *C. horizontalis*, but it has white-margined leaves that color red in the fall.

pencils and columns

The starkest columnar forms in plants are found in large cacti such as the saguaro (*Carnegiea gigantea*) of Arizona, southern California, and northwestern Mexico. But there are numerous trees, many of them conifers, that are narrowly vertical, sometimes with short branches of nearly equal length the whole height of the tree, sometimes with branches swept upward and hugging the trunk. The form can be columnar or pencil-like, but there is almost invariably a degree of taper, and many fastigiate trees, that is those with erect branches, have a slender, flame-like outline.

These tightly vertical forms inevitably suggest the hand of the gardener. They are rarely encountered in communities of wild plants, and most of those we have in gardens are exceptions, sports of more generously proportioned trees that have been perpetuated (they are usually propagated from cuttings or by grafting) because they fit into restricted spaces and do not cast shade over large areas. A downside to the fastigiate forms of beech (*Fagus sylvatica*), oak (*Quercus robur*), and other substantial trees is that they have lost the grace of generous curving masses. But in large gardens the gathered foliage of these and columnar conifers such as *Chamaecyparis lawsoniana* "Wisselii" can make telling contrasts with freer forms as well as standing out impressively on the skyline.

The close regularity of the columnar shape, at its most extreme a kind of topiary without shears, lends itself to formal treatment. The avenue, an impressive formal feature for a landscape or garden, relies on the repetition of trees or shrubs planted in pairs. In a landscape there may even be room for broad-crowned trees, but a classic of columnar form is the Lombardy poplar (*Populus nigra* "Italica"), also widely used as a windbreak and screen. Its soaring height and the beautiful movement of the foliage, indeed of the whole tree, in a strong breeze make an avenue or screen a glorious feature. But this is a tree to appreciate on someone else's land. It is often not long lived, and its extensive root system can cause problems to the foundations of buildings and drains. The Italian cypress (*Cupressus sempervirens* Stricta Group) is another tree strongly associated with the landscapes of southern Europe, but in a mild climate its slim pencil outline, the gray-green to dark foliage forming dense sprays, makes it suitable for gardens, too.

My choice for an avenue of imposing solemnity in a large garden is the Irish yew (*Taxus baccata* "Fastigiata"). It starts life as a pencil, but develops into a somewhat irregular and broad column, weighty with the black-green of its foliage. A smaller and brighter version, rarely exceeding 5ft/1.5m miniature, is the golden *T. b.* "Standishii." A useful selection of junipers ranges down to the dwarf, slow-growing *Juniperus communis* "Compressa," which is tall when it eventually reaches 32in/80cm.

Compact and upright forms of deciduous trees are another option for formal arrangements. The ornamental cherry *Prunus* "Amanogawa" is mainly grown for its lavish display of shell-pink flowers, but the foliage is an attractive bronze green in spring, and for a brief period the leaves color well in the fall. Another narrow flowering tree is the ornamental pear *Pyrus calleryana* "Chanticleer." Wreathed in white blossoms in spring, glossy dark green in summer, it becomes a purple-red exclamation mark in the fall. Most of the maples are grown for the beauty of their leaves, not for their flowers, but they are generally trees and shrubs of broad outlines. Bucking the trend, *Acer* "Scanlon" makes a broad column that ignites dramatically in the fall.

Top left: The Irish yew (*Taxus baccata* "Fastigiata") is a female selection of the common yew, of dense upright growth, hence the scarlet-fleshed fruits. Here the tree's shape has been accentuated by clipping.

Right: The Italian cypress (*Cupressus sempervirens* Stricta Group) is the classic narrow upright tree of the Mediterranean region. A single specimen of this evergreen conifer often looks inadequate, but rows and double rows can make important landscape features.

shuttlecocks
and fountains

SELECTION

TREES & SHRUBS *Betula pendula • Fagus sylvatica "Dawyck" • F. sylvatica "Dawyck Purple"*

CONIFERS *Larix decidua*

PERENNIALS *Cynara cardunculus • Phormium cookianum*

GRASSES *Arundo donax • Cortaderia selloana "Aureolineata" • Fargesia murieliae • F. nitida • Miscanthus sinensis "Gracillimus" • M. sinensis "Grosse Fontäne" • M. sinensis "Zebrinus" • Phalaris arundinacea var. picta "Feesey" • Phyllostachys viridiglaucescens*

FERNS, PALMS, & CYCADS *Asplenium scolopendrium • Dryopteris affinis • D. wallichiana • Matteuccia struthiopteris • Polystichum aculeatum • P. munitum • P. setiferum*

Shuttlecocks and fountains may seem only distantly connected, but both conjure up symmetrical forms, restricted at the base but then spreading, the shuttlecock consisting of components all set at the same angle, fountains with components arching over more casually after an initial near-vertical surge. The shuttlecock is a specialty of the ferns. In a number of these, the fronds develop from the crown in a symmetrical rosette, extending and splaying outward slightly so that when fully developed they look like the feathered crown stuck into the stub of a shuttlecock. The ultimate shape is highly distinctive, but in almost all ferns so, too, is the steady unfurling of the fronds. "Circinate vernation" is a dry technical term for one of the most beautiful slow-motion processes in the development of plants, the rolled-up fronds assuming, as they unfold, the shapes of croziers or the necks and heads of fiddles – the imagination runs wild, for one can see them, too, as uncoiling furry caterpillars risking themselves in an uncertain world.

The classic shuttlecock arrangement of fronds is best seen in the fancifully named ostrich-plume fern (*Matteuccia struthiopteris*), also known as the shuttlecock fern. This is a moisture-lover needing shelter from drying winds. In damp ground or bog, it makes a short stem from which the fronds, spaced with perfect regularity, make their well-defined shape in lacy bright green. The fronds start to flag in late summer, but short dark fertile fronds in the center of the shuttle persist even in winter. Although this fern is invasive, with new crowns growing from the spreading rhizomes, it is reasonably easy to control and is certainly one of the loveliest of its kind for temperate gardens. In many other ferns, the shuttlecock formation is obscured by the dense growth of fronds, but it shows clearly in several that are evergreen, including the golden male fern (*Dryopteris affinis*), and the hard and soft shield ferns (*Polystichum aculeatum* and *P. setiferum*). "Dahlem" is an impressive form of the soft shield fern, with nearly upright fronds making a narrow shuttlecock that creates an effective contrast with more horizontal and arching shapes.

Fountain-like growth is found in a wide range of plants. The tight structure of columnar trees often loosens with age. A mature specimen of the Dawyck beech (*Fagus sylvatica* "Dawyck"), for example, can look like a giant fountain, and even when it is young, the narrower but more open *F. s.* "Dawyck Purple" makes a dark jet of foliage in the landscape. The most sensational of the perennial foliage fountains is produced by the cardoon (*Cynara cardunculus*). Its purple thistle-heads, sometimes a good 8ft/2.5m above ground level, are in themselves impressive, but it is the soaring jagged leaves, arching over elegantly, that suggest phenomenal artesian vitality. There is the same vigor in the upright canes of bamboos such as *Fargesia nitida*, the foliage spilling away like broken showers of water.

Although they may be less vigorous, many deciduous grasses also suggest the upward movement of water in their vertical stems and falling water in their arching leaves. Good examples can be found throughout the genus *Miscanthus*, of which some, such as the fine-leaved *M. sinensis* "Gracillimus," are lightly silvered. But fountains do not all soar dramatically, and many small plants with arching stems and leaves evoke more gently purling water.

Opposite: An unusual perspective on the ostrich-plume fern (*Matteuccia struthiopteris*) shows the lacy intricacy of its shuttlecock. This species spreads by rhizomes in moist soil.

Below: The boldly cut arching leaves of the perennial cardoon (*Cynara cardunculus*) form a silver-gray fountain that is topped in summer by violet thistle flowerheads.

the garden

There are as many ideas of what makes the perfect garden as there are gardeners. Whatever your ideal, there is a place for foliage in it, easily justified on grounds of practicality and economy quite apart from its decorative attributes. Leaves have varied and exceptional ornamental qualities of their own, distinct from, but often complementary to, those of flowers. Foliage is the living architecture of gardens designed on austerely formal lines. It is the calm greenery of intimate enclosures. It is the substance, and sometimes the focus, of loosely naturalistic and more regimented plantings in which flowers often play a significant role. And it can be dramatically exotic, giving a seasonal tropicality even to gardens that in winter may be covered by frost and snow.

The golden rule of selecting plants is to make your choice to suit the growing conditions. Therefore, the more you know about your own plot, the better. Although you can improve your soil by drainage and by digging in plenty of well-rotted organic matter, you have to come to terms with its basic character. A simple soil-testing kit will tell you whether your soil is acid, neutral, or alkaline, and by digging holes at several points in the garden, you can find out how much topsoil there is and whether it is light and free-draining or heavy and lump-forming. Note how areas of sun and dappled shade change through the seasons, and choose leafy plants that enjoy the particular conditions. Every garden has difficult areas, perhaps chilled by lingering frost, savaged by wild winds, or deeply shaded and dry. But most gardens also have sunny, warm, and sheltered corners that are worth reserving for more tender subjects. The range of plants with ornamental foliage is so diverse that a choice is available for almost every set of conditions.

Right: A tropical summer garden can be created by planting out tender exotics such as cannas and bananas (*Musa*) when there is no longer a risk of frost.

broad effects

A useful way to think of your garden is as a space with three dimensions as real as those of the house. Windbreaks, hedges, and screens mark the perimeter, creating shelter and privacy, but with openings for access and to give views into the world beyond the garden. There may be internal divisions, too, so that the overall space is broken up into a sequence of rooms. Even if much of the garden is open to the sky, the canopies of trees and shrubs partly roof it and create areas of shade. Structures such as arbors and arches clothed with plants may perform the same role, but in a more defined way. Grass and low plants, usually in combination with hard surfaces, floor it. Flowerbeds allow the garden to be furnished from a vast selection of shrubs, perennials, bulbs, ferns, grasses, and edible plants, all of which have leaves and many whose foliage is their chief merit.

Ground cover

The promise of ground-cover plants is that they will quickly produce enough attractive foliage, one plant knitting together with another, to exclude weeds and so relieve the gardener of work. There are several reasons for disenchantment. First, many plants have been inappropriately described as good ground cover, sometimes because their sprawling growth is too open to suppress weeds, sometimes because the savior becomes an invading enemy, sweeping through the garden or seeding itself so freely that it is as troublesome as the weeds it is supposed to suppress. Beware of plants such as *Lamium galeobdolon*, *Vinca major*, and *Pleioblastus variegatus*! Second, although well-planted ground cover will eventually be labor saving, some hard work is needed to remove perennial weeds and prepare the ground well before planting. And the ground between plants needs to be kept weed free until the ground cover grows together. Finally, this low maintenance solution is tainted by its spiritless use in many municipal plantings.

If suitable plants have been chosen and the preparation has been done properly, using ground cover is genuinely labor saving. It offers a sensible way of dealing with difficult areas of the garden, including steep slopes where exposed soil erodes and where mowing is hazardous, awkward gaps between buildings and walls, and shaded areas, even areas of dry shade. Despite its possible associations with dull institutional planting schemes, there is a place for extensive ground cover. In an impressive massing of vertical and horizontal forces, it creates confident planes of foliage abutting walls and hedges, running into distant vistas of trees and forming a podium for thrusting uprights and sculptural forms. The mixture of grasses in lawn sod makes up a specialized ground cover, but one that requires a high level of maintenance. Wildflower meadows and prairie gardens are other ground-covering mixtures of plants in which grasses play a major role. They require much less maintenance than lawns once they are established, but there is a lot of work to be done during the initial stages.

The broad approach is less successful in small and medium-sized gardens. On a modest scale, a patchwork of interlocking foliage plants is more appropriate. It can create a highly effective weed-suppressing cover without detracting from the garden's intimate character. And the choice of suitable plants is so extensive that there are endless possibilities for subtle and sophisticated combinations, as well as for dramatic effects.

The choice must be dictated by the growing conditions. Gray-leaved plants such as artemisias and lambs' ears (*Stachys byzantina*) give a good mixture of textures for sunny, well-drained areas. And I have a great liking for woodland plants such as epimediums, dicentras, geraniums, heucheras, pulmonarias, and tiarellas that adapt well to the shady conditions of town

Left: In fertile moist soil, joined clumps of the perennial *Ligularia* make an impressive cover of large heart-shaped leaves. In the second half of summer they are topped by tall spikes of orange-yellow daisies.

Above: In a sunny, well-drained garden, a weathered stone repeats the domed shapes of the green-leaved aromatic *Santolina rosmarinifolia* subsp. *rosmarinifolia* and French lavender (*Lavandula stoechas*), low shrubs that need an annual trim to remain neat and compact.

gardens. Ferns and hostas are also good in shade and are naturals to mix with moisture-loving astilbes and rodgersias.

Climbing cover

Not every wall is blank and boring. But many gardens do have stretches of wall and fences that are better clothed in foliage than left bare. The cover is a camouflage and is also a way of making the boundaries seem less like an imposition from outside and more like an extension of the garden within. Climbers fall into two broad categories. There are those, like the ivies (*Hedera*) and the Boston ivy (*Parthenocissus tricuspidata*), that are equipped with specially adapted roots or suckers to cling to their support. Provided the support itself is sound, they will not cause damage, although they will mark painted surfaces. Many of these self-clingers are superb foliage plants, an attractive feature being the way the leaves fit together and are angled to catch the light. They may take some time to get started, but then generally grow vigorously and need little looking after. The familiar ivy leaves are, in fact, a juvenile stage. Mature ivy produces top growths with no aerial roots and leaves that are unlobed. These are best removed from plants on walls, but cuttings from them will take and make bushes that retain the adult form of the leaf.

A large number of climbers are equipped in various ways to attach themselves to supports. If vigorous plants such as the startlingly variegated *Actinidia kolomikta* are to be grown on a wall, it is essential to have a support system in place. This usually consists of horizontal wires at intervals of about 16in/40cm, the wires standing clear of the walls for air circulation, which helps reduce the risk of disease. Climbers that twine, such as honeysuckle (*Lonicera japonica* "Aureoreticulata"), those that are supported by tendrils (*Vitis coignetiae*), and those with twisting leaf stalks (*Clematis armandii*), can all work their way up through trellis or other open support, filling in gaps and forming canopies to arches and arbors. Whatever support they are grown on, they may need some training to make sure growths are well spaced. Few need regular pruning, but many of these climbers are vigorous and require periodic overhaul to remove excessive and tangled growth. Yet another way of growing them, and the most natural of all, is to train them through other plants.

The yellow leaves of the golden hop (*Humulus lupulus* "Aureus") insinuating themselves among purple or even deep green foliage can make very beautiful contrasts. This perennial climber is, however, difficult to keep in check and, like so many other climbers, needs a robust partner as support. A number of lax shrubs that are not strictly climbers – *Abutilon vitifolium* and *Buddleja crispa* are good examples – are also often grown against walls, and they, too, need to be trained to structures and supports.

Windbreaks, hedges, and screens

Planted protection for habitation probably goes back to a very early stage in the history of human settlement. In the modern garden hedges and windbreaks still perform useful practical roles, but their aesthetic value also counts for a lot. The framework of branches and their cover of leaves make many trees and shrubs highly effective as windbreaks. They do not form a solid barrier, but, if they are planted thickly enough, filter the wind, reducing its force and diverting it without causing excessive turbulence. Those most widely planted are fast growing, one of the most popular being x *Cupressocyparis leylandii*. It is easy to see that the conifer has a value in this role, but it is a pity that it is also so widely planted as a fast-growing hedge. Other large trees grown as windbreaks include larches (*Larix*), spruces (*Picea*), pines (*Pinus*), and poplars (*Populus*). Shrubs that are especially useful near the sea because of their tolerance of salt include escallonias, *Fuchsia magellanica*, and *Griselinia littoralis*.

Hedges, which consist of trees or shrubs grown in line to form a barrier, have the same practical advantage as windbreaks in that they filter wind. They are also often livestock-proof; they can be used to block out unsightly views, and they make the garden private – or at least give it the feeling of being a secluded place. Evergreen hedges have the advantage of retaining their leaf cover throughout the year, and deciduous hedges of hornbeam (*Carpinus betulus*) and beech (*Fagus sylvatica*) hold onto their dead leaves. Boundary hedges in rural areas usually consist of a mixture of plants, and even a more sophisticated garden hedge can be made up of different species. A frequently seen version of the mixed hedge consists of green- and purple-leaved forms of beech. A more subtle combination consists of mixed clones of a tree such as yew, where slight differences in the habit of growth can create attractive patterns. For absolute uniformity and consistency of texture, a formal hedge should be planted using a single clone of whatever plant is chosen. Hedges are generally much cheaper than walls or fences as a barrier, but they take time to reach maturity, so they are not fully functional for several years, and nor are they complete aesthetically until they have reached their desired height.

Informal hedges, often of flowering shrubs, require only light trimming. In fact, there is a large number of foliage plants that can be lined out and treated as an informal hedge. Non-running bamboos and large clump-forming grasses can be used this way. Most perennials lose their leaves in winter, but nonetheless can be used to make an ornamental summer barrier. Formal hedges need to be trimmed often enough to keep the foliage dense: that is, at least once in the growing season or up to three times for fast-growing hedges. The character of the free-growing tree or shrub is lost, and what you have instead is an architectural form clearly defined by foliage.

Edgings in a garden often consist of low hedges, for example of box (*Buxus sempervirens*). But you can aim for a much looser approach, with perennials that have good foliage making a fluid boundary between borders and paths. Suitable plants to choose from include acaenas, ajugas, bergenias, *Geranium macrorrhizum*, and tiarellas.

Left: Despite its common name Boston ivy, the self-clinging climber *Parthenocissus tricuspidata* is an Asiatic species. Its interlocking leaves make a bright green curtain for high walls in summer, with a transition in the fall to brilliant crimson and purple.

Right: In an unusual suburban garden, the design is based on open areas of water and decking surrounded by dramatic foliage plants such as palms and bamboo.

Below: The combination of plain- and purple-leaved forms of beech (*Fagus sylvatica*) make strong contrasts in a mixed hedge.

details

Left: Although seen here as an isolated detail, this specimen of *Gunnera manicata*, with its few stems and cone of flowers, will develop into a dramatic clump that will obscure the lake beyond.

Right: The blades of the variegated succulent *Furcraea foetida* var. *mediopicta* rise iris-like from among the rounded leaves of *Tropaeolum majus* 'Alaska,' a speckled-leaf nasturtium.

It is the quality of the detail that gives a garden its distinctive character, marking it out from others that are competently but unimaginatively planted. There is no doubt that some gardeners have an exceptional flair for assembling plants in an interesting way, but something approaching their skill can be acquired by any observant gardener. A good beginning is to try planting foliage as you have seen it used to telling effect in other gardens. The success of a tested formula in your own space will encourage you to experiment with a selection of plants that suit your garden's conditions.

Accents

A coherent garden design must rely to some extent on dramatic accents. They draw the eye so the garden is experienced in a particular way. When used in pairs, framing a view, they also are a way of manipulating space. And they complete vistas, which is especially important when there is no worthwhile view beyond the garden. On a small scale, an accent gives point to a grouping of objects or a collection of plants. A sculpture, a fountain, a painted door, an interestingly shaped stone – these are all possible accents or eye-catchers. And so, too, are plants, those of distinctive shape and color being especially useful. The most commonly used shapes are the symmetrical forms of trees and shrubs, but asymmetry, for example in a strawberry tree (*Arbutus*) or a weathered pine, can be even more full of character. Because trees and shrubs have a permanent framework, they are often the automatic choice for planted focal points in the garden. It is worth casting the net wider, though. A clump of bamboo has a lively grace, as do stands of large grasses such as *Miscanthus sacchariflorus*, beautiful even when the foliage is dead. Think, too, of large perennials of the kind frequently described as sculptural. A good example is the cardoon (*Cynara cardunculus*); although it loses its leaves in winter, the jagged fountain of summer foliage puts it into the top flight of eye-catchers.

Topiary, the art of clipping plants to shape, controls the development of foliage in a very severe way. A familiar repertoire of geometric shapes, including balls, cones, columns, and spirals, is a legacy of the Renaissance garden. So, too, are fantastical shapes, some representational, some curious composites. The solidity of a well-trimmed topiary specimen contributes to its effectiveness as an accent in the garden, perhaps as part of a paired arrangement or even grander schemes. Another kind of topiary, cloud pruning, has its origins in oriental traditions of gardenmaking, but is increasingly popular in Western gardens. The aim of pruning and trimming is to develop balanced masses of foliage, clipped in the form of cloud-like puffs, with the structure of the stems supporting them fully exposed. The armature of the plant and the pruned foliage combine to make a highly individual entity that, when treated as an accent, can impose a distinctive character on a garden.

The silver-gray of the cardoon is one of this plant's great assets. It is certainly true that some of the best plants to use for accents have foliage outside the normal green range. To make their effect, though, they need a background that shows them off, and the greens are often most reliable for this purpose. You see its effectiveness when variegated plants make a highlight in shade and also when an accent suddenly becomes powerful with the turning of its fall foliage. Maples such as *Acer* "Scanlon," the crabapple (*Malus tschonoskii*), and the scarlet oak (*Quercus coccinea* "Splendens") all stand out magnificently when they are seen against a backdrop of broad-leaved or coniferous evergreens.

Planting in a container can be a highly effective way of isolating and giving prominence to fine foliage plants, including perennials and grasses. This is a superb way to show off some of the large hostas. Even though you may see it planted this way many times, *Hosta sieboldiana* var. *elegans* is so lavishly quilted and of such a sumptuous blue-gray that it never disappoints. Among the best grasses for containers are *Hakonechloa macra* "Alboaurea" and *H. m.* "Aureola." Although they differ in the depth of their gold or cream variegation and in the hints of bronze, they both have ribbon-like leaves about 12in/30cm long that arch over gently to form a soft clump. Larger plants for pots and tubs include shrubs such as the Japanese maple (*Acer palmatum*). Isolating and raising them displays their form, often weeping, as well as the exquisitely colored and shaped leaves. Growing in containers is the obvious solution for important tender shrubs and perennials. After a winter under cover, the Japanese sago palm (*Cycas revoluta*) can be moved out and made a focal point in the garden. Working on a much smaller scale, you might do the same with impressive succulents, including aeoniums, agaves, and aloes. Cacti fit the bill, too, although their foliage takes the form of spines. They are the most impressive accents, in or out of pots, in true desert gardens, their unique shapes highlighted by the sparseness of the vegetation around them.

Harmonies and contrasts

Harmony in the garden is easy on the eye, but the effect of plants growing together without contrast is bland. Among the simplest contrasts are those created when plants of different shape are brought together. You see this in woodland, with the pyramidal shape of conifers set against the rounded crowns of oaks (*Quercus*) and the upright columns of a tree like the Dawyck beech (*Fagus sylvatica* "Dawyck"). Not many of us have the opportunity to plant woodland trees, but similar contrast are possible on a much smaller scale. A small weeping tree such as *Buddleja alternifolia* can be partnered with a rounded shrub such as *Choisya ternata*, or a slow-growing upright conifer, for example, *Juniperus communis* "Hibernica," can be matched with another juniper of horizontal form such as *J. sabina* var. *tamariscifolia*. Even in a raised bed planted with rock garden plants, you can combine hummocks and mats, low mounds and pencil uprights.

Contrasts of leaf size and shape often have an intimate character, mosaics of small plants being particularly beautiful. Imagine the minute silvery leaves of a raoulia trickling over stones and between mats of thyme (*Thymus*), spiky tufts of blue fescues (*Festuca*), and rosettes of sedums and sempervivums. Or think of the simple contrast between the light and feathery green of young love-in-a-mist (*Nigella damascena*) and the blades of a variegated iris.

In tropical gardens and in waterside plantings, the contrasts can often be highly dramatic. Tropical gardens are by no means confined to the tropics, for many large-leaved plants can be pot-grown, kept under glass from fall to spring, and moved out in summer to make star performers in the garden. Cycads, bananas, and palms are just the sort of plants to make bold contrasts. By the waterside and in bog gardens, you can set the bold verticals of irises and reeds against the large paddles of skunk cabbages (*Lysichiton*), the rounded leaves of the umbrella plant (*Darmera peltata*), the lobed foliage of Chinese rhubarb (*Rheum palmatum*), and the giant parasols of *Gunnera manicata*.

Left: The swords and straps of yuccas and New Zealand flaxes (*Phormium*) provide a strong theme in a sunny garden that includes aromatic plants such as sage (*Salvia officinalis*) and rosemary (*Rosmarinus officinalis*).

Above: The trickle of flowers is almost irrelevant, for this calm and coherent ensemble of plants uses shades of green, and contrasts of foliage texture and shape to create a perfected version of a woodland fringe.

Mosaics of leaves often show marked contrasts of texture. In a well-drained sunny garden, you might have the large woolly rosettes of a mullein (*Verbascum*) and the spiky rosettes of a thistle such as *Silybum marianum* set against shiny and leathery bergenia leaves and the succulent and glaucous foliage of sedums. In this assembly the surface quality of the leaves counts for a lot. But leaf shape and size can contribute something, too, the shadowed depths of layered leaves adding another dimension to the surface qualities. Contrasts of foliage texture are often left to chance, but they make such a difference to the garden they deserve to be given a higher priority in planting schemes.

Gardeners are more accustomed to orchestrating color harmonies and contrasts than they are to dealing with texture. In one of the classic harmonies, that based on silver-gray and pastel colors, foliage is a key player, although often thought of as simply performing in a supporting role. The shabbiness of gray plants such as artemisias, helichrysums, and santolinas in winter gives little hint of the way they are transformed in summer. Their silver foliage makes a perfect foil for dianthus, but is just as effective calming a border, linking one area with another, and serving as a buffer between strong and even clashing colors. The silvers and grays come into their own in hot, sunny weather, bleaching as the summer advances. In dull weather they can give the garden a sullen cast,

and it is then you feel the lack if there is no strong design element giving the garden a focus. You might find a suitable solution in the grays themselves by including a dramatic clump of the thistle *Onopordum acanthium*. Silver and gray leaves are also useful in container gardening. Densely planted pots and windowboxes need foliage to dilute the effect of congested flowers. One of the most successful grays is *Helichrysum petiolare*, whose wayward stems work their way through other plants so its soft gray shows them off with nonchalant charm.

Other quiet harmonies that are beautiful seen up close can be based on blues, with foliage plants such as hostas; on creams and yellows, using variegated irises and grasses; or with a deeper bias, using as a foliage plant the purple-leaved loosestrife *Lysimachia ciliata* "Purpurea." For drama you need to use strong contrasting colors. A stark effect can be achieved with white and black-purple, say with the variegated grass *Holcus mollis* "Albovariegatus" set against the nearly black lilyturf *Ophiopogon planiscapus* "Nigrescens," a plant with strap-like leaves that seems to be scuttling across the garden. On this small scale, the contrast is wonderfully arresting, but translated into trees and shrubs it might be more disconcerting than pleasing. There is endless scope for experimentation, although, if you are planting trees and shrubs, you want to be confident of the effect before committing yourself. For that reason alone it is always worth looking at what other gardeners have done and noting failures as well as the more common successes. Contrasts that have particularly appealed to me include some based on silver and purple foliage (an uncomplicated version consisting of a purple-leaved *Berberis thunbergii* with *Elaeagnus* "Quicksilver"), others with yellow and purple (a ground-cover mixture that is especially good in winter combines the ivy *Hedera colchica* "Sulfur Heart" and *Bergenia cordifolia*), and red against green (a stunning example for the fall being the maple *Acer japonicum* "Vitifolium" among green conifers such as pines).

Patterns

The use of plants to create pattern has a long history and is evident even in wall paintings showing the well-ordered gardens of dynastic Egypt. At a modest and unaffected level, we can see how pleasing patterns can be even in a working vegetable garden, with the foliage of lines of vegetables presenting beautiful contrasts of color, texture, and shape even though the order is dictated by the cultivation requirements of crops. The self-conscious elaboration of this artisan simplicity in the potager or ornamental kitchen garden is not necessarily more beautiful, despite the self-conscious gathering together of the most remarkable vegetables and herbs.

The traditional patterns of knot gardens and embroidered parterres are commonly formed by low hedges of dwarf box (*Buxus sempervirens* "Suffruticosa"), but many other plants were used in the past, including small aromatic shrubs such as hyssop (*Hyssopus officinalis*). The legacy of the Renaissance garden continues to exert a strong influence in these designs and in the grouping of formally planted trees in avenues, blocks, and quincunxes (arrangements of five like the dots of the five on dice). The predictability of these plantings is part of their appeal. The same could be said of bedding schemes, including carpet bedding and combinations of flowers and dotted foliage plants such as *Senecio cineraria*. However, there is no need to be always looking back for inspiration. You could create your own original designs or draw on repertoires that have so far been underused. Art Deco motifs offer many possibilities, as do patterns in folk art. An altogether freer approach is possible in long beds, and there bold perennials such as bear's breeches (*Acanthus mollis*) and clump-forming grasses planted at intervals could be used to create rhythms that energize the garden and hold it together.

Left: Aromatic plants such as hyssop (*Hyssopus officinalis*) have traditionally been used to form the planted patterns of knot gardens, often, as here, in combination with dwarf box (*Buxus sempervirens* "Suffruticosa").

Below: Rows of vegetables of contrasting shapes, textures, and colors make appealing patterns in the vegetable garden. Here the rows are filled with leeks, and purple and gray-green forms of brassicas.

Right: The Mediterranean garden, in which aromatic plants such as lavender (*Lavandula*) and rosemary (*Rosmarinus officinalis*) play a prominent role, remains a classic model for sunny, well-drained sites.

Aromatic plants

We are as susceptible as pollinating insects to fragrant flowers, but often overlook the spicy, even pungent scent of aromatic leaves. This is partly because most foliage keeps the secret of its aromatic richness until the volatile oils are released by friction or bruising. We can walk around the garden unaware of the full extent of its scent dimension. Once we have discovered it, the garden takes on a new enchantment, charged with sensations unpredictably but usually happily linked to chains of associations that are all our own.

Many of the plants with aromatic foliage have long been cultivated as culinary or medicinal herbs. Sixteenth- and seventeenth-century gardeners, having to make do with a relatively limited range of plants, frequently incorporated herbs in the patterned layouts of knot gardens. There has been a revival of interest in these and also in slightly less formal arrangements in which the herbs are brought together in allusion to a cottage style of gardening. These options have their advantages. The pattern, particularly if outlined in a clipped evergreen such as box (*Buxus sempervirens*), is pleasing in all seasons, although the herb content will start to look tired in the second half of summer. From a special herb garden positioned close to the kitchen door, it is easy to gather aromatic sprigs as and when they are wanted. In spring and early summer, when the herbs are fresh and vigorous, the whole collection can look very attractive. There are some disadvantages, too. There are so many good plants to include in a garden that it is a shame to devote more than a small compartment to schemes of such finite interest. Furthermore, not all herbs will thrive in the same conditions.

My preference is to see aromatic plants of all kinds distributed throughout the garden. Position rosemary (*Rosmarinus officinalis*) where you brush against its linear leaves, grow thymes (*Thymus*) wherever they will be crushed by light treading, surround a seat with lavender (*Lavandula*) so you can pinch the leaves as well as enjoy the flowers, and cherish the alpine mint bush (*Prostanthera cuneata*) in a warm sunny spot where you yourself will want to linger. Do not plant your own balsam poplar (*Populus balsamifera*), but enjoy, if you can, the exquisite invasion of your privacy as the unfolding leaves of a neighbor's tree scent the air. Whether your garden is large or small, it is worth having a collection of aromatic plants in containers. The stars for this are the scented-leaved pelargoniums, which are easy plants, although they need winter protection. The range of fragrances in the beautifully textured and colored leaves holds many surprises – a refined rose scent in *Pelargonium* "Attar of Roses," lavender in *P. dichondrifolium*, and orange citric in *P.* "Prince of Orange."

Movement

We do not generally pay much attention to the self-generated movements of plants. The most important are those relating to growth: at an elemental level the roots respond to gravity and grow downward while the stems and leaves respond to light and grow skyward. More sophisticated is the coiling of tendrils, with touch stimulation prompting one side of a stem to grow more rapidly than another. Unseen, the stomata or breathing pores open and close, controlling the passage of gases in and out of the leaves. Other movements include the orientation of leaves to the light and the drooping or rolling of leaves in heat to slow down water loss. A small number of plants go one step farther toward animal-like movement. The Venus flytrap (*Dionaea mascipula*) snaps shut its hinged leaves when triggered by the movement of an insect, and the sensitive plant (*Mimosa pudica*), an annual or short-lived perennial, closes the segments of its four leaflets when touched.

These movements are all in their way remarkable, but what counts most for effect in the garden are leaves moving in wind. I have already made the point that a drawback of some planting schemes, notably combinations of dwarf conifers, heaths, and heathers, is that they are so static, even a rate of growth being difficult to register. This is a shortcoming, too, of bedding schemes using compact flowering and foliage plants. Fortunately, most mixed plantings include different kinds of foliage, some or all of which yields to a breeze. The movement, sometimes in unison, more often wavelike and sometimes even syncopated, is pleasing in itself. But it also creates shifting patterns of light and shade, and a sudden gust turning leaves all one way to show their underside can make contrasts as dramatic as those produced by the flashing movement of schools of fish or flocks of birds.

Leaves hanging by slender leaf stalks move in the lightest breeze. The aspens (*Populus tremula* and *P. tremuloides*) are quivering landscape trees. So, too, is the pendulous silver linden (*Tilia* "Petiolaris"), the silver backing of the leaves flashing as they turn in the wind, an effect of great beauty on many trees and shrubs where the reverse of the leaves is lighter than the upper surface. The birches (*Betula*) are more suitable for gardens, and they have light foliage that moves freely. In weeping trees, including *B. pendula* "Tristis," the foliage is carried by the sweeping movement of the trailing branches. Autumn gales denude deciduous trees and shrubs of their finery, but odd pennants fluttering gallantly are vivid markers of woody skeletons.

The scale of trees and shrubs makes the movement of their leaves very conspicuous. Among the smaller plants animating the lower levels of the garden, the grasses stand out, their fluid blades moving at a different tempo from the stiffer flowering stems, and seething in a stiff breeze. My choice for lively movement are species of the grass *Miscanthus*, a superb giant being *M. floridulus*. The pampas grasses (deserving more than a suburban reputation) make heaving clumps, the cross-

Below: The fans of the palm *Trachycarpus wagnerianus*, like those of the better-known Chusan palm (*T. fortunei*), rattle drily when they are stirred by a breeze.

Above: Choosing the right bamboo is important, for some forms spread rampantly. The larger species produce some of the most pleasing effects of movement and sound in the garden.

cutting arches of *Cortaderia selloana* "Aureolineata" enlivened by the yellow margins of the leaves. Nearer to ground level, the ribbons of Bowles' golden grass (*Milium effusum* "Aureum") flutter brightly.

Sound

With movement comes sound. The most remarkable noises produced by plants are caused by growth. It is said that in ideal conditions, a grove of the giant timber bamboo (*Phyllostachys bambusoides*) is filled with weird groans and shrieks produced by friction between the rapidly growing shoots and their sheaths and bracts. In the garden it is foliage, stirring lightly or heaving tumultuously, that provides the chamber music or symphonic background to the sounds of falling water or birdsong. It can also help to blank out the intrusive noise of traffic. Most of us are content to accept the sound values of foliage that we have chosen for reasons of color, texture, shape, and size. But it is not too fantastical to imagine an "audio garden" planted with more deliberation to exploit differences between, say, the murmuring of bamboos, the swishing of New Zealand flaxes (*Phormium*), the dry rustling of grasses, the sighing of pines, and the rattling of the palm *Trachycarpus fortunei*.

Left: The emerging leaves of *Paeonia mlokosewitschii*, at first like purple-pink clenched fists thrusting through the ground, are eye-catching for several weeks, and the foliage is attractive even in its more sober maturity. Molly-the-witch, as this species is sometimes known, bears short-lived but exquisite pale yellow goblet flowers.

Below: *Sorbus sargentiana*, a small-to-medium deciduous tree, has conspicuous winter buds that are red and sticky. When the leaves are fully developed, they can be 14in/35cm long. In fall they turn from dark green to vivid red.

the seasons

In the garden, as in natural landscapes, changes to foliage are decisive markers of the seasons. Outside the tropics and subtropics, all the developments in the garden, including the dam-burst of spring blossom and the sustained crescendo of summer flowering, are in some sense overshadowed by the primal drama of deciduous leaf growth and leaf fall. These great climaxes are not, in fact, events, but processes made up of innumerable little incidents, some synchronized, others apparently out of step, set against the slower, almost imperceptible pace at which evergreen plants change. The challenge for gardeners is to make a concert in which many different rhythms work as a pleasing whole through all four seasons.

Spring

If only one concentrated hard enough, surely it would be possible to see spring growth in action. That is the feeling I get as seedlings green the rows of the vegetable garden, perennials heave in the bed, ferns uncoil in shady corners, and the buds of deciduous trees and shrubs break. The process is as measured and miraculous as the emergence of a butterfly from its chrysalis. For each species the compression and intricate folding of the leaf tissues is unique, as is the way the meticulous pleats loosen, the tight balls unravel, or the leaflets open out like the pages of a book. It is rejuvenating simply to observe. And it is as beautiful in a flowerbed, where bare earth is steadily covered by expanding clumps of foliage, as in deciduous woodland.

No greens are ever more tender than those of spring. Uncertain but brilliant flashes of sunshine show the translucent vulnerability of an expanding deciduous canopy. In evergreen trees and shrubs, the new growth forms a light green overlay on the darker substratum of old growth. Spring green often has a marked yellow bias, the correcting process occurring as the leaves gain body.

Above: A simple formula in a summer garden exploits contrasts in color between plants with similar leaf shapes. In the foreground is a purple-leaved form of the New Zealand cabbage palm (*Cordyline australis*) and behind it the red-flowered *Crocosmia* "Lucifer."

Sometimes there is an overlay of bronze, pink, or red tints. These are most appealing when there is a contrast between green and the masking pigment. Most of the barrenworts (*Epimedium*) show this well. One of the loveliest of these shade-tolerant perennials, *E.* x *rubrum*, has green veins that seem to feed their color into the copper-red of the new leaves. Delicate pink, as found in *Acer negundo* "Flamingo," is usually a prelude to cream variegation. The reds and purples are the strongest of the spring foliage colors, verging on vivid overstatement in shrubs such as *Pieris* "Forest Flame."

Summer

Summer is the season when we risk not seeing foliage for the flowers, even though it is when most leaves achieve their ultimate fullness. Nonetheless, it is a time of the year when foliage is of great practical value and where its ornamental qualities can be at their peak. It is the season when we are most grateful for shade. Trees are not necessarily the answer; indeed, it is quicker and easier to create a finite area of shade by training climbers over an arbor or arch. And in this outdoor season, we are always grateful for the privacy that can be afforded by clipped foliage or dense informal hedges.

A week or two after midsummer is a good moment to make judgments about summer foliage, preferably in someone else's garden and before you have made planting decisions you might regret. You would expect the gray foliage of artemisias, santolinas, and other silvery plants to come into its own, calming strident flower color and making peace where there might be color clashes. The grays do well in dry, sunny gardens, but you can use greens just as effectively as linking and buffer plants, and it will be easier to find a choice of these for moist and shady areas of the garden. Check the performance of plants that delighted early in the season with their clean variegation or clear yellows. If they have faded, does their short season warrant giving them frontal or dominant positions? Look at the way the color and texture of foliage affects the balance of tones. Yellow foliage may seem too bright while the richness of purple foliage may weigh down parts of the garden and intensify the gloom of gray days.

Fall

When deciduous trees and shrubs color well, fall is a splendid culminating moment in the foliage year, although one that always has a keen edge to it. Even on a calm bright day when the brilliant disintegration seems in a state of suspension, there is a sense that time is ticking away. The broadest range of colors, the clearest yellows and the most intense scarlets, reds, purples, and oranges occur on acid rather than alkaline soils, especially where a continental climate gives hot summers and an early start to night frosts. In these conditions you can plant many deciduous trees and shrubs, confident that their summer green will catch fire and blaze before falling.

In a relatively mild maritime climate, cool moist summers followed by wet and windy falls can make for disappointing color changes, with a short-lived climax. There are reliable trees and shrubs, among them *Euonymus alatus*, and several outstanding climbers such as the Boston ivy (*Parthenocissus tricuspidata*) and *Vitis coignetiae*. But even allowing for these brilliant performers, in a soggy climate you cannot plan for a sensational fall garden, as you might, say, in eastern North America. It may be better to give preference to plants that might dazzle, but have other qualities that make them worth having even if their autumnal display fizzles out. The cherry *Prunus sargentii* is just the sort of small tree to look for. The young foliage is bronze red, making a good contrast to

Above: The particulars of the Japanese garden rarely translate well into Western gardens, but the originals contain valuable ideas for contrasts of deciduous and evergreen, here in a subtle autumnal phase, as well as natural and clipped shapes.

Right: The forms of *Acer japonicum* are less widely planted than those of another Japanese maple, *A palmatum*, but include superlative shrubs such as *A. j.* "Aconitifolium." Its leaves are deeply cut, and in the fall they glow with an inner fire.

the pink flowers. After a deep green summer phase, the leaves are among the first to turn and, at their best, are an intense orange or crimson. If you are lucky, there will be notable color changes at a lower level, too, with russet and brown livened by the yellow of hostas and crimson tints in *Ceratostigma plumbaginoides*.

Winter

The dearth of flowers in winter means that this is the season when you cannot help noticing foliage or the lack of it. Evergreens really do count, partly because of their value as windbreaks and material for hedging, partly because the character of their foliage and the form in which it is presented are so impressive ornamentally. Most are trees and shrubs, but there are good evergreen perennials such as bergenias and the hart's-tongue fern (*Asplenium scolopendrium*). A striking perennial to mix with the earliest bulbs is *Arum italicum* subsp. *italicum* "Marmoratum," the arrow- or spear-shaped leaves veined in ivory.

I feel perfectly happy with a winter garden dominated by shades of green. The range can include the finely textured dark green of yew (*Taxus baccata*), the glittering dark green of hollies such as *Ilex* x *altaclarensis* "Camelliifolia," the brighter greens of bamboos and the cherry laurel (*Prunus laurocerasus*), not to mention that of lawns and the tawny greens of longer grass. If you want a wider range of colors, there is plenty to choose from among trees and shrubs, many of them conifers, with variegated, gold, silvery, or blue foliage. In cold weather yellows may take on old-gold tints and greens turn purple-bronze, as they do in *Cryptomeria japonica* "Elegans." Contrasts of foliage color are easily overdone, and my preference is to see them used sparingly within a context of calm greens.

Two trees, hornbeam (*Carpinus betulus*) and beech (*Fagus sylvatica*), if clipped as hedges in later summer, retain their leaves throughout winter. Their russet makes a less forced contrast with greens than other colors, warming the garden even in bleak weather. This color theme can be extended by retaining until late winter the dead foliage and seedheads of perennials, especially grasses, and the brown fertile fronds of ferns such as *Matteuccia struthiopteris*. Low lighting shows up their rich textures, most tellingly when they are powdered with snow or rimmed with frost.

Right: Despite its name, the heavenly bamboo (*Nandina domestica*) is not a bamboo at all, but an evergreen flowering shrub. Even without its flowers and fruit, the species and its compact forms are handsome plants, with leaves that color bright red in the fall and winter.

selected foliage plants

The following is a selection of more than one thousand plants that are worth growing for the ornamental value of their leaves. In many cases the foliage is appealing on several counts and a high proportion of the plants described warrant a place in gardens because they display a range of decorative qualities. Most of the plants described are readily available from nurseries and garden centers. The relatively small number than are less common are usually no more difficult to grow than familiar plants and are likely to be seen more widely as they become better known. Gardeners interested in propagating their own stocks should remember that in most cases selected forms will not come true from seed and these forms must be propagated vegetatively, for example by division or from cuttings. There are plants here for a wide range of conditions. The most demanding for those in cool regions are the borrowings from tropical and subtropical gardens which will need protecting from frost between fall and spring.

Plant hardiness zones are given in [ ] after each entry; [A] indicates annual.

Left: The faceted depths of *Agave victoriae-reginae* are composed of keeled succulent leaves outlined in white.

Trees & shrubs

This section covers broad-leaved plants with a woody frame (for Conifers, see page 136). A surprising number of the plants listed develop as either small trees or large shrubs, which is a good reason for bringing together these important groups of ornamentals.

ACER Mainly deciduous trees and shrubs of woodland, most with leaves consisting of a fan of lobes or leaflets. The "Japanese maples" belong to two elegant species, *A. japonicum* [5–8] and *A. palmatum* [5–8], which are large shrubs or small trees. *A. japonicum* has relatively large flowers for the genus but the leaves, with rounded lobes, are the main feature and color red in fall. "Aconitifolium" has deeply divided and cut foliage while the leaves of "Vitifolium," the lobes shallow and toothed, provide some of the richest fall colors. All cultivars of *A. palmatum* color well in fall. "Osakazuki" turns brilliant scarlet; "Sango-kaku" yellow on coral stems. Those with finely dissected leaves are mound-shaped, var. *dissectum* Dissectum Viride Group with bright green leaves in summer. Dissectum Atropurpureum Group has purple foliage. Other purple-leaved cultivars include *A. p.* "Tamukeyama," a good choice where there is a risk of leaf scorch in hot summers; the larger-leaved "Bloodgood," and several with very finely cut leaves, including "Burgundy Lace" and "Garnet". "Corallinum" has young leaves of arresting pink. "Butterfly," of rather feeble delicacy, is variegated white and pink on gray-green. The slow-growing *A. shirasawanum* "Aureum" [5–7] is in the same mold as *A. japonicum*, each pale yellow leaf a fan of 7-11 shallow lobes, turning red in fall. The box elder, *A. negundo* [5–8], is a small to medium-sized tree with striking variegated forms, "Variegatum" having white-edged leaves, "Flamingo" a mixture of pink and white. The Norway maple, *A. platanoides* [3–7], a large tree with broad leaves that have 3-5 lobes, has a striking white-variegated form, "Drummondii," and several with purple foliage, including "Crimson King." *A. pseudoplatanus*

"Brilliantissimum" [4–7] is a small to medium-sized sycamore, leaves bright pink in spring, then yellow and green. Many maples provide magnificent fall color, among them the red maple, *A. rubrum* [3–9], the closely related and columnar *A.* "Scanlon" [3–9] and the larger sugar maple, *A. saccharum* [4–8]. Other fine species include the Cappadocian maple, *A. cappadocicum* (FH), yellow in fall; the large-leaved *A. macrophyllum* [5–7]; the striped maple, *A. pensylvanicum* [(3–7], and the paper-bark maple, *A. griseum* [4–7], both with attractive bark and foliage.

AEONIUM Succulents, some with woody bases, the stems terminating in attractive leaf rosettes. Good container plants to move outdoors in summer. *A.* "Zwartkop" [9–10], 2ft/60cm high, has rosettes of spoon-shaped black-purple leaves radiating from a green ember-like center.

AESCULUS Horse chestnuts and buckeyes are deciduous shrubs and usually large trees, often magnificent in flower and with handsome foliage, the compound leaves of most consisting of a fan of 5-7 leaflets. The horse chestnut, *A. hippocastanum* [3–8], sets the pattern, with splendid upright flower candles and large leaves; conspicuously veined leaflets often over 12in/30cm long. The size of this tree and most other species rules them out for general planting. The sunrise horse chestnut, *A. x neglecta* "Erythroblastos" [5–8], is a more manageable small to medium tree, its red-stalked compound leaves opening brilliant pink, then turning yellow and later green. The bottlebrush buckeye, *A. parviflora* [5–9], is a suckering shrub to 10ft/3m high, with attractive leaves bronze when young; white flowers.

AILANTHUS The fast-growing deciduous tree of heaven, *A. altissima* [4–8], has pinnate leaves up to 2ft/60cm long. Reddish fruits like those of ash. Can be cut back and kept as a large-leaved shrub.

ALNUS Alder Deciduous trees and shrubs tolerant of wet conditions. *A. glutinosa* "Imperialis" [4–7], graceful mid-height version of common alder, conical in shape with feathery, deeply cut leaves.

AMELANCHIER Snowy mespilus Deciduous shrubs and small trees showing strong family resemblance; prefer lime-free soil. Masses of white flowers in spring accompanied by bronze young leaves; blue-black edible fruit with foliage that turns orange and red in fall. *A. lamarckii* [5–8] usually develops into a small tree; copper-red young leaves covered with silky hairs.

ARALIA Japanese angelica tree Compound leaves, doubly divided and up to 4ft/1.2m long, are the outstanding feature of the spiny *A. elata* [4–9], with frothy clusters of cream flowers in fall. Plain-leaved form, up to 30ft/9m high, eclipsed by less vigorous "Variegata" and "Aureovariegata". Both have creamy white leaf margins later in season but in spring the former's variegation is yellow.

ARBUTUS Strawberry tree Characterful evergreen large shrubs and trees of irregular outline, some with attractive bark. *A. unedo* [7–9], gnarled shrub or small tree with leathery toothed and glossy leaves which stand out against trunks of shredding red-brown bark. Pink or white pitcher-shaped flowers and strawberry-like fruit. The Grecian strawberry tree, *A. andrachne* [8–9], usually has dark green entire leaves; those of hybrid *A.* x *andrachnoides* [8–9] are closer to those of *A. unedo*. All lime-tolerant to some degree. Shrubby Californian madrono, *A. menziesii* [7–9], needs acid soil; dark green leaves set against shiny red-brown bark.

ARCTOSTAPHYLOS Evergreen shrubs and small trees for lime-free soils. Low mat-forming species include the dune manzanita, *A. pumila* [8–10], with small, downy, spoon-shaped leaves, and the common bearberry, *A. uva-ursi* [2–6], with leathery dark green leaves. Fruits often 12ft/3.7m, has sea-green leathery leaves, red-brown flaking bark, and small pitcher-shaped white or pink flowers.

AUCUBA Spotted laurel, *A. japonica* [7–9], evergreen shrub up to 10ft/3m high that survives in wide range of conditions. Bright red berries on female contrast with large, glossy mid-green leaves, lightly toothed. Best-known cultivars are variegated: female "Crotonifolia" has yellow-speckled leaves. The male "Lance Leaf" and female f. *longifolia* "Salicifolia" are plain and lance-leaved, "Rozannie" compact and rounded.

BALLOTA Shrubby bushes about 30in/75cm high with attractive felted leaves, suitable for sunny gardens with well-drained soil. Flowers inconspicuous. *B. pseudodictamnus* [8–9] has woolly white stems and round to ovate leaves, the upper surfaces gray-green with a yellow tint, undersides white. *B. acetabulosa* [[8–9] has less woolly stems and heart-shaped leaves. *B.* "All Hallows Green" [8–9] is compact, heart-shaped leaves lime-green.

BERBERIS Barberry Large group of deciduous and evergreen shrubs, mostly spiny. Leaves arranged in rosette-like clusters and flowers in narrow color range, yellow to orange. Many bear large crops of colorful fruits. Several evergreens have glossy foliage: *B. calliantha* [7–9], has holly-like spiny leaves nearly white on the underside and makes a bush 30in/75cm high. The foliage of many deciduous species colors well in fall. Outstanding is *B. thunbergii* [5–8], a compact shrub for lime-free soil whose light green leaves turn vivid red, followed by long-lasting scarlet berries. Purple-leaved f. *atropurpurea* richly colored in fall, as is dwarf, dome-shaped "Bagatelle." "Rose Glow" has purple leaves flecked pink and white; "Golden Ring" has purple leaves with a narrow green-yellow margin.

BETULA Birch Graceful deciduous trees and shrubs. Leaves, often diamond-shaped, usually turn yellow in fall. The conical monarch birch, *B. maximowicziana* [6–8], up to 70ft/22m high; its large, heart-shaped, deep green leaves turn butter-yellow in fall and its bark, gray-white with tints of orange and pink, peels in horizontal strips. Silver birch, *B. pendula* [3–6], is a slightly taller conical tree whose branchlets hang elegantly; diamond-shaped, toothed leaves move freely in a breeze. Dark cracks and crests show up against startling white bark. Variations in shape include stiffly upright "Fastigiata," narrowly symmetrical and weeping "Tristis" and mushroom-headed, weeping "Youngii." The weeping Swedish birch, "Laciniata," has deeply cut leaves.

BRACHYGLOTTIS Sun-loving evergreen trees and shrubs, very useful in seaside gardens. *B.* (Dunedin Group) "Sunshine" [9–10], a sprawling shrub with silver-gray, later gray-green leaves, downy white undersides. White-felted flower buds and brash yellow daisies. *B. repanda* [9–10], to 10ft/3m, has white felting on all young growths; large green leaves, wavy and jagged at the margins, downy white on the underside. *B. monroi* also has wavy leaves.

BUDDLEJA Most are deciduous shrubs grown for their densely clustered, often fragrant flowers. Interesting foliage species include *B. alternifolia* [5–9], with leaves unusually arranged alternately; makes attractive small weeping tree when trained as standard, with arching stems wreathed in mauve flowers in early summer. *B. fallowiana* [8–9], a spreading shrub up to 8ft/2.5m high, makes a soft gray fountain of arching growth; gray-white lance-shaped leaves have dense white-felted undersides. Cones of blue-mauve flowers with orange

eyes in late summer and fall; var. *alba* a study in white and grays. Hybrid *B.* "Lochinch" [6–9], similar in scale and leaf color. *B. crispa* [8–9], often wall-trained, is more markedly white woolly with cylindrical spikes of strongly scented mauve flowers. All like full sun and well-drained soil, and tolerate lime. Butterfly bush, *B. davidii* [5–9], will even grow on building rubble. Variegated "Harlequin" has yellow-margined leaves and red-purple flowers.

BUXUS Box Unclipped specimens of the common box, *B. sempervirens* [6–8], can make untidy bushes over 15ft/4.5m tall but its small leaves make classic material for hedging and topiary; regular trimming results in dense, deep green shapes. Variegated forms include "Elegantissima," with narrow leaves edged in white, and "Latifolia Maculata," whose large leaves are yellow when young, later green blotched yellow. "Rotundifolia" has rounded leaves; "Suffruticosa" is slow-growing and compact. Small-leaved box, *B. microphylla* [5–8], very slow-growing; "Green Pillow" makes tight mounds or domes.

CALLUNA Heather or ling *C. vulgaris* [5–7], colonizes vast areas of heathland. In late summer and fall the dark evergreen linear foliage, lying flat along stems, is overwhelmed by a tide of purple flowers. Hundreds of cultivars, 10-18in/25-45cm high, much used as ground cover on lime-free soils. "Darkness," dark green with crimson flowers; "Foxii Nana," tidy mounds 6in/15cm high of bright green foliage with sparse mauve flowers. "Silver Knight" has gray foliage that turns purplish in winter; many, like "Sir John Charrington," have yellow leaves turning orange-red in winter.

CAMELLIA In the first rank of flowering shrubs, their beauty is completed by highly polished evergreen leaves. *C. japonica* [7–9], which eventually forms a tree 20ft/6m or more high, is represented in gardens by numerous cultivars, compact or spreading. Dark green leaves broadly elliptic, pointed at the tip and finely toothed. Flowers vary in form, the color range covering white, pinks, and reds. *C.* x *williamsii* cultivars [7–9] have similar leaves of brighter green. Those of *C. reticulata* [7–9] are less polished and show a network of veins. All need humus-rich acid soil, moist but well-drained, and do best in sheltered dappled shade.

CARPINUS Hornbeam Deciduous trees with prominently veined leaves borne on zigzag twigs and hop-like fruit clusters in late summer and fall. Common hornbeam,

C. betulus [4–8], superb for hedges, clipped plants retaining their russet-brown dead leaves all winter. Trees can reach 80ft/25m, but attractive as specimens or in woodland for gray-fluted bark and copious foliage, the ovate mid-green leaves ribbed and unequally toothed. "Fastigiata" starts as a narrow column but becomes neatly conical. American hornbeam, C. caroliniana [3–9], a small to medium tree with smooth gray bark, has polished blue-green leaves that turn yellow and orange in fall.

CATALPA Indian bean tree C. bignonioides [5–9] makes a round-headed tree 50ft/15m high, with large heart-shaped leaves, foxglove flowers in midsummer and long drooping beans to follow. Leaves of "Aurea" bronze, then yellow and, by flowering time, lime green. Does best in sheltered position in sun and moist soil. Cut back to near ground level in early spring for extra-large leaves.

CERCIDIPHYLLUM C. magnificum [4–8], a deciduous tree that succeeds in woodland conditions on neutral to acid soils; grows to 25ft/7.5m, tiny red flowers. Heart-shaped leaves, up to 5in/12cm long with serrated edge, open bronze and color yellow, orange and red in fall. C. japonicum [4–8] also colors well in fall.

CERCIS Small genus, most species with heart- or kidney-shaped leaves and thickly clustered pink or mauve flowers in spring. Eastern redbud, C. canadensis [4–9], heart-shaped leaves, pointed at the tip; they open bronze before turning green, then color yellow in fall. "Forest Pansy" gives a stronger foliage effect, the leaves deep reddish purple. Cut back in early spring to encourage extra-large leaves.

CHOISYA Mexican orange blossom, C. ternata [7–9], evergreen aromatic shrub making dark green mound up to 8ft/2.5m high, spangled in spring and fall with scented white flowers; polished leaves are divided into 3 leaflets; "Sundance" has sickly yellow foliage. C. "Aztec Pearl" [7–10], slightly smaller, has leaves composed of 5-7 narrow segments.

CONVOLVULUS Many species are trailing perennials but C. cneorum [8–10] an evergreen shrub, up to 3ft/90cm high, for full sun on well-drained soil. Its refinement lies in the silvery silkiness of its foliage and its elegant, funnel-shaped flowers, pink tinted in bud and white with yellow centers.

CORDYLINE Several species, particularly C. fruticosa [10–11], much used in tropical and subtropical gardens for their bold lance-shaped leaves and range of color forms. New Zealand cabbage palm, C. australis [9–10], strikes a tropical note in temperate gardens; can grow to 30ft/9m or more but generally much shorter, especially when container grown. Mature specimens have plumes of heavily scented white flowers. Leaves sword-like, matte green, making large tufts at ends of branches. Variegated forms: "Torbay Dazzler," with leaves striped cream; "Albertii," green, cream, red, and pink. Purpurea Group have purple leaves and there are red-leaved forms like "Torbay Red." C. indivisa [9–10] has broader leaves.

CORNUS Dogwoods Deciduous trees and shrubs needing neutral to acid soils but offering varied ornamental qualities; they include several fine variegated plants. C. alba "Elegantissima" [2–7], medium-sized shrub, white-edged gray-green leaves; "Spaethii" has a warmer variegation. Variegated pagoda dogwood, C. alternifolia "Argentea" [4–7], one of the finest small deciduous trees; tiered branches carry layers of silvered foliage. C. controversa "Variegata" [5–8], slightly larger tree with tiered branches and distinct contrast of green and white. Bracts surrounding flowers a major ornamental feature. Flowering dogwood, C. florida [5–8], a large shrub or small tree with 4 white to pink bracts surrounding insignificant flower clusters; foliage colors well in fall. "Cherokee Chief" has red-pink bracts with darker veining. Foliage of C. kousa [5–8], a shrub of similar scale, also takes on rich fall tones and flower clusters are surrounded by white or, in "Satomi," pink bracts; var. chinensis has tapered bracts. Conspicuous bracts also a feature of the Pacific dogwood, C. nuttallii [7–8], a medium-sized tree, and C. "Eddie's White Wonder" [5–8], usually a large, multi-stemmed shrub with foliage that colors well in fall.

CORYLUS Hazel C. avellana [3–9], a deciduous large shrub or small tree, with heart-shaped leaves that turn yellow in fall and, before the leaves develop, dangling catkins. "Contorta," corkscrew hazel, has twisted shoots and leaves; "Aurea" is brighter, with yellow young leaves. A striking contrast is the filbert's purple-leaved form, C. maxima "Purpurea" [5–8]. Cut both back hard in early spring for extra-large leaves. Turkish hazel, C. colurna [5–7], a medium-large tree remarkable for its pyramidal shape. All thrive on alkaline soils.

COTINUS Smoke bush Deciduous shrubs or trees owing common name to the wispy plumes, often pink-tinged, surrounding flowers and fruit. C. coggygria [4–8] bushy shrub up to 15ft/4.5m tall, with oval mid-green leaves that color brilliantly in fall. "Royal Purple" deep red-purple changing to vivid scarlet before leaf fall, as does the hybrid C. "Grace" [5–8], growing to 20ft/6m high, and C. "Flame" [5–8], light green in summer and furnace-red in fall. Cut back hard in spring to get maximum foliage effect.

COTONEASTER Many grown for their colorful berries, but the foliage and habit of growth add to their appeal. Deciduous C. horizontalis [5–7] has a herringbone arrangement of branches; stems neatly set with small, rounded dark green leaves, which turn red in fall when berries are glowing. C. atropurpureus "Variegatus" [5–7] is similar, with white-edged leaves. C. dammeri [6–8], one of several evergreen prostrate species; C. congestus [7-8] another, forming a tight mound 2ft/60cm high, studded with red berries in fall.

CRATAEGUS Hawthorn Genus with many small to medium-sized trees that tolerate a wide range of conditions. C. persimilis "Prunifolia" [6–7], all-rounder, makes a thorny, rounded tree up to 30ft/9m high; densely covered with glossy oval leaves, deep green in summer, orange and red in fall. White blossoms in early summer and red fruit in fall.

DAPHNE The stars are shrubs with sweetly scented flowers, some with variagated leaves. Evergreen D. odora [7–9] makes a dark green mound less than 5ft/1.5m high, brightened by purple-pink and white flowers in winter; "Aureomarginata" has glossy leathery leaves with an irregular yellow margin. Spurge laurel, D. laureola [7–8], a shorter but spreading evergreen, makes good ground cover, even in deep shade; its leathery glossy leaves are inversely lance-shaped. Clusters of slightly scented yellow-green flowers and black berries.

DAVIDIA Dove tree, handkerchief tree D. involucrata [6–8], an elegant medium-sized deciduous tree with conspicuous white bracts lining its branches when the leaves have already opened. Insignificant flowers are surrounded by 2 bracts of unequal size.

DISANTHUS D. cercidifolius [5–8], a woodland shrub up to 10ft/3m high that thrives in moist, well-drained, lime-free soil with tiny purplish flowers in fall. Heart-shaped leaves blue-green in summer and in fall yellow, soft crimson and wine red.

ELAEAGNUS Evergreen and deciduous shrubs with attractive foliage and small bell-shaped flowers, in most species fragrant. Young leaves, the undersides of mature leaves and sometimes stems and flowers have a silver or bronze scaliness. Evergreens do well in coastal gardens. Deciduous *E.* **"Quicksilver"** [3–10] like a very silvery form of the oleaster, *E. angustifolia* [2–10]. A spiny shrub or small tree with tapered, willow-like leaves and as a standard a good substitute for *Pyrus salicifolia* "Pendula" [5–7]. *E. x ebbingei* [7–9], an evergreen spreading shrub with scaly leaves that are particularly silvery on the underside; scented flowers in fall. Fine cultivars include **"Gilt Edge,"** with yellow edging to the green center, and **"Limelight,"** with silvery young leaves, later splashed with yellow and soft green. Evergreen *E. pungens* [7–9], a slightly spiny shrub to 12ft/3.7m, densely covered with polished dark green oblong to elliptic leaves, usually with a wavy margin; small flowers followed by red fruits. Best known for variegated forms such as **"Goldrim,"** with yellow leaf margins, and **"Maculata,"** leaves with rich yellow centers. **"Frederici,"** a compact version with small narrow leaves, yellow centered.

ENKIANTHUS Small genus of deciduous trees and shrubs, all needing lime-free soil, with flowers of subtle beauty and leaves coloring richly in fall. *E. campanulatus* [5–8], tree-like with creamy yellow pink-veined flowers whose leaves cover the red to yellow spectrum in fall. *E. perrulatus* [6–8], smaller, with white flowers and foliage turning brilliant red.

ERICA Heath Genus includes many dwarf evergreen shrubs with linear leaves and numerous small bell-shaped flowers; most require lime-free soil. Winter heath, *E. carnea* [5–7], makes dense mound or mat spreading up to 20in/50cm, its leaves dark green and flowers purple-pink. Numerous cultivars include some with foliage in shades of yellow, orange, red and bronze, the stronger colors developing in fall and winter. **"Foxhollow,"** yellow-green in summer, orange-red in cold weather; unfortunately pink-flowered. **"Vivellii,"** with carmine flowers and bronze leaves in winter. The cross-leaved heath, *E. tetralix* [5–7], dwarf species with gray-green leaves; **"Alba Mollis,"** silver-gray leaves and white flowers.

ERIOBOTRYA Loquat *E. japonica* [8–10], medium-sized tree producing orange-yellow edible fruit but in cooler regions grown as a large shrub for its evergreen foliage, which conveys an impression of subtropical luxuriance. Coarse stems making an open framework bear glossy leathery leaves, up to 12in/30cm long, and heavily veined.

EUCALYPTUS Eucalypts, Gums Evergreen trees and shrubs with hundreds of species, mostly natives of Australia. Many have beautiful aromatic foliage, in warm climates produce masses of white flowers, and the patchwork or shredding bark is often attractive. Young leaves often different in form from mature leathery leaves. Tasmanian blue gum, *E. globulus* [8–10], superb large tree, young leaves silvery blue and circular, mature leaves deep green and sickle-shaped. The cider gum, *E. gunnii* [8–10], with blue-green rounded young leaves and sickle-shaped sage-green mature leaves, also suitable for this regime. The snow gum, *E. pauciflora* subsp. *niphophila* [8–10], a small tree remarkable for its patchwork bark, forms a light canopy of blue-green lance- or sickle-shaped leaves. Many species, including *E. perrineana* [9–10], have lance-shaped mature leaves.

EUONYMUS The winged spindle, *E. alatus* [4–9], small deciduous tree that gets its common name from corky phlanges to its stems. Toothed leaves, dark green in summer, vivid dark red in fall, hang vertically. Fruits red-purple, splitting to show orange inside. Evergreen *E. fortunei* [4–9] cultivars different in character; can climb but usually grown as small shrubs. **"Emerald Gaiety"** and larger **"Silver Queen"** have dark green leaves with white variegation, often tinged pink in winter. **"Emerald 'n' Gold"** has yellow-variegated green leaves.

FAGUS Beech Deciduous trees suitable for planting in woodland or as isolated specimens. At 100ft/30m, a mature common beech, *F. sylvatica* [5–7], is too large for most gardens but has an impressive spreading crown. Ovate wavy-edged leaves, delicate pale green on opening, turn dark and lustrous and, in fall, yellow and copper-brown. The hanging branches of **"Pendula"** (weeping beech) make floor-length curtains of dense foliage. Fern-leaved beech (var. *heterophylla* "Aspleniifolia") has deeply cut foliage. **"Dawyck," "Dawyck Gold,"** and **"Dawyck Purple"** are columnar or flame-shaped cultivars. Other purple-leaved forms include very dark **"Riversii"** and cut-leaved **"Rohanii."** Common beech excellent for hedging, trimmed plants retain dead copper-brown leaves all winter.

FATSIA *F. japonica* [7–9], a spreading evergreen shrub up to 12ft/3.7m high, often grown in temperate gardens to create a subtropical atmosphere. Thrusts out large, dark green, fingered leathery leaves, wavy at the margins; **"Variegata,"** lobes have irregular cream tips. Tiny off-white flowers

form globular clusters in fall, followed by black berries. Tree ivy, x *Fatshedera lizei* [7–9], a cross between this species and an ivy, has glossy leathery leaves with 5 or 7 distinct lobes; **"Annemieke"** and **"Variegata,"** splashed or margined with creamy white.

FICUS see Fig (Edible plants)

FOTHERGILLA Witch hazel, *F. gardenii* [5–9], a deciduous woodland shrub of acid soils that grows to 3ft 3in/1m. Toothed oval leaves dark green until coloring brilliant shades of red, orange, and yellow in fall; bottlebrush clusters of petal-less white flowers appear before the leaves. **"Blue Mist"** develops its cool summer tone best when grown in shade but the species, and the taller *F. major* [5–8], flower most freely and produce the richest fall colors if grown in well-lit positions.

FRAXINUS Ash Fast-growing trees, mainly deciduous, that succeed in a wide range of conditions. *F. ornus* [6–9] and the Ornus Group have conspicuous flowers but other ashes grown principally for their attractive pinnate foliage. The claret ash, *F. angustifolia* **"Flame"** [6–9], which grows dense and upright to 60ft/18m, dark green in summer then plum-purple. The common ash, *F. excelsior* [5–8], a magnificent large tree with several interesting forms, including vigorous **"Jaspidea,"** with yellow shoots and clear yellow leaves in fall, and the weeping ash, **"Pendula,"** less tall but wide spreading, with trailing branches to the ground. *F. pennsylvanica* **"Summit"** [4–9], medium-sized upright tree with glossy leaves, rich yellow in fall.

FUCHSIA Most hybrid fuchsias in general cultivation are deciduous shrubs, valued for their ballerina-shaped dangling flowers. Several cultivars, including *F.* **"Genii"** [9–10], have yellow to lime-green foliage; hybrids of *F. triphylla* have purple-backed leaves, in the case of *F.* **"Gartenmeister Bonstedt"** [9–10] bronze-red on upper surface. *F. magellanica* **"Versicolor"** [7–9], variegated shrub that can be treated as a perennial growing to 3ft 3in/1m in a season. The arching stems are well-covered with tapered leaves, soft pink when young and when mature subdued gray-green, livened by cream and pink. The flowers are crimson. *F. m.* var. *molinae* **"Sharpitor"** [7–9] has pale mauve and white flowers and gray-green leaves with white edging.

GLEDITSIA Deciduous thorny trees with insignificant flowers but conspicuous seed pods; ferny foliage is beautiful in several cases. The honey locust, *G. triacanthos*

[3–7], a handsome large tree, drought-tolerant when mature, with dark green leaves 10in/25cm long, divided into numerous leaflets; they turn yellow in fall. In cultivation often replaced by less vigorous cultivars, though even these can grow to 40ft/12m, including thornless f. *inermis.* "Rubylace," leaves open bronze-red, later turning bronze-green. Thornless "Sunburst," yellow young leaves that become progressively greener.

GRISELINIA Broadleaf, *G. littoralis* [8–10], an evergreen shrub, tree-like in mild areas and suitable as a hedge plant; especially useful in sunny seaside gardens. Ovate leathery leaves bright green and glossy; "Dixon's Cream" leaves have irregular pale yellow centers.

HAMAMELIS Witch hazel Deciduous woodland shrubs valued for their fragrant spidery flowers in winter. The large Virginian witch hazel, *H. virginiana* [3–8], widely used as a rootstock for selected clones; has round leaves turning yellow in fall when yellow flowers have already opened. Best for fall color is *H. x intermedia* "Diane" [5–8], with dark red winter flowers.

HEBE Shrubby evergreens with ground-covering foliage and attractive flowers in summer, clustered in spikes or small heads. Several grown mainly for foliage; those with strong variegation, such as cream and green *H. x franciscana* "Variegata" [9–10], popular in container gardening. Several species under 2ft/60cm high are useful as edging. *H.* "Red Edge" [9–10], blue-gray leaves with red margins and veining which intensifies in winter. In early summer mauve flowers, which fade to white. Other compact hebes have blue-green leaves without contrasting red edge, including *H. pimelioides* "Quicksilver" [9–10], blue-mauve in flower, and *H. pinguifolia* "Pagei" [8–10], white. *H.* "Pewter Dome" [9–10], tight and compact, studded in spring and early summer with white flowers. Whipcord hebes have small scale-like leaves that hug the stems. *H. cupressoides* "Boughton Dome" [8–9] makes a regular shape packed with bright green leaves; slightly taller with more arching growth is *H. ochracea* "James Stirling" [8–10], with ocher-yellow leaves and small white flowers in late spring.

HELICHRYSUM Genus includes numerous evergreen shrubs and perennials with woolly or hairy leaves, adapted to hot, dry habitats. *H. italicum* [7–10], tidy aromatic plant 2ft/60cm high, its downy stems covered with narrow gray leaves and topped in summer with mustard-yellow flowers; more

compact curry plant, subsp. *serotinum,* even more aromatic. *H. petiolare* [10–11], trailing shrub with almost heart-shaped leaves, woolly and gray on upper surface, lighter on underside; used as an annual in bedding schemes and in containers. Other versions include "Limelight," with lime-green leaves, and "Variegatum," a subtle blend of cream and gray-green.

HYDRANGEA Flattened or dome-shaped flowerheads are an important feature of hydrangeas but some also have distinctive foliage. Those described all deciduous shrubs needing moist but well-drained soil; the larger-leaved species do best in partial shade. *H. aspera* subsp. *sargentiana* [6–9], upright bristly shrub growing to 10ft/3m, stems sparsely furnished with large dark green leaves, velvety on upper surface, paler and bristly on underside; heads of pink-mauve flowers. *H. a.* Villosa Group [7–9], more rounded, with narrower, lance-like leaves, dull green and bristly on upper surface, downy and gray on underside; flowers pale mauve. More marked color difference between upper and lower leaf surface found in *H. arborescens* subsp. *radiata* [4–9], a white-flowered erect shrub growing to 6ft/1.8m whose dark leaves have a dense cover of white hairs on undersides. The oak-leaved hydrangea, *H. quercifolia* [5–9], a medium shrub with distinctive lobed leaves up to 8in/20cm long that color bronze-purple in fall, as white cone-like flowerheads take on pink tints.

IDESIA Tiered deciduous tree *I. polycarpa* [6–9], to 40ft/12m, has glossy egg-shaped leaves on long reddish stalks. Green-yellow flowers and red berries on female plants.

ILEX Holly Large genus, including many evergreen trees and shrubs with spine-toothed or spiny leaves. Female plants need male nearby to produce berries. Common or English holly, *I. aquifolium* [7–9], an exceptionally versatile evergreen, tolerant of a wide range of conditions and excellent for hedging or uncomplicated topiary shapes. Makes a large shrub or tree, often pyramidal, with glossy dark green leaves with wavy margins and spines. Many cultivars, some among the most pleasing of variegated evergreens. "Golden Milkboy" (male), rich yellow splashes in leaf centers; "Golden van Tol" (female), leaves edged yellow. Purple-stemmed "Handsworth New Silver" (female), gray-mottled and and white-edged leaves. Hedgehog holly, "Ferox" (male) and its variegated forms, very prickly leaves. Hybrid *I. x altaclarensis* [5–9], similar to common holly, with variants including handsome plain-leaved "Camelliifolia" (female), more or less

spineless, and brightly variegated "Golden King" (female) with leaves edged in yellow. Horned holly, *I. cornuta* [7–9], to 12ft/3.7m, has almost rectangular spined leaves. Japanese or box-leaved holly, *I. crenata* [5–7], small or medium-sized shrub, good as a low hedge, with tiny glossy dark green, lightly scalloped leaves and black berries; "Convexa" (female) has bulging leaves. Blue hollies, *I. x meserveae* [5–9], medium-sized shrubs that do best in a continental climate; bear strong resemblance to common holly but spiny glossy leaves have a blue cast.

KALOPANAX Single maple-like species, *K. septemlobus* [5–9], small to medium-sized deciduous tree for a sheltered position in moist, well-drained soil. Leaves up to 12in/30cm across cut into fans, each with up to 7 sharply defined lobes; white flowers.

KOELREUTERIA The golden rain tree or pride of India, *K. paniculata* [5–9], small to medium-sized deciduous tree with a broad head of arching pinnate leaves, up to 18in/45cm long, composed of up to 15 leaflets; reddish pink on opening, mid-green through summer and clear yellow in fall. In areas with hot summers, yellow flowers and bladder-like seedpods.

LAURUS see Bay laurel (Edible plants)

LAVANDULA Lavender Evergreen shrubs or sub-shrubs mainly from Mediterranean region, showing strong family resemblance and preference for well-drained soil and sun. Rarely more than 3ft 3in/1m high, with spikes of fragrant, usually purple flowers, attractive to bees, and aromatic, more or less gray foliage. Trim in early spring. *L. x intermedia* [5–8] covers a range of hybrids between narrow-leaved *L. angustifolia* [5–8] and *L. latifolia* [6–8], with broader, often spoon-shaped leaves. Vary in height from 12in-3ft 3in/30-100cm and in hardiness; in shape, their gray-green leaves tend toward one or other parent. *L. x i.* Dutch Group [5–8], relatively broad gray leaves with long spikes of pale purple flowers. *L. lanata* [8–10], woollier and whiter, conspicuously so in hot dry summers, with violet-purple flowers. French lavender, *L. stoechas* [7–8], arrow-leaved, with ear-like bracts topping flower spikes. *L. dentata* [8–9] has gray-green toothed leaves.

LEUCOTHOE Switch ivy *L. walteri* [5–8], small to medium-sized evergreen shrub with arching stems carrying leathery, elegantly tapered green leaves which in fall and winter develop red and bronze tints; white lily-of-the-valley flowers in spring. Leaves of "Rainbow" mottled cream and pink. *L.* "Zeblid" similar but young foliage red-purple and turns bronze after green summer phase. All good ground cover for acid soils.

LIGUSTRUM Privet Genus includes some excellent foliage plants, though poorly maintained hedges of semi-evergreen *L. ovalifolium* [7–9] have tarnished their reputation. Golden privet, *L. o.* "Aureum" [5–7], usefully fast-growing, with broad yellow margins to the leaves, sometimes obliterating the green centers. Evergreen Chinese privet, *L lucidum* [7–10], best seen as a round-headed, symmetrical medium-sized tree growing to 30ft/10m. Oval pointed leaves, glossy dark green, show off sprays of white flowers late summer or early fall; fruits blue-black. "Excelsum Superbum" an eye-catching yellow-variegated form.

LIQUIDAMBAR Sweet gum, *L. styraciflua* [5–9], large tree making a symmetrical broad cone, with maple-like lobed leaves, though alternate not opposite, hanging more or less vertically from framework of branches and twigs. Their glossy summer green transformed into a brilliant fall display of orange, red, and purple, especially when grown in full sun. "Lane Roberts" has reliable fall color; "Worplesdon," deeply lobed leaves. Sweet gum unsuitable for shallow chalky soils.

LIRIODENDRON Tulip tree *L. tulipifera* [5–9], fast-growing specimen tree of conical to columnar shape to 100ft/30m. Three-lobed leaves cut across at tips to give a saddle-like outline; "Aureomarginatum," leaves have a broad yellow margin that becomes greener as summer advances. "Fastigiatum," narrow, upright branches. Distinctive leaf shape also found in Chinese species, *L. chinense* [7–9].

LOTUS Mixed group of plants with pea flowers includes several evergreen sub-shrubs of dry stony ground with distinctive foliage. Hairy canary clover, *L. hirsutus* [8–10], delightful lightweight usually less than 3ft 3in/1m high, notable for the silvery silkiness of its gray-green leaves, each composed of 5 leaflets; off-white flowers with a pink tinge followed by bronze seed-pods. Coral gem (*L. berthelotii*) [10–11], trailing plant, silver-gray leaves with 3-5 needle-like leaflets, much used in containers for its foliage and scarlet beak-like flowers.

LUPINUS Lupine Group of sub-shrubs or shrubs, also annuals and perennials, most with fingered leaves, often covered with fine hairs so that water drops on them turn to quicksilver. Evergreen tree lupine, *L. arboreus* [8–9], beautiful quick filler in sunny gardens with fast-draining soil, has silky gray-green leaves and yellow flower spikes; can grow to 6ft/1.8m. Smaller shrubs with leaves even more silvered by silky hairs include blue- or purple-flowered *L. albifrons* [9–10] and *L. chamissonis* [9–10], with flowers mixed white and blue-purple.

MAGNOLIA In many magnolias, leaves play a subordinate role to flowers of superlative quality but in a few species leaves and flower evenly matched. Wall-trained or freestanding, *M. grandiflora* [7–9] is a handsome tree with scented creamy white flowers, up to 10in/25cm across, nestling among large, leathery leaves of glossy dark green. Thick fine hairs on underside are rust-colored, markedly so in "Exmouth" and "Ferruginea." Deciduous great-leaved magnolia or umbrella tree, *M. macrophylla* [6–9], a giant in leaf and flower; thin leaves, light green with a silvery underside, up to 3ft 3in/1m long, with creamy white flowers more than 12in/30cm across; grows to 30ft/10m.

MAHONIA Evergreen shrubs, most with spiny pinnate leaves and yellow flowers followed by purple or blue-black berries. The Oregon grape, *M. aquifolium* [6–9], a suckering shrub useful as ground cover in sun or shade. Glossy, leathery leaves with up to 9 spiny leaflets dark green in summer, often purple-bronze in winter, markedly so in "Atropurpurea." *M.* x *wagneri* [5–8] similar to species but taller; "Undulata" has polished leaflets with wavy margins. *M. japonica* [7–8], upright shrub growing to 10ft/3m; from whorls of graphically jagged leaves spill sprays of scented yellow flowers in winter; holly-like leaflets may color bright red.

MALUS Crab apples Deciduous trees and shrubs with attractive spring blossom and colorful fruit; in some instances also colorful foliage, especially in fall. *M.* "Royalty" [5–8], small, wide-spreading tree with glossy red-purple leaves, the red coming through strongly in fall; purplish crimson flowers followed by deep red fruit. *M. trilobata* [5–8], medium-sized tree of upright growth, unusual among crabs in having lobed leaves with a toothed margin, glossy green in summer, yellow to red in fall. White flowers in early summer followed by green, sometimes red-flushed, fruit. *M. tschonoskii* [5–8], also upright and of conical shape, with mid-green glossy leaves that color brilliantly in fall; white blossoms and yellow-green fruit both tinged red-pink.

MELIANTHUS *M. major* [7–10], evergreen shrub capable of reaching 10ft/3m, sometimes treated as herbaceous plant. Its great beauty lies in jagged complexity of the large, glaucous-blue, pinnate leaves. Brown-red flowers in late spring.

MELIOSMA *M.veitchiorum* [9–10], slow-growing deciduous tree of great character to 30ft/9m. Prominent winter buds develop into large pinnate leaves, with up to 11 dark green leaflets, carried on red stalks; white flowers and violet fruit. Plant in a sheltered position in lime-free soil.

MUSA Bananas and plantains are evergreen perennials but their trunk-like stems give the appearance of trees. Most edible kinds are forms of *M. acuminata* [9–10]. Japanese banana, *M. basjoo* [8–10], produces unpalatable fruit but it is one of the hardiest, and its large paddle-like leaves, up to 10ft/3m long, distinctively tropical. It needs a sheltered position to reduce risk of wind damage to leaves. Creamy yellow flowers have brown bracts.

MYRTUS Myrtle Common myrtle, *M. communis* [8–9], aromatic shrub to 10ft/3m, with dark green glossy leaves. At margin of its range, worth growing at foot of a sunny wall. White flowers followed by purple-black fruits. "Variegata," gray-green leaves with creamy white margins; subsp. *tarentina* compact and free-flowering, with small narrow leaves; responds to trimming.

NANDINA Heavenly bamboo, *N. domestica* [6–9], an evergreen or semi-evergreen shrub with unbranched stems and large leaves divided into many narrow leaflets. Foliage purplish when young and richly burnished in fall and winter. Sprays of small white flowers in summer but showy red fruits produced after a hot summer. "Firepower," compact cultivar 18in/45cm high with red leaves in winter.

NYSSA Tupelo *N. sylvatica* [5–9], slow-growing deciduous tree that eventually makes a large cone or column with dense covering of glossy dark green leaves. Brilliant shades of yellow, orange and scarlet in fall. Chinese tupelo, *N. sinensis* [7–9], deciduous large shrub, its foliage, bronze-red when young, vivid shades of red in fall. For moist, lime-free soil.

OLEA Olive *O. europaea* [8–10], drought-tolerant and long-lived, eventually making a tree 30ft/9m high with a gnarled trunk supporting a rounded head of leathery gray-green leaves, silver-white on undersides.

OLEARIA Daisy bush Evergreen shrubs or small trees that stand up well to coastal conditions. White or cream flowerheads in profusion; several have distinctive foliage. The aromatic arorangi, *O. macrodonta* [8–10], growing to 20ft/6m, has white felted stems and sharply toothed gray-green leaves with silvery down on undersides.

OSMANTHUS Evergreen shrubs, several with wonderfully fragrant small white flowers; woodland plants but tolerant of sun as well as partial shade. Some have holly-like leaves, like *O. heterophyllus* [7–9] which can grow to 15ft/5m but is usually smaller and can be clipped for topiary or hedging. Leathery, shiny dark green leaves usually have sharp teeth but may have none at all. Leaves of "Variegatus" have white margins; young foliage of "Purpureus" is black-purple.

PARROTIA Persian ironwood, *P. persica* [5–8], deciduous spreading large shrub or short-trunked tree with glossy dark green pendulous leaves, up to 5in/12cm long and wavy at the margins. Rich orange-yellow and red-purple in fall. Small, spidery crimson flowers on bare stems in winter and attractive patchwork of flaking bark. Compact "Pendula" makes a dome of weeping branches, 10ft/3m high.

PAULOWNIA Foxglove tree *P. tomentosa* [5–8], gets common name from violet-purple flowers borne by mature trees in late spring. Large leaves, covered with a velvet pile, are a more certain ornamental feature. If cut back in early spring and generously fed, plants produce leaves up to 2ft/60cm across.

PHILADELPHUS Mock orange Richly scented white flowers in early summer are a hallmark but *P. coronarius* "Aureus" [5–8], a medium-sized deciduous shrub, also has bright yellow young leaves. These "burn" in full sun. "Variegatus" is compact; leaves have conspicuous white margins.

PHILLYREA Phillyria Once popular evergreens, now unfashionable because understated. *P. latifolia* [7–9], large shrub or small tree whose branches bow gracefully under the weight of dark green glossy foliage. Individual leaves small, oval and inconspicuously toothed. *P. angustifolia* [7–9], more compact with very narrow leaves.

PHLOMIS Sage-like low shrubs and perennials. Jerusalem sage, *P. fruticosa* [7–9], makes a broad mound up to 3ft 3in/1m high, well covered with gray-green leaves whose wrinkled edges hint at felted gray-white undersides. Stiff stems also downy gray; whorled yellow flowers leave attractive seedheads.

PHOTINIA Medium-sized to large shrubs, attractive in own right and alternatives to *Pieris* where there is lime in the soil. The young foliage of several evergreen photinias is richly colored. Compact hybrid *P.* x *fraseri* "Red Robin" [8–9], one of the most brilliant in spring and early summer, with bright red lustrous new leaves turning glossy dark green when mature. *P.* "Redstart" [7–9], also with bright red young foliage, can make a small tree. *P. davidiana* "Palette" [7–9] a curiosity, slowly forming medium-sized shrub with leathery leaves, blotched and streaked with cream and pink.

PHYSOCARPUS *P. opulifolius* "Dart's Gold" [3–7], a yellow-leaved form of the ninebark; a suckering shrub that reaches up to 6ft/1.8m. Three-lobed leaves hold color well, though plant does not thrive in shallow soils on chalk.

PIERIS Group of evergreen shrubs, several whose leathery leaves are bright red when young. White lily-of-the-valley flowers in spring, often attractive during winter bud stage. All intolerant of lime and foliage vulnerable to damage by cold winds and late frosts, so plant in sheltered positions with light overhead cover. *P.* "Forest Flame" [6–9], growing to 12ft/3.7m, with finely toothed leaves that progress through red, pink, and creamy white before turning green. *P. formosa* var. *forrestii* [7–9] has several clones with bronze to red young leaves; "Wakehurst" very brightly colored.

PITTOSPORUM Evergreen shrubs and small trees with leathery leaves; good near sea. Japanese mock orange, *P. tobira* [9–10], a slow-growing large shrub with small white flowers of bewitching scent, is one of most drought-tolerant. Polished dark green leaves arranged in whorls; more compact "Variegatum" has leaves with an irregular white margin. Kohuhu, *P. tenuifolium* [8–10], makes a tree to 30ft/9m high but responds well to clipping and is a useful hedge. Leaves have wavy margins and their mid-green contrasts with the nearly black stems; cut foliage useful in flower arrangements. Small red-brown flowers borne late spring and early summer. Several cultivars of compact growth: "Irene Paterson," leaves white with green speckling and mottling; "Silver Queen," gray-green foliage with white variegation. Purple-leaved forms include "Tom Thumb," a low shrub whose leaves have a bronze luster, and "Purpureum." *P.* "Garnettii" [9–10], large shrub with gray-green leaves randomly spotted pink and with white wavy margins.

PLATANUS Plane Large deciduous trees with maple-like leaves. London plane, *P.* x *hispanica* [5–8] has very variable bright green leaves, 12in/30cm or more long with 3-5 lobes. Mottled bark and strings of long-lasting rounded fruit clusters are other major features. Oriental plane, *P. orientalis* [7–8], equally magnificent, with deeply lobed leaves.

POPULUS Poplar Fast-growing large trees, mostly deciduous with wide-spreading roots. Many make good windbreaks but few suitable for close confines of a garden. White poplar, *P. alba* [4–9], an eye-catching landscape tree when a breeze reveals the white woolly underside of the leaves; leaves variable in shape but often consist of a fan of 3-5 lobes; turn yellow in fall. "Raket" has upswept branches making narrow cone. Chinese necklace poplar, *P. lasiocarpa* [6–9], has largest leaves of species; dark green, heart-shaped and up to 12in/30cm long, carried on red stalks. Several poplars have sweetly aromatic leaves as they unfold, including the balm of Gilead, *P.* x *jackii* [5–9]; its striking variegated form, "Aurora," with young leaves that show a splashy white, cream, and pink variegation on green, grows to 50ft/15m.

PRUNUS Ornamental cherry A large genus of evergreen and deciduous trees and shrubs, including the flowering cherries and some choice fruits. The common or cherry laurel, *P. laurocerasus* [7–9], is a versatile evergreen shrub but not suitable for shallow soils on chalk. Eventually wide-spreading and attaining a height of 20ft/6m. Large leathery leaves dark green and polished; upright sprays of white spring flowers are followed by red, then black cherry-like fruits. An excellent screen and a good hedge. Cultivars include compact "Otto Luyken," narrow leaves; "Rotundifolia," one of best for hedging, with vigorous upright growth; narrow-leaved "Zabeliana," good for ground cover because of its horizontal growth. The Portugal laurel, *P. lusitanica* [7–9], another good evergreen for screening and hedging, better on chalk; also makes a fine standard. Dark green leaves held on red-tinted stalks. Some deciduous cherries have new leaves tinted red-brown or bronze, including vigorous and stiffly upright *P.* "Kanzan" [6–8] and *P.* "Amanogawa" [5–7]. Others color well in fall, the best being *P. sargentii* [5–9], a round-headed tree to 50ft/15m high, leaves copper-red, summer green, then early turn brilliant orange-red. Several forms of the myrobalan or cherry plum, *P. cerasifera* [5–9], have purple leaves in summer; foliage of **"Nigra"** near black, that of **"Pissardii"** deep red-purple. Useful for hedging. The leaves of *P. x blireana* [6–8] are a more subtle purple, with a coppery luster; a large shrub or small tree whose double pink flowers open with the leaves.

PYRUS Pear Ornamental pear, *P. salicifolia* **"Pendula"** [5–7], small deciduous tree with weeping branches. After initial training develops into a graceful tree with narrow willow-like leaves, very silvery early in the season, later gray-green. White spring blossom followed by small brown fruits. *P. calleyerana* **"Chanticleer"** [5–8], with toothed leaves, turning red in fall, is narrowly conical.

QUERCUS Oak Deciduous and evergreen shrubs and trees. Evergreens include the shrubby Kermes oak, *Q. coccifera* [7–9], with dark glossy leaves, often prickly. A much larger evergreen, the Holm Oak [7–9], *Q. ilex*, is a sober, round-headed tree with glossy dark green leaves, downy gray on underside. Tolerates clipping and good near the sea. Several large deciduous oaks color magnificently in fall. The scarlet oak, *Q. coccinea* [7–9], its outstanding cultivar **"Splendens,"** and the pin oak, *Q. palustris* [5–8], with smaller, more elegantly lobed leaves, are glossy green on both sides before coloring scarlet. The large lobed leaves of the red oak, *Q. rubra* [3–7], are matte. All 3 species need lime-free soil. The long-lived English oak, *Q. robur* [5–8], a rugged broad-headed tree with almost stalkless, shallow-lobed leaves. Columnar f. *fastigiata* less space-consuming. **"Concordia"** grows to 30ft/9m; foliage bright yellow when young, later green.

RHAMNUS Italian buckthorn, *R. alaternus* [8–9], an evergreen shrub to 15ft/4.5m, has glossy dark green that are ovate to oblong. **"Aureovariegata"** has gray-green leaves with bright white margins.

RHODODENDRON Rhododendrons and azaleas are a major group of flowering ornamental trees and shrubs for acid soils. Hundreds of species and cultivars, many with dull and mournful foliage, but others attractive in leaf and flower. Some, such as *R. orbiculare* [6–8], to 10ft/3m, have rounded leaves. A covering of dense hairs (indumentum), sometimes suede-like, on the underside of leaves a marked feature of many species, including several large-leaved evergreens that often develop into small trees. *R. sinogrande* [8–9], one of most magnificent; lance-shaped leaves up to 30in/75cm long, pale buff indumentum

contrasting with glossy dark green of the upper surface; trusses of creamy yellow flowers. *R. rex* [8–10], also impressive, with smaller leaves; indumentum is rust-brown and present on upper surface of young foliage. Flowers pink with crimson spotting. Other large-leaved species include *R. falconeri* [8–9], with brown indumentum, and *R. maccabeanum* [7–9], with beige underside, both with creamy yellow or yellow flowers. Some rhododendrons have blue-tinted foliage. Red-flowered *R. cinnabarinum* [7–9], large shrub whose foliage has metallic blue sheen. Smaller, slow-growing *R. campanulatum* subsp. *aeruginosum* [7–9], of startling blueness. Many smaller rhododendrons make neat mounds or domes. *R. yakushimanum* [5–8], tightly packed leaves with fawn indumentum on upper surface when they first open and retained in a darker tone on undersides; pink flowers. The parent of similar compact rhododendrons.

RHUS Sumac Mainly deciduous suckering shrubs with impressively large pinnate leaves, coloring vividly in fall. Insignificant flowers often followed by conspicuous fruit clusters. Sap can cause strong allergic reactions. Scarlet or smooth sumac, *R. glabra* [3–9], medium-sized shrub with hairless leaves up to 18in/45cm long, composed of numerous blue-green leaflets that turn orange-red in fall. Leaves of larger *R. x pulvinata* **"Red Fall Lace"** [2–8] similarly smooth, but leaflets deeply cut and ferny, splendid in their intense fall colors. Stag's horn sumac, *R. typhina* [3–8], can make a small irregular tree; velvety red shoots. Divided leaves, up to 2ft/60cm long, color brilliantly in fall; **"Dissecta,"** with finely cut leaves, turns vivid yellow and orange.

RICINUS Castor oil plant *Ricinus communis* [A], fast-growing evergreen shrub which can in a season reach 5ft/1.5m high. Often grown as an annual for its foliage. Leaf fans of 5-12 toothed lobes, glossy green or, in several cultivars, red-purple; **"Impala"** compact, young bronze-purple leaves with a metallic luster.

ROBINIA Locusts and acacias are fast-growing, often spiny, deciduous trees and shrubs with attractive ferny leaves and pea-like flowers. Branches brittle but useful ornamental trees for dry, sunny gardens. Black locust, *R. pseudoacacia* [4–8], to 50ft/15m, with dark green pinnate leaves and white flowers. In gardens generally replaced by less vigorous (and less free-flowering) cultivars, especially mop-headed **"Umbraculifera"** and yellow-leaved **"Frisia,"** latter becoming green as summer

advances but the yellow intensifying again in the fall.

ROSA The foliage of many highly bred roses is susceptible to disease and attractive to pests and best enjoyed in an early red-purple phase. Purple-flowered *R. rugosa* [2–9] and its progeny are among those least affected by disease; shining crinkled leaves bright green, turning gold in fall, when the large hips are scarlet. Albas have gray-green leaves composed of finely toothed leaflets, in **"Céleste"** [3–9] making a perfect foil for soft pink flowers. *R. glauca* [5–8], cool purple-gray leaves carried on glaucous purple stems, making it a superb foliage plant; starry pink flowers of fleeting interest.

RUTA Rue Common rue, *R. graveolens* [5–9], an acridly aromatic evergreen shrub making a rounded blue-green bush with small yellow flowers in summer. Compact **"Jackman's Blue,"** 2ft/60cm high and crowded with numerous leaflets of its glaucous divided foliage.

SALIX Willow Genus of deciduous trees and shrubs, with several hundred species found in a wide range of habitats. Plenty of exceptions, but characteristic willow leaf is lance-shaped; many species have attractive catkins in spring and some have colorful stems. Larger willows unsuitable for small to medium-sized gardens but include some beautiful trees. Golden weeping willow, *S. x sepulcralis* var. *chrysocoma* [6–8], bright green tapered leaves trailing to the ground on slender pliant shoots, yellow when young. *S. babylonica* var. *pekinensis* **"Tortuosa"** [6–9], a tree up to 50ft/15m high, grown for its general appearance of a puzzle of more or less upright contorted branches and bright green twisted leaves. White willow, *S. alba* [2–8], a fast-growing landscape tree, with masses of silky leaves giving billowing trees a silver luster; var. *sericea*, a tree usually less than 50ft/15m high, has an effect of more finely finished metal. Coyote willow, *S. exigua* [3–7], a large suckering shrub with silky and silvery leaves, narrow and tapered, with minuscule teeth along the margins. Woolly willow, *S. lanata* [3–5], a more compact bushy shrub for mixing with rock-garden plants; rounded leaves felted and gray-white. Dwarf *S.* **"Boydii"** [4–7], a characterful upright shrub to grow among alpines; small gray-green leaves rough-textured and deeply veined. A dwarf of dense prostrate growth, *S. reticulata* [2–6] has rounded dark green leaves that are white and hairy on the underside and attractively net-veined; small catkins stand above the leaves.

SAMBUCUS Elder Among these large, rather coarse deciduous shrubs, color variations and cutting of the leaves makes some useful foliage plants for mixed borders. Common or European elder, *S. nigra* [5–7], with pinnate leaves composed of 5 toothed leaflets; purple-leaved variants include "Guincho Purple," whose heads of white flowers have a pink tint that blends to perfection with the foliage; "Madonna" has yellow-variegated leaves. Red-berried elder, *S. racemosa* [3–7], has forms with finely cut leaves: "Plumosa," with young growths tinted purple; "Sutherland Gold," yellow-green leaves, less susceptible to sun scorch than the more golden "Plumosa Aurea."

SANTOLINA Natives of sunny dry habitats, most are small evergreen shrubs, many with dense gray foliage topped by yellow buttons. Cotton lavender, *S. chamaecyparissus* [6–9], with felted stems and finely dissected silvery leaves; dwarf version, var. *nana*, makes a neat mound. *S. pinnata* subsp. *neapolitana* [7–9], whose feathery aromatic foliage bleaches silvery white in dry conditions. Bright green aromatic *S. rosmarinifolia* subsp. *rosmarinifolia* [7–9] makes a good contrast in dry gardens.

SENECIO A large genus including some gray-leaved woody-based plants. *S. cineraria* [8–10] often grown for its foliage as an annual in bedding schemes and containers. Gray-green woolly leaves, almost white in "White Diamond," with stiff, deeply cut foliage, like felted fern fronds; yellow flowers best removed. Height 2ft/60cm. *S. viravira* [8–10] is a laxer sub-shrub, its silver-white leaves elegantly cut

SKIMMIA Evergreen *S. japonica* [7–9], a low woodland shrub making compact dome of leathery aromatic leaves. Female plants produce long-lasting red berries if a male plant is nearby; male "Rubella" has red stalks, narrow red rim to its dark green leaves, and red tint in overwintering flower buds; scented white flowers in spring.

SORBUS Large genus of deciduous trees and shrubs includes several good trees for small to medium-sized gardens. In many species, fruits highly ornamental, as is the foliage; creamy white flowers often the least interesting feature. Whitebeam, *S. aria* [6–8], with simple leaves, makes a small to medium-sized tree with rounded head. Oval to ovate leaves at first gray-white, later bright green on the upper surface but downy white on underside; turn shades of yellow and warm brown in fall; "Lutescens" a radiantly beautiful tree in spring, almost white leaves with a dense

covering of fine hairs. Rowan or mountain ash, *S. aucuparia* [4–7], representative of species with pinnate leaves which have up to 19 finely toothed leaflets; dark green in summer, coloring well in fall after berries have turned orange-red; "Aspleniifolia" has deeply cut fern-like foliage. *S. sargentiana* [5–7], a superb medium-sized tree with conspicuous crimson buds in winter that develop into large pinnate leaves; foliage and berries orange-red in fall. *S. vilmorinii* [6–8] is a more compact tree or shrub. *S. reducta* [5–8] is a small suckering shrub with pinnate leaves, rich purples and reds in fall.

SPIRAEA Deciduous or semi-evergreen *S. thunbergii* [5–8], a medium-sized shrub mainly grown for its early display of white flowers; light green narrow leaves an attractive feature, turning orange in fall. *S. japonica* "Goldflame" [4–9], a dwarf deciduous shrub more brashly eye-catching; orange-red young leaves turn bright yellow before becoming green; dark pink flowers in summer. "Gold Mound" has yellow leaves and pale pink flowers.

THYMUS see Thyme (Edible plants)

TILIA Lime or linden Deciduous trees, many of impressive size, well clothed with attractive leaves, in summer bearing small creamy yellow flowers with a sweet and pervasive scent. They tolerate hard pruning, the large species often being pleached. Several have more or less heart-shaped leaves, among them the small-leaved lime *T. cordata* [4–8] and a beautiful large tree, the pendulous silver lime, *T.* "Petiolaris" [5–9] whose branches sweep down gracefully; long-stalked dark green leaves with white-felted undersides. Flowers narcotic to bees. *T. henryana* [6–8], medium-sized, slow-growing tree with young foliage tinged red, mature leaves glossy green, paler and downy on the underside, their edges fringed with conspicuous bristly teeth.

ULMUS Elm Good resistance to usually fatal Dutch elm disease in several Asiatic species, including the Chinese elm, *U. parvifolia* [5–9], a medium-sized to large tree with small toothed leaves, glossy green and leathery. "Frosty," shrubby form growing to about 6ft/1.8m, its neat, tiny leaves fringed with white teeth; "Geisha" similar, the teeth creamier.

VIBURNUM A large genus of deciduous and evergreen shrubs showing a range of ornamental features. Laurustinus, *V. tinus* [8–10], large shrub long cultivated for its dark evergreen foliage and heads of pink-

tinted white flowers in winter and early spring. Compact forms with small leaves include "Eve Price" and "Gwenllian;" "Lucidum" and "Lucidum Variegatum" have very glossy leaves. Other interesting forms include the creamy margined "Variegatum" and "Purpureum," the latter with young leaves that are bronze-purple. *V. davidii* [7–10], a low spreading evergreen useful as ground cover; oval dark green leaves, paler on undersides, are leathery and glossy, 3 conspicuous veins running lengthwise. To produce lustrous turquoise berries, females must have a male plant close by. Deciduous viburnums worth growing for foliage color include a compact form of the guelder rose, *V. opulus* "Aureum" [3–8]. Bright yellow leaves burn in full sun. Several viburnums color well in fall. *V. sargentii* "Onondaga" [4–7], vigorous and upright, has maple-like leaves, rich maroon when young, red-purple in fall; pink-tinged white lacecap flowers followed by red berries. *V. plicatum* "Mariesii" [5–9], tiered branches decked with white flowers in late spring and colorful, deeply veined leaves hanging almost vertically in fall.

VINCA Periwinkle Two evergreen trailing periwinkles make useful ground cover. Greater periwinkle, *V. major* [6–10], with ovate, dark green glossy leaves, an aggressive colonizer in sun and shade and hard to confine to awkward parts of the garden where it is really useful; "Variegata," with irregular creamy margins and gray-green markings, also rampant. Lesser periwinkle, *V. minor* [4–8], less of a bully; "Argenteovariegata" a pretty variegated form. All have neat blue flowers.

WEIGELA Easy, free-flowering deciduous shrubs of small to medium size, some with added interest of variegated or purple foliage. *W. florida* "Variegata" [5–8], creamy white edges to the leaves that work well with pink flowers. Compact "Foliis Purpureis" has purple leaves to go with the pink. *W.* "Olympiade" [5–8], with red flowers and yellow-green or yellow-variegated leaves, which tend to burn in full sun.

XANTHORHIZA Yellowroot, *X. simplicissima* [3–9], a suckering deciduous shrub suitable for ground cover in sun or shade; gray shoots up to 3ft 3in/1m high bear sprays of tiny purple-brown flowers as foliage develops. Leaves, composed of up to 5 deeply lobed leaflets, start bronze, turn bright green, and in fall purple or brown.

YUCCA Yuccas Some tree-like, others stemless, yuccas are natives of parched and rocky landscapes. Their rosettes of sword-like leaves and spikes of drooping bell-shaped cream flowers are jaggedly exotic. Stemless Adam's needle, *Y. filamentosa* [5–10], has stiff dark green leaves with curled white threads at the edge; leaves of "Bright Edge" have a yellow margin. *Y. flaccida* [5–9], also stemless and with a fringe of curling filaments, but the blue-green leaves more lax, the end sometimes bending abruptly; "Golden Sword" has yellow margins to the leaves. Our Lord's candle, *Y. whipplei* [7–9], another stemless species, one of the most beautiful in flower, dying after its superb performance; in the years it may take to reach flowering maturity the gray-green leaves are a threatening cluster of spine-tipped stiletto blades. Spanish dagger, *Y. gloriosa* [6–9], develops several trunks and can grow to over 6ft/1.8m; it has stiff, spiked gray-green leaves, a palm-like appearance when old leaves are removed.

ZELKOVA Caucasian elm, *Z. carpinifolia* [5–9], a magnificent large tree, usually with a short trunk and many erect branches supporting a rounded head; dark green elliptic leaves notched with rounded teeth, their surface rough to the touch, turn orange-brown in fall. Japanese zelkova, *Z. serrata* [5–9], a large, wide-spreading tree with narrow tapered leaves turning from dark green to rich fall colors; "Green Vase" has upright then arching branches and good fall color; "Goblin" is a bushy dwarf form.

Conifers

The conebearing trees and shrubs include some of the largest and oldest living things, but there are also numerous dwarf conifers, some interesting for their foliage and form. Most are evergreen but a few, including some of great ornamental value, are deciduous.

ABIES Silver fir Evergreen and in many cases magnificent large trees that are symmetrically conical in form, with whorls of branches in ascending tiers. Leaves scale-like, female cones sometimes an attractive feature. Species of impressive size include the giant fir, *A. grandis* [5–6] and the noble fir, *A. procera* [5–6]. There are smaller species and compact cultivars more suitable for gardens. A form of the balsam fir, *A. balsamea* Hudsonia Group [3–6], makes a curious spherical dark green

mound eventually little more than 3ft 3in/1m high. White fir, *A. concolor* [3–7], a striking large tree with silver-gray foliage, has a dwarf gray-blue cultivar, "Compacta," height and spread 6-10ft/ 1.8-3m. Korean fir, *A. koreana* [5–6], is neat and slow-growing to 30ft/9m, producing violet-blue cones when 5-10 years old. The spiky foliage is dark green on the upper surface, bright silver beneath, the contrast conspicuous in the very slow-growing "Silberlocke," whose leaves twist upward. Blue-gray *A. lasiocarpa* "Arizonica Compacta" [5–6] densely conical, slow-growing to 15ft/5m.

ARAUCARIA Mainly tropical evergreens, the remarkably tiered and symmetrical Norfolk Island pine, *A. heterophylla* [9–10], sometimes being grown as a conservatory plant. Monkey puzzle, *A. araucana* [7–10], grows to more than 60ft/18m, producing whorls of spidery branches densely clothed in spine-tipped dark green leaves arranged spirally. For moist but well-drained soils.

CEDRUS Cedar Majestic evergreen conifers, usually conical when young but with age the outline becomes picturesquely broad and irregular. The cones are erect, the female ones barrel-like. The species described can all grow to 100ft/30m or more. Atlas cedar, *C. atlantica* [6–8], initially has ascending branches but later the growth is more horizontal; the short needle-like leaves are gray or gray-green. The blue cedars, **Glauca Group**, are markedly silver-blue. "Glauca Pendula" is of moderate height, with weeping branches and gray-blue foliage. Cedar of Lebanon, *C. libani* [6–9], is a similar though slower-growing tree, remarkable when mature for its tiered and horizontal branches; foliage gray-green. "Sargentii" is a slow-growing prostrate form that can be trained up to make a small weeping tree. The deodar cedar, *C. deodara* [7–9], is distinguished by its drooping leader, and the pendent tips of its branches give the whole tree a languid air; relatively long leaves gray-green to mid-green. "Aurea" is slow-growing, the foliage yellow-green at first, greener with age.

CHAMAECYPARIS Cypress Evergreen, usually large conical or columnar trees, the foliage in broad flattened sprays. The adult leaves are scale-like. Lawson cypress, *C. lawsoniana* [5–8], to more than 100ft/30m, has bright green or gray-green foliage and the leading shoot is drooping. Great variety in its numerous cultivars. Dome-shaped or rounded dwarf kinds under 6ft/1.8m include: "Aurea Densa," gold and very dense; "Minima Glauca," almost rounded

and gray-green; and "Pygmaea Argentea," rounded, blue-green with silver tips. "Ellwoodii," columnar, to 10ft/3m, is feathery gray-green, metallic blue in winter. Taller columnar or conical cultivars include: "Green Hedger," foliage rich green; "Wisselii," blue-green, and "Pembury Blue," with silver-blue foliage sprays. Nootka cypress, *C. nootkatensis* [4–7], has a fine weeping form, "Pendula." Hinoki cypress, *C. obtusa* [5–8], is tall and fast-growing, making a broad-based, deep green cone. Yellow-leaved cultivars include "Crippsii," a loose column up to 50ft/15m high; and "Tetragona Aurea," angular and with foliage tinted bronze. Sarawa cypress, *C. pisifera* [5–8] is a large tree with dark green foliage but "Boulevard," under 20ft/6m, has dense steel-blue foliage, soft to the touch.

CRYPTOMERIA The Japanese cedar, *C. japonica* [6–9], tall-growing evergreen column-like or conical in shape, with deep green leaves and shredding reddish bark. **Elegans Group**, which rarely exceeds 25ft/7.5m, retains its feathery juvenile foliage, making a blue-green column in summer, but taking on purplish or red-brown tints in fall and winter; "Elegans Compacta" a smaller version.

X CUPRESSOCYPARIS A hybrid genus between *Chamaecyparis* and *Cupressus*. Leyland cypress, x *C. leylandii* [6–9], a fast-growing tree, eventually more than 100ft/30m high, making a dense column of dark green or gray-green foliage; scale-like leaves held in flat sprays. Useful as a shelter belt. "Castlewellan" less vigorous, the young foliage gold, maturing to bronze green.

CUPRESSUS Cypress Evergreen conifers usually of moderate growth and dense columnar shape, the foliage arranged in plume-like sprays, the leaves scale-like. The Italian cypress, *C. sempervirens* [7–9], long cultivated in the Mediterranean region, is most commonly seen as a narrow dark green column, **Stricta Group** being a pencil-like form growing to 26ft/8m or more, but only 5-10ft/1.5-3m across. As a young tree the Monterey cypress, *C. macrocarpa* [7–10], is a narrow cone or column but old specimens are large, spreading, and cedar-like; tolerant of salt winds. "Goldcrest" makes a medium-sized column of feathery yellow foliage. Other good species include conical gray-green *C. arizonica* var. *glabra* [7-9], and the Kashmir cypress, *C. cashmeriana* [7–9], capable of growing to 100ft/30m; sometimes planted in conservatories for its weeping blue-green sprays of foliage.

GINKGO Maidenhair tree An astonishing living fossil, *G. biloba* [5–9], is a deciduous tree that can grow to 100ft/30m. Bright green leaves of distinctive shape, forming a notched fan up to 5in/13cm across, turn clear yellow in fall. Females bear yellow plum-like fruits. "Fastigiata" is columnar, "Pendula" spreading and weeping.

JUNIPERUS Juniper Versatile evergreen trees and shrubs, most tolerant of a wide range of conditions, with needle-like young leaves, scale-like mature leaves. The Chinese juniper, *J. chinensis* [3–9], is a somber gray-green columnar small tree; "Obelisk" a narrow blue-green version to 8ft/2.5m. "Blue Alps," up to 12ft/3.7m and almost as wide, has shoots arching at the tips and silver-blue juvenile leaves. The common juniper, *J. communis* [3–8], aromatic, very variable spreading or upright shrub with silver-backed gray-green leaves; "Hibernica" is pencil-like to 15ft/4.5m and "Compressa" a smaller version, under 3ft/90cm high. *J. scopulorum* "Skyrocket" [3–8] is similar but narrower than either, up to 16ft/5m high. Green-leaved junipers of low spreading growth include *J. horizontalis* "Emerald Spreader" [3–7] and *J. sabina* "Tamariscifolia" [3–8]. The cultivars of *J.* x *pfitzeriana* [4–8], such as the bright green "Mint Julep," are taller shrubs with tiered branches rising at an angle. The numerous junipers with blue-gray foliage include: *J. horizontalis* "Blue Chip" [3–7], a vigorous prostrate shrub with an ultimate spread of 10ft/3m, *J. squamata* "Blue Carpet" [5–8], half this in extent, and *J. s.* "Blue Star," a compact silvery blue mound.

LARIX Larch Large deciduous conifers of handsome conical form, the lower branches growing downward but curving up at the ends. Needle-like leaves fresh green in spring, yellow and russet in fall. Pretty "flowers" followed by neat persistent cones. European larch, *L. decidua* [3–6], and Japanese larch, *L. kaempferi* [5–7], similar but the latter a more solid tree when young, the winter shoots waxy and purplish red, leaves broader and lighter green.

METASEQUOIA Dawn redwood, *M. glyptostroboides* [5–10], a living fossil, is deciduous, conical when young, eventually over 100ft/30m. Feathery bright green foliage turns rusty pink and yellow in fall. For moist but well-drained soil. "Gold Rush" has yellow foliage.

PICEA Spruce Evergreen trees, mainly conical or columnar, with short needle-like leaves. Several handsome species, including Serbian spruce, *P. omorika* [5–8], and oriental spruce, *P. orientalis* [5–8], too large for most gardens. Similarly the Norway spruce, *P. abies* [3–8] but "Nidiformis" is a dwarf bush with tiered foliage up to 6ft/1.8m high with a dip in the center. Another dwarf, *P. glauca* var. *albertiana* "Conica" [3–6], ultimately 10ft/3m high, is a slow-growing, extremely dense mid-green cone. Even smaller is the blue-gray mound of *P. mariana* "Nana" [3–6], height and spread 20in/50cm. Brewer's spruce, *P. breweriana* [5–8], an elegant tree of medium height, its blue-green needles weeping from trailing branchlets. Morinda spruce, *P. smithiana* [7–8], tall and with dark green leaves, also weeping. Colorado spruce, *P. pungens* [3–8], usually represented in gardens by its eye-catching silver-blue cultivars; two of medium size are "Koster" and "Hoopsii."

PINUS Pine Evergreen trees and shrubs, many fast-growing, so widely used in forestry. Some are astonishingly long-lived; specimens of the bristle cone pine, *P. aristata* [4–8], of south-western USA are said to be more than 4000 years old, their needle-like leaves bundled in clusters of 2-5. Several interesting for their shape, notably the stone or umbrella pine, *P. pinea* [9–10], a picturesque medium-sized tree with a dense mushroom-domed canopy. Several have attractive needles. Montezuma pine, *P. montezumae* [6–8], has needles up to 12in/30cm long, grouped usually in fives, the end of a branch looking like a chimney brush. The Mexican weeping pine, *P. patula* [8–9], is a graceful medium-sized tree with long bright green needles, usually in threes, gathered in drooping clusters. Another graceful species is the Bhutan pine, *P. wallichiana* [6–9], needles blue-green and hanging, in bundles of fives. Some of the most useful pines in gardens are compact or dwarf. The dwarf mountain pine, *P. mugo* [3–7], has several compact cultivars under 3ft/90cm, among them "Mops," a dense green globe; and "Ophir," bun-shaped and turning yellow in winter. In the same class is a gray-green compact version of the Scots pine, *P. sylvestris* "Beauvronensis" [3–7].

PSEUDOLARIX Deciduous golden larch, *P. amabilis* [5–7], is a slow-growing conical tree to about 65ft/20m, with bright green needle-like leaves that turn orange-yellow in fall; green female cones ripen to brown. For sheltered sunny sites and lime-free soil.

TAXODIUM Swamp cypress Young trees of the deciduous *T. distichum* [5–10] conical but older specimens, sometimes over 100ft/30m high, make untidy columns. Small, scale-like leaves bright green in summer, rust-brown in fall; fibrous bark is red-brown and, in wet conditions, knee-like growths extend above ground level from the roots. This and the more narrowly columnar, less vigorous var. *imbricatum* "Nutans" need moist to wet conditions and preferably acid soil.

TAXUS Yew Common yew, *T. baccata* [6–8], is an evergreen conifer of somber beauty and one of the best plants for architectural hedges and topiary. Slow-growing to 50ft/15m or more and long-lived, usually conical when young, later spreading. The foliage is dense and the short, spirally arranged leaves black-green. Female plants bear fruits with a fleshy red-pink covering around the poisonous seed. Irish yew, "Fastigiata," makes a column, initially narrow, of densely packed upright branches. "Repandens" is prostrate. Several forms have yellow-green to gold foliage: "Elegantissima" and Fastigiata Aurea Group are upright, "Dovastonii Aurea" horizontally branched with weeping branchlets, "Summergold" a spreading shrub, and "Repens Aurea" prostrate. The pick is the upright "Standishii," slow-growing to 5ft/1.5m. *T.* x *media* [5–7] is similar to the species but hardier and tends to make a spreading large shrub; "Hicksii" forms a broad column.

THUJA Arborvitae Evergreen trees and shrubs with aromatic leaves, juvenile foliage soft and feathery, mature leaves scale like and held in flat sprays, with shredding reddish brown bark and small cones; represented in gardens by compact forms. White cedar, *T. occidentalis* [2–7], is a slow-growing columnar tree of medium size, the leaves glossy yellow-green above and matte underneath, usually bronzed in winter. Numerous cultivars include: "Holmstrup," a dense conical bush to 13ft/4m high with rich green leaves in upright sprays; "Rheingold," a cone of golden amber, usually under 6ft/1.8m; and "Smaragd," an even more compact bright green cone. Western red cedar, *T. plicata* [5–8], a columnar or conical tree growing to more than 100ft/30m, has glossy green leaves in drooping sprays; "Atrovirens" rich green and an excellent hedging plant. The green foliage of "Zebrina" is banded pale yellow; "Stoneham Gold" is a compact dome of copper-tinted yellow over green.

TSUGA Hemlock Evergreen trees of elegant conical outline, branchlets drooping and linear leaves banded silver on the underside. Small cones, which hang from the branches, may persist for 3 years. Eastern hemlock, *T. canadensis* [4–8], a large tree, often branching near the base, is usually represented in gardens by cultivars such as **"Jeddeloh,"** a small hummock of bright green foliage 12in/30cm high, and **"Pendula,"** a shrub up to 12ft/3.7m high with wide-spreading branches and weeping foliage. Western hemlock, *T. heterophylla* [6–8], an elegant symmetrical tree to more than 100ft/30m, with slightly ascending branches from which the foliage hangs; beautiful as a specimen, excellent hedging.

Climbers

Climbers and scramblers have turned to other plants or rocky outcrops for support, some twining, others catching on by tendrils, some having aerial roots, and others with small adhesive pads. In the garden they are often seen at their best clothing buildings, or pergolas and arches.

ACTINIDIA Twining deciduous climbers, including Chinese gooseberry or kiwi fruit, *A. deliciosa* [7–9]. This vigorous plant, growing to 33ft/10m or more, has dark green leaves, bristly at the margins, set against stems and leaf stalks covered with a fuzz of reddish hairs. Female plants with a male nearby produce edible fruit bristling with red-brown hairs. *A. kolomikta* [5–8] is a more slender, variegated climber to 15ft/4.5m high. Leaves ovate, heart-shaped at the base, finely tapered at the tip, and where they are touched by sun the tip or even all of the leaf is white with a pink flush; the color later fades.

BOUGAINVILLEA The evergreen and semi-evergreen thorny scramblers in the genus are grown for the showy, long-lasting flower-like bracts, 3 "petals" surrounding 3 tiny true flowers, bracts and flowers being arranged in large clusters. The most widely grown is the hybrid *B.* x *buttiana* [9–11], which in favorable conditions can grow to over 30ft/9m. The color range includes magenta, scarlet, pink, white, and gold.

CLEMATIS Most of the evergreen and deciduous climbers in the genus are grown for their showy flowers but some have pleasing foliage. Their leaves are compound, consisting often of 3 leaflets; the long stalks of these act as tendrils. The deciduous *C. montana* [6–9] is one of the most versatile, often growing to more than 30ft/9m; **var. rubens,** purplish foliage and pink flowers, borne in profusion. The evergreen *C. armandii* [6–9] needs a sheltered

position. White flowers and leathery, lustrous leaflets in threes, the longest about 6in/15cm long; new foliage is copper-colored.

HEDERA Ivy Evergreen climbers, in their initial phase clinging to surfaces by aerial roots, and usually bearing lobed leaves. The mature branches at the top of the plant are non-clinging and bear unlobed leaves and spherical clusters of small flowers. Canary Island ivy, *H. canariensis* [6–10], which grows to more than 16ft/5m, has large leaves of variable shape, often only slightly lobed; most commonly seen in the variegated form **"Gloire de Marengo,"** with irregular creamy white margins and gray patches. The Persian ivy, *H. colchica* [5–10], even more vigorous, has large dark green leaves, heart-shaped at the base and either unlobed or shallowly lobed; **"Dentata,"** an outstanding plain-leaved evergreen climber, bright green, prominently veined and sparsely toothed; **"Dentata Variegata"** [6–10] a superb match with creamy yellow margins, gray mottling, and green center; **"Sulfur Heart"** has yellow splashes on light and dark green. The common or English ivy, *H. helix* [5–10], with 3- or 5-lobed, dark green glossy leaves, 1-2in/2.5-5cm long, represented in gardens by numerous cultivars of varying vigor, many growing to over 20ft/6m. Attractive green-leaved cultivars include: **"Duckfoot,"** small-leaved and compact, the 3 lobes in the shape of a duck's foot; **"Green Ripple,"** with 5 jagged forward-pointing lobes; **"Ivalace,"** the 5-lobed leaves very shiny, their margins waved and curled; **"Pedata,"** with 5 lobes, the central lobe elongated, others backward-pointing; **"Parsley Crested,"** leaves with crimped margins. Among the many with cool variegation are: **"Adam,"** leaves small, 3-lobed, gray and gray-green with creamy white margins; **"Glacier,"** small leaves with 3-5 lobes, green, gray-green, and creamy white, and **"Little Diamond,"** compact and slow-growing, the leaves nearly triangular, gray-green and creamy white. **"Buttercup"** [5–7], with large 5-lobed leaves, is yellow in sun, green in shade; **"Oro di Bogliasco"** has pink stems and 3-lobed dark green leaves with an irregular central yellow splash. Irish ivy, *H. hibernica* [6–10], vigorous and similar to *H. helix* but the dark green leaves, with 5 triangular lobes, are larger; **"Deltoidea"** is slow-growing and the lobes at the base of leaves overlap to give them a heart shape.

HUMULUS Hop Twining herbaceous perennials. The hops used in brewing are the bracted cones produced by female plants of *H. lupulus* [4–8], which climbs about 20ft/6m in a season. The leaves, with

3-5 lobes and toothed margins, are an attractive yellow green in **"Aureus;"** best in full sun; tends to turn green in warm summers. Can be a beautiful nuisance but less overwhelming than the plain-leaved form.

JASMINUM Jasmine Common jasmine, *J. officinale* [9–10], twining deciduous climber up to 40ft/12m high noted for its sweetly scented white flowers. The leaves have 5, 7, or 9 leaflets, margined creamy white in **"Argenteovariegatum,"** blotched yellow in **"Aureum,"** and yellow in **"Fiona Sunrise."**

PARTHENOCISSUS Virginia creeper Deciduous climbers, all those described clinging to supports by adhesive disks at the tips of tendrils. Virginia creeper itself, *P. quinquefolia* [3–9], often growing over 50ft/15m, has hand-like leaves, the leaflets sharply toothed, turning vivid red in fall. Boston ivy, *P. tricuspidata* [4–8], even more vigorous, has leaves with 3 lobes or 3 leaflets, intense crimson in fall; foliage of **"Veitchii"** purple-bronze in spring, blood red in fall. Chinese Virginia creeper, *P. henryana* [7–8], has leaves with 3-5 toothed leaflets with silver veins, sometimes tinged pink, conspicuous when the leaves color red in fall.

SCHIZOPHRAGMA Self-clinging deciduous climbers with dark green leaves, and in summer heads of small creamy white flowers with conspicuous marginal bracts. *S. hydrangeoides* [6–9] has coarsely toothed leaves of metallic green and long-lasting ovate bracts, pink in **"Roseum."** The leaves of *S. integrifolium* [5–9] are bright green, gray-green beneath, its creamy bracts larger than those of *S. hydrangeoides*. Both can grow to more than 30ft/9m, and do best in rich moist soil and partial shade.

TRACHELOSPERMUM Evergreen twining climbers for warm sunny walls. The confederate or star jasmine, *T. jasminoides* [7–10], grown principally for its fragrant white flowers, reaches to 25ft/7.5m; it is well covered with oval leaves that are glossy rich green in summer, reddish bronze in winter. **"Variegatum"** [8–10] has leaves prettily margined and splashed creamy white, tinged pink in winter; **"Wilsonii"** is purplish in winter with lighter veins.

VITIS Vine Deciduous climbers with tendrils. All the following are best in sun and capable of growing more than 20ft/6m. Cultivars of the grapevine, *V. vinifera* [6–9], have highly ornamental lobed foliage, in the case of **"Purpurea"** 6in/15cm long, claret red and in fall crimson; grapes unpalatable. The parsley vine, "Apiifolia," has very divided leaves; "Incana" and "Ciotat," the latter fruiting reliably, have white woolly shoots and young leaves. V. "Brant" [5–9], very close to the grapevine and bearing small sweet grapes, is striking in fall, when leaves turn dark red or purple but the veins remain green or yellow. V. coignetiae [5–9], which can streak 50ft/15m into trees, is the most handsome vine, its large, coarsely toothed leaves heart-shaped at the base but with 3 or more shallow lobes, rusty-felted on undersides, turning rich shades of red, yellow, and purple-crimson in fall. V. amurensis [4–9] is similar to V. vinifera.

WISTERIA Deciduous twining climbers with a strong family resemblance, best in well-drained but moist soil. Noted for their cascades of pea-like, usually mauve flowers, produced most freely in full sun, but also having attractive pinnate leaves. The classic is the Chinese wisteria, W. sinensis [5–9], easily exceeding 50ft/15m, the elegant leaves with 7-13 leaflets. The Japanese wisteria, W. floribunda [5–9], has some impressive flowering forms, and leaves with 11-19 lance-shaped leaflets. Less vigorous than these species, the silky wisteria, W. brachybotrys "Shirokapitan" [6–9], has fine silvery hairs on young stems and foliage.

Perennials

Perennials are non-woody flowering plants that live for several years. A few, such as bergenias, are evergreen, but the herbaceous perennials follow a seasonal cycle—the annual growth dies down in fall before a period of winter dormancy. The growth of bulbous plants, included here, has a slightly different rhythm, and their leaves often die down in the summer. Many selected forms are most easily propagated by division.

ACAENA New Zealand burr Mat-forming evergreens for sun or partial shade; some spread aggressively. Pinnate leaves, the leaflets often prettily toothed, and spiny burrs, more showy than the flowers. A. microphylla "Kupferteppich" [6–8], bronzed blue-green foliage and bright red-brown burrs. A. saccaticupula "Blue Haze" [7–9], with metallic blue-green

leaves, tinged purple, and dull red-brown burrs.

ACANTHUS Bear's breeches Impressive mounds of large, glossy leaves variously lobed or cut, topped by stems packed with tiers of lipped flowers surrounded by spiny bracts in a color scheme of white, purple, and green. For sun or partial shade. A. mollis [6–9], broad leaves, in the Latifolius Group up to 8in/20cm across. A. spinosus [5–9], deeply cut, spiny arching leaves up to 3ft/90cm long, the gray-green leaves of Spinosissimus Group nearly cut to the ribs.

ACHILLEA Yarrow Clump-forming plants for sunny, well-drained borders, their ferny foliage complementing flat or rounded flowerheads. A. "Moonshine" [4–8] and A. "Taygetea" [3–8] both to 2ft/60cm, have finely cut gray-green leaves and yellow flowers. A. tomentosa [4–8], an edging plant to 6in/15cm, has ferny gray-green leaves covered with fine wool.

ACORUS The sweet flag, A. calamus [5–10], is a waterside plant with sword-like leaves to 3ft/90cm; "Argenteostriatus" [7–9] has white or cream stripes running lengthwise and a basal pink flush in spring. The more slender Japanese rush, A. gramineus [7–9], grows in shallow water, producing linear-leaf fans, in "Ogon" [7–9] striped pale green and cream.

AEGOPODIUM Ground elder The pestilential weed A. podagraria [3–9] has an attractively white-variegated form, "Variegatum," up to 2ft/60cm high.

AGAPANTHUS African blue lily Clump-forming, with strap-shaped leaves, and stout stems bearing blue or, more rarely, white trumpet-shaped flowers. Evergreen kinds, like A. africanus [9–10] and A. praecox subsp. orientalis [9–10], both to 3ft/90cm, usually with broad, deep green leaves but less hardy than deciduous kinds with narrower leaves, like the more compact A. campanulatus [7–10]. Numerous, mainly deciduous hybrids, like A. "Blue Giant" [8–10], to 4ft/1.2m, with broad leaves and large heads of blue flowers. All for sunny borders and containers.

AGAVE Rosette-forming succulents suitable for outdoors in sunny, frost-free gardens or for containers. Rosettes usually die after plants flower. A. americana [8–10], sculpted rosettes of broad, spined, blue-gray leaves up to 5ft/1.5m long, inner leaves imprinted with the outline of older leaves. Flower spike, to 25ft/8m, produced after 30 years or more. "Marginata" and "Variegata" have cream or yellow and

gray foliage. Smaller species include the spined sea-green A. parryi [9–10] and A. victoriae-reginae, with faceted leaves.

AJUGA Bugle, A. reptans [3–8], is useful ground cover in shade, forming colonies of low rosettes, the evergreen leaves more or less spoon-shaped. Spikes of blue flowers in spring and early summer. Forms with colorful leaves include: "Atropurpurea," metallic purple-bronze; "Burgundy Glow," mixture of wine-red and cream; and "Multicolor," agitated splashes of bronze-green, pink and cream.

ALCHEMILLA Lady's mantle The low clump of A. mollis [3–7] consists of rounded light green leaves, velvety in texture and with serrated and wavy margins. Frothy sprays of lime-green flowers. For sun or shade and an excellent skirt for shrubs. Pretty species usually less than 6in/15cm high include A. erythropoda [3–7] and A. conjuncta [8–10], the latter's leaves a fan of up to 9 lobes, covered with silky hairs on the underside and showing at the margins.

AMICIA Purple-veined, bract-like stipules enclose the young leaves of A. zygomeris [8–10] which develop as paired leaflets, inversely heart-shaped and notched. Yellow and purple pea flowers.

ANAPHALIS Gray-leaved plants, untypical in needing moist conditions and succeeding in partial shade. A. triplinervis [3–8] forms a clump 2ft/60cm high of spoon-shaped leaves, undersides covered with white hairs, topped by "everlasting" flowerheads with white bracts.

ANEMONE The larger anemones, often invasive, are suitable for moist soils in sun or partial shade. The dark green 3-lobed leaves of the Japanese anemones, A. x hybrida [5–7], such as white-flowered "Honorine Jobert," become the base for flowers floating at 4-5ft/1.2-1.5m. A. tomentosa [4–8], to 5ft/1.5m, has large divided leaves, deeply veined and white woolly on the underside; flowers pale pink.

ANTHEMIS Daisies for well-drained soil and sun. A. punctata subsp. cupaniana [5–9] forms mats of finely cut foliage, silver-gray in summer when there are long-lasting white flowerheads, gray-green in winter.

AQUILEGIA Columbine Often short-lived but freely self-seeding plants making clumps of prettily divided leaves, topped in late spring or early summer by spurred flowers. Several are suitable for the rock garden, such as A. flabellata var. pumila [4–9],

4in/10cm high, the leaves with a blue cast, the flowers blue with white. Larger columbines, 18-36in/45-90cm tall, suitable for borders and shrubberies in sun or partial shade include, at the shorter end, *A. alpina* [4–7], with blue-green leaves, developing purplish tints in summer, and blue flowers. Forms of granny's bonnet, *A. vulgaris* [3–8], include **"Nivea"** [3–8], with cool gray-green foliage to partner white flowers, and **Vervaeneana Group** [3–8], with foliage marbled yellow and white, flowers purple or pink.

ARABIS Rock cress Mat-forming evergreen perennials from mountainous regions, some species with variegated forms. *A. alpina* subsp. *caucasica* **"Variegata"** [4–8] has rosettes of toothed leaves outlined in creamy yellow while the rosettes of *A. procurrens* **"Variegata"** [5–8] consist of shiny leaves more white than green and sometimes tinted pink. *A. ferdinandi-coburgi* **"Old Gold"** [5–8] makes low cushions packed with little rosettes variegated rich yellow. All have white flowers in spring.

ARISAEMA Tuberous woodland plants with arum-like flower parts and handsome leaves composed of fingered leaflets. *A. sikokianum* [5–9], to 20in/50cm, produces 2 dark leaves, one with 3 leaflets, the other with 5. A club-like white spadix protrudes from the spathe's white center below a white-striped purple-black hood.

ARMERIA Thrift Low plants of rocky mountains or seashores form mats or mounds of evergreen grass-like leaves. The flowers, usually pink, are carried in tight rounded clusters above the foliage. For well-drained soil in sun. Sea thrift, *A. maritima* [4–7], forms mounds 12in/30cm across, packed with linear dark green leaves. *A. juniperifolia* **"Bevan's Variety"** [4–7], is a tiny hummock about 2in/5cm high of sharp-tipped leaves; flowerheads almost stemless.

ARTEMISIA Mainly gray- or silver-leaved plants for sunny, well-drained gardens. Usually aromatic, as is tarragon, *A. dracunculus* [3–7]. Flowers, typically dull yellow, relatively insignificant. Some have very finely cut leaves, like *A.* **"Powis Castle"** [6–9], a shrubby bush to 2ft/60cm, with soft pelt-like silver-green foliage. There is finer silky filigree in *A. schmidtiana* [5–8], 12in/30cm high, and in its miniature, **"Nana."** The more wispy divided leaves of *A. alba* **"Canescens"** [4–8] are carried on upturned stems growing to 18in/45cm. The western mugwort, *A. ludoviciana* [4–8], makes a clump 4ft/1.2m high with willow-

like leaves of silver whiteness, those of **"Valerie Finnis"** jagged. *A stelleriana* **"Boughton Silver"** [3–8] is an edging plant of felted whiteness, with sprawling stems carrying leaves cut fastidiously into many rounded lobes.

ARUM In winter the tuberous *A. italicum* subsp. *italicum* **"Marmoratum"** [6–9] makes clumps to 12in/30cm of arrow- or spear-shaped, glossy dark green leaves, heavily veined in green-tinted ivory. Spikes of lustrous red berries.

ARUNCUS Goatsbeard, *A. dioicus* [3–9], makes a broad clump of light green ferny leaves, a perfect base for the summer plumes of tiny white flowers. The finely divided leaves of **"Kneiffii,"** in a smaller clump about 3ft 3in/1m high, thread-like.

ASARUM Mainly creeping evergreens. Asarabacca, *A. europeum* [4–8], with kidney-shaped satin-glossy leaves, makes rich green ground cover in shade. The leaves of *A. hartwegii* [6–8] heart-shaped and bronzed, but with silvered veins.

ASTELIA *A. chathamica* [8–9] is a tussock about 4ft/1.2m high of sword-like, although sometimes limp, leaves that are silvered by minute scales, markedly so when young.

ASTILBE Many have highly ornamental ferny foliage and a long-lasting display of airy flower plumes, attractive even dead in winter. For sun or shade where the soil is moist. The numerous hybrids, many with beautifully tinted young foliage, include: *A.* **"Straussenfeder"** [4–8], 3ft/90cm high, with bronze-tinted young foliage building up to large clumps topped in late summer by arching sprays of pink flowers; *A.* **"Bronce Elegans"** [4–8], to 12in/30cm, dark shadows on rich green leaves and red-tinted stems carrying cream and salmon-pink flowers.

ASTILBOIDES A woodland plant for moist soils, *A. tabularis* [5–7] has light green leaves up to 3ft/90cm across; the stalk attachment, slightly off-center, supports the leaf from underneath. Rounded, softly hairy leaves lobed and toothed, veins conspicuous. Plumes of tiny white flowers.

ASTRANTIA Masterwort Most with pleasing foliage, the leaves of the basal clump consist of a fan of lobes or leaflets. The impact of the flowers is enhanced by the ruff of papery bracts surrounding them. *A. major* subsp. *involucrata* **"Shaggy"** [5–7], to 30in/75cm, has dramatically cut leaves and long bracts that are white with a pink flush and green tips. The foliage of

"Sunningdale Variegated" [5–7] is streaked and splashed creamy white.

BEGONIA Mainly tropical and subtropical plants, including many with beautifully shaped, colored, and marked leaves. Many evergreen perennials about 12in/30cm high, resulting from crosses between the painted-leaf or king begonia, *B. rex* [10], and related species. The leaves, spirally lopsided and wrinkled or quilted, are dark green, patterned and zoned with silver, red, purple, and cream. *B. scharfii*, to 3ft/90cm, has reddish furry leaves and pink flowers. For summer displays in sheltered gardens.

BERGENIA Elephants' ears Evergreens with bold rounded to spoon-shaped leaves that are usually glossy, leathery, and deep green in color, although often turning shades of purple in fall and winter. Tolerate a wide range of conditions in sun and shade and many make excellent ground cover 12-24in/30-60cm high; flowers borne in spring. *B. cordifolia* **"Purpurea"** [3–8], with large rounded or heart-shaped leaves that turn purplish red in winter; flowers magenta. *B. purpurascens* [3–8], with elliptic deep green leaves, purple-red on the underside, and purplish all over in winter; flowers red-purple. *B.* **"Ballawley"** [3–8], one of the largest of the numerous hybrids, with lustrous fresh green leaves coloring rich purples and red-brown in winter; flowers crimson. *B.* **"Sunningdale"** [3–8], with mid- to deep green rounded leaves, purplish red on the underside, turning copper red in winter; flowers magenta. *B.* **"Beethoven"** [4–8], large, and *B.* **"Rosi Klose"** [4–8], small, both have spoon-shaped leaves. *B. ciliata* [5–8], 12in/30cm, often deciduous and with unusual bristly leaves; pink flowers.

BRUNNERA The large, heart-shaped and softly hairy basal leaves of *B. macrophylla* [3–7] make good ground cover, 18in/45cm high, in partial shade; blue forget-me-not flowers in spring. **"Dawson's White,"** with leaves deep green and creamy white, and **"Hadspen Cream,"** with narrower richer cream margins, both vulnerable, especially the former, to sun scorch and wind damage. **"Langtrees,"** leaves dark green with a regular pattern of metallic gray spots.

CALADIUM Tuberous tropical perennials that die back in winter for indoors, and in subtropical bedding in lightly shaded but bright conditions. Hybrids, up to 20in/50cm high, have arrow- or spear-shaped leaves, the leaf stalk attached underneath. Thin leaves often almost white with variegation, and suffused, speckled, or mottled pink or red. Conspicuous veins. For outdoors choose hybrids with thick leaves, like "White Christmas"[10].

CALTHA Marsh marigold A plant for shallow water or bog to 16in/40cm, *C. palustris* [3–9] is also known as kingcup for its glistening yellow flowers in spring. Kidney-shaped toothed leaves of glossy dark green. The giant marsh marigold, var. *palustris* [3–7], has more rounded and more numerous leaves and fewer flowers.

CANNA Indian shot plant Half-hardy and frost-tender plants with large paddle like leaves, often strongly colored, and flowers that are usually gaudy yellow, orange, or red. They need full sun and fertile moist soil in prepared beds or containers. For subtropical bedding, plant in spring and lift rhizomes in fall. The numerous hybrids, most 4–6ft/1.2–1.8m high, include: "Durban" [7–10] and "Striata" [7–10], with conspicuously veined leaves.

CIMICIFUGA Bugbane Several medium-sized to large perennials suitable for moist soil in partial shade. *C. simplex* "Brunette" [3–8], 4ft/1.2m, has purple-brown foliage; the irregularly lobed leaflets are arranged in threes; off-white bottlebrushes. The promising *C. ramosa* "Hillside Black Beauty" [4–8] is a larger form with darker colored foliage.

CONVALLARIA Lily-of-the-valley Where content, *C. majalis* [2–9] spreads rampantly, broadly lance-shaped or elliptic leaves making close ground cover to 10in/25cm, with sprays of white waxy flowers scenting the air in spring. A more striking foliage plant, "Albostriata," has leaves with longitudinal cream stripes.

CRAMBE Seakale The wavy leaves of *C. maritima* [6–9] are 12in/30cm long, blue-green and waxy; small white flowers. The blanched stem is considered a delicacy.

CROCOSMIA Bulbous plants producing fans of blade- or sword-like leaves topped in mid to late summer by sprays of funnel-shaped flowers in shades of red, orange, and yellow. *C.* "Lucifer" [6–9], to 4ft/1.2m, with pleated leaves, the flowers inferno red. Smaller and more grassy, x *crocosmiiflora* "Solfatare" [6–9] has bronze leaves setting off apricot-yellow flowers.

CYCLAMEN Low tuberous plants with shuttlecock flowers in shades of pink and magenta or white. Ivy-like leaves of fall-flowering *C. hederifolium* [5–8] appear with flowers in fall, often patterned silver. *C. coum* [5–8], winter-flowering and leaves

rounded, sometimes with silver or duller metallic coloring, as in **Pewter Group**. In both species underside of leaves red-purple.

CYNARA The cardoon, *C. cardunculus* [6–8] is the ultimate silver-gray perennial, a fountain of arching jagged leaves to 4ft/1.2m long, topped by violet thistle flowerheads. The blanched shoots are a culinary delicacy.

DAHLIA Tuberous-rooted plants, numerous hybrids. The pinnate leaves are typically rich green but in some cases their deep coloring is highly ornamental. In frostprone areas plant in spring and lift the tubers in fall. "Bishop of Llandaff" [8–10], to 43in/110cm, purple-black foliage and bright red semi-double flowers. Compact hybrids to 2ft/60cm with purple or bronze leaves include: "Bednall Beauty" [8–10], flowers rich red; "Ellen Houston" [8–10], flowers orange-red; "Yellow Hammer" [8–10], flowers yellow.

DARMERA The rhizomatous *D. peltata* [6–8] is suitable for moist soils in sun or partial shade. Dense heads of pink flowers followed by leaf stalks supporting parasol leaves up to 12in/30cm across. Margins scalloped and veins radiate conspicuously from the center. Rich fall colors.

DIANTHUS Pink Numerous tough dwarf plants from mountainous terrain, all with linear or narrowly lance-shaped leaves, dark green to blue-gray, often with a waxy bloom. Grown mainly for their single or double flowers, often richly scented. Mats or cushions of tight foliage are attractive among other dwarf plants that like sun and well-drained neutral to alkaline soil. The hedgehog pink, *D. erinaceus* [4–9], a cushion 2in/5cm high of stiff gray-green leaves; flowers, often sparse, are pink.

DICENTRA Mainly woodland plants, with delicate ferny foliage and heart- or locket-shaped flowers. For humus-rich moist soils in partial shade. *D. eximia* "Snowdrift" [4–8], and *D. formosa* [4–8] both have elegant, much divided leaves but the best for foliage are plants with distinctively gray-blue to silver leaves such as "Langtrees" [4–8], cream and pink flowers, and "Stuart Boothman" [3–8], deep pink flowers; both grow to 12in/30cm.

DISPORUM Fairy bells Quiet woodland plants dangling small white bells in spring. For humus-rich soils in partial shade. *D. sessile* "Variegatum" [4–9], to 18in/45cm, coolly elegant with broad, lance-shaped leaves irregularly striped clean white. *D. smithii* [5–7] with wavy leaves.

ECHINOPS Globe thistle Bold thistles with spherical flowerheads, for well-drained soil and full sun. *E. ritro* [4–8] has a framework of silver-white branching stems with stiff, prickly dark green leaves, white and downy on the back. "Veitch's Blue," to 3ft 3in/1m, the flowerheads metallic indigo then a softer blue when starry flowers open.

EPIMEDIUM Barrenwort Low-growing evergreen or deciduous perennials with refined compound leaves on wiry stems, the leaflets heart-shaped and usually sharply toothed. Foliage often subtly or richly tinted pink, red, or bronze in spring and fall; airy sprays of small flowers in spring. Steadily form carpets 8–12in/20–30cm high. Tolerant but especially good in humus-rich soil in partial shade. Deciduous kinds include: *E. grandiflorum* "Rose Queen" [5–8], bronzed leaves becoming light green, pink flowers; *E.* x *rubrum* [5–8], leaves retained through winter, reddish tints in spring and fall, yellow-spurred crimson flowers; *E.* x *versicolor* "Sulfureum" [5–9], green leaves tinted delicate shades of chocolate brown and marbled bronze in fall, flowers yellow; and *E.* x *youngianum* "Niveum" [5–9], short-growing and with white flowers, leaves red-tinted in spring and flushed orange-red in fall. *E.* x *perralchicum* "Frohnleiten" [4–8] and *E. perralderianum* [5–9], evergreen, glossy deep green in summer, marbled in spring and fall; flowers yellow. *E. pinnatum* subsp. *colchicum* [5–8], yellow-flowered evergreen, with leaves having 5 leaflets.

EQUISETUM Horsetail Spore-bearing and primitive plants, usually dreaded as ineradicable weeds, but with attractive plumes consisting of erect stems and whorls of what look like green needles or threads. The great horsetail, *E. telmateia* [4–8], has stems to 15ft/1.5m and threads 4–6in/10–15cm long. Best in moist heavy soil that is neutral to alkaline.

ERODIUM Stork's bill Many are compact sun–loving plants of rocky habitats making small mats or tufts of attractively lobed and cut leaves, and producing neat 5-petaled flowers. *E. chrysanthum* [7–8] makes a silver–gray mound of finely dissected leaves with pale yellow flowers floating well above it. *E. manescaui* [6–8], 18in/45cm high, suitable for border edge, has hairy, ferny, light green leaves, magenta–pink flowers.

ERYNGIUM Sea holly Misleadingly thistle-like plants falling into two broad categories. Many of the deciduous European species, all plants for full sun and well-drained soils, have conspicuous prickly bracts surrounding the heads of tiny flowers, the bracts and upper parts of the stems often metallic blue. *E. alpinum* [5–8], to 75cm/30in, has almost heart–shaped and spiny basal leaves and frills of softly spiny bracts, deep blue in **"Blue Star."** *E. bourgatii* [5–9] has jaggedly curled and prickly basal leaves veined with silver, the stems, up to 2ft/60cm high, bearing blue flowerheads and silver-gray bracts. *E. x oliverianum* [5–8], *E. x zabelii* [5–8], and evergreen *E. variifolium* [5–9] with white-veined basal leaves, are good variations on the spiny metallic theme. Most of the evergreen South American species, with dramatic rosettes of strap-shaped leaves, require moist conditions. The leaves of *E. agavifolium* [6–9] are rich green, sword-like and sharply armed, making a fierce base from which to launch stems to 5ft/1.5m bearing green-white thimble flowerheads. The smaller *E. proteiflorum* [9–10] has narrower spiny leaves; white bracts surround the cone-shaped flowerheads.

ERYTHRONIUM Dog's-tooth violet Bulbous plants of woodland and alpine meadows for dappled shade and humus-rich soil. The foliage, in some species heavily mottled, dies down in early summer but is at its peak when the pendent flowers are out. Foliage of European dog's-tooth violet, *E. dens-canis* [3–9], 4in/10cm high, and of the larger American trout lily, *E. revolutum* [5–9], are heavily mottled maroon, the latter's leaves having a wavy margin; pink flowers.

EUPATORIUM Hemp agrimony Among the herbaceous species are heavyweights such as Joe Pye weed, *E. purpureum* [3–8]. White snakeroot, *E. rugosum* [4–9], is more refined and in **"Chocolate"** the nettle-like toothed leaves are purple-bronze; white flowerheads. For moist, preferably alkaline soil and partial shade.

EUPHORBIA Spurge A large and varied genus, ranging from flimsy annuals to large shrubs and tree-like succulents. Many species have attractive foliage. The much reduced floral parts are cradled by conspicuous, long-lasting bracts, highly colored in the popular Christmas plant, poinsettia, *E. pulcherrima* [10–11]. Another shrubby species, *E. characias* [7–9], has gray-green leaves and large heads of yellow-green bracts with dark or, in the case of subsp. *wulfenii*, yellow glands at the center. Perennial spurges with richly colored foliage include: *E. amygdaloides* **"Purpurea"** [5–9], a form of the evergreen wood spurge, 18in/75cm high with maroon stems, bright red new shoots and yellow-green bracts; *E. dulcis* **"Chameleon"** [6–9],

12in/30cm high, with purple-tinted bracts and purple oval leaves, in fall turning red and orange; and *E. griffithii* **"Dixter"** [5–9], 3ft/90cm high, with lance-shaped, copper-tinted leaves and brick-red bracts. The form of many spurges is pleasing. *E. myrsinites* [6–8] is a sprawler, with whorls of waxy blue-green leaves spiraling the length of radiating prostrate stems, in spring terminating in heads of lime-green bracts. *E. polychroma* [4–9] makes a neat dome or mound 16in/40cm high, radiant in spring with green-yellow bracts.

FARFUGIUM The large, kidney-shaped leaves of *F. japonicum* [7–8] are most striking in variegated forms: **"Argenteum,"** irregularly blotched creamy white; **"Aureomaculatum,"** with irregular yellow markings. Long-stalked leaves to 2ft/60cm make good ground cover in moist soils.

FERULA The giant fennel, *F. communis* [6–9], makes large mounds of dark green, finely cut leaves and after several years pushes up a stout flower stalk about 10ft/3m high, branching to carry numerous rounded heads of small yellow flowers.

FILIPENDULA Mainly moisture-loving plants, most with attractive divided foliage. *F. ulmaria* **"Aurea"** [3–9], a meadowsweet 18in/45cm high, makes clump of rich yellow, deeply veined leaves in spring; scorches in full sun. Remove flowers to encourage new growth.

FOENICULUM see Fennel (Edible plants)

GALAX Wandflower The evergreen *G. urceolata* [3–8] has rounded toothed leaves about 4in/10cm across, glossy dark green in summer but burnished in winter. Stems of tiny white flowers stand 12in/30cm high. For moist and lime-free soil.

GERANIUM Cranesbill Important genus of ornamentals, many with attractive foliage and flower, some outstanding as ground cover. Leaves, rounded or 5-pointed, often further lobed and toothed. *G. madarense* [8–9] and *G. palmatum* [8–9] are giants about 4ft/1.2m high with deeply cut leaves; they die after producing a profusion of purple-pink flowers. The hardier *G. x magnificum* [4–8] makes large, deep green clumps that tint attractively in fall; violet-blue flowers. *G. phaeum* **"Samobor"** [5–7], to 30in/75cm, is particularly good in shade, the large leaves with a central brown blotch, the flowers sulky purple. Aromatic *G. macrorrhizum* [3–8] makes dense and nearly evergreen cover 16in/40cm high, the leaves lightly felted and scalloped; flowers white or pink. In light shade *G.* **"Anne**

Folkard"** [5–9] trails lemon-yellow leaves, later darker green, and dark-eyed magenta flowers. *G. renardii* [6–8], best in sun, forms a mound under 12in/30cm of quilted, velvety sage-green leaves with a scalloped edge; purple-veined white flowers.

GLAUCIDIUM In moist soil and woodland shade *G. palmatum* [6–9] makes a clump 18in/45cm high of large, light green leaves, prominently veined, lobed, and toothed; poppy-like mauve flowers.

GLECHOMA The variegated ground ivy, *G. hederacea* **"Variegata"** [5–9], evergreen or semi-evergreen, trail stems as much as 5ft/1.5m long carrying kidney- to heart-shaped leaves variegated white, especially around the scalloped edge. Good in containers.

GUNNERA The stout bristly stalks of *G. manicata* [7–9] support vast leaves, some more than 6ft/1.8m across. They are jaggedly lobed, bristly, and prominently veined. Cone-shaped green-brown flower spikes lurk within the clump. *G. tinctoria* [9–10] is similar but its dense clump is only 5ft/1.5m high. *G. magellanica* [8–9] forms mats only 6in/15cm high of kidney-shaped, scalloped leaves. All for waterside and boggy ground.

HELLEBORUS Hellebore Shade-tolerant perennials combining handsome evergreen leaves with long-lasting flowers. The shrub-like *H. argutifolius* [6–8] makes a mound to 4ft/1.2m high, its leathery leaves composed of 3 conspicuously toothed leaflets, dark gray-green and noticeably veined, lighter on the underside; pale green flowers in late winter and early spring. *H. x sternii* **"Boughton Beauty"** [6–9] slightly smaller, stems purple-pink, leaves veined silver, and flowers pink in bud, opening green. Stinking hellebore, *H. foetidus* [5–9], a dark green clump 2ft/60cm high, with fingered leaves and bell-shaped green flowers, sometimes maroon rimmed, in winter and spring; in **Wester Flisk Group** the stalks and leaf bases are tinted red.

HEMEROCALLIS Daylily Mostly clump-forming plants with arching strap-shaped leaves and stems in summer bearing numerous trumpet-shaped flowers, individually short-lived. The foliage of thousands of hybrids [dormant varieties 3–9; evergreen varieties 6–9] at its fresh best when emerging.

HEUCHERA Coral flower Good edging plants and ground cover for sun and partial shade, doing best in moist but well-drained soils. The lobed leaves, often beautifully shaded and mottled, form mounds usually less than 12in/30cm high, above which in spring or early summer stems about 18in/45cm high carry spikes of small bell-shaped flowers. Ivy-like leaves of *H. americana* [4–8] lustrous dark green, tinted and veined tan, especially when young; flowers brown and green. Almost used to excess, *H. micrantha* var. *diversifolia* "Palace Purple" [4–8] has jagged and shiny metallic purple leaves, magenta pink on the underside; sprays of creamy pink tiny flowers followed by pink seedheads. Hybrids with less jagged leaves include *H.* "Plum Pudding" [4–8], deep purple with darker veins, and *H.* "Pewter Moon" [4–8], with a subdued metallic luster, except for the veins, over purplish green. Red flowers of *H. sanguinea* [3–8] show in "Snow Storm," with ruffled leaves that are white, speckled, and margined green, and "Taff's Joy," with variegated creamy yellow leaves tinged pink.

HOSTA Plantain lily Popular clump-forming plants, the species and numerous hybrids interesting principally for their foliage, although many have stems of lily-like flowers in white or mauve. Leaves heart-shaped, lance-shaped, rounded, or ovate, variously textured, and the broad color range includes all shades of green, gray-blue, yellow, and many subtle and bold variegations. Some turn tawny gold in fall. For lush, immaculate leaves grow in partial shade and moist, fertile soil; protect plants from slugs and snails. Many make dense ground cover. The larger kinds, with clumps 2–3ft/60–90cm high, are superb container plants. The greens range from the dark glossiness of *H. lancifolia* [3–9], with a clump 2ft/60cm high of narrow pointed leaves, to the light freshness of *H.* "Royal Standard" [3–9], with a clump 3ft/90cm high of heart-shaped leaves that are puckered, deeply veined, and wavy at the margins. *H.* "Sum and Substance" [3–9] has large, heart-shaped leaves of yellow-green. A stronger yellow bias is seen in several, including *H.* "Zounds" [3–9], which has thick puckered leaves forming a clump about 2ft/60cm high. An irregular yellow-green margin makes a subtle variegation on the large puckered leaves of *H.* "Frances Williams" [3–9]. In the much bolder warm variegation of *H.* "Gold Standard" [3–9], the large leaves are almost completely yellow except for an irregular heart outline in green. In *H. fortunei* var. *aureomarginata* [3–9] the margin is yellow, the heavily veined center rich green. White and creamy white outlines give a crispness to narrow-leaved *H.* "Ginko Craig" [3–9] and *H.* "Francee," with large

puckered leaves. In some, including *H. undulata* var. *univittata* [3–9], a dense clump 18in/45cm high of twisted leaves, the creamy white forms a central splash. Examples with blue-green waxy foliage include *H.* "Krossa Regal" [3–9], with a clump 3ft/90cm high of pointed and rather narrow, deeply veined leaves, and *H.* "Halcyon" [3–9], 18in/45cm high, deeply veined and pointed, with a strong blue cast. *H. sieboldiana* var. *elegans* [3–9] supreme, with a commanding clump about 3ft/90cm high of deeply veined and quilted heart-shaped leaves that are waxy blue-green; they are amber-gold in fall.

HOUTTUYNIA In its plain-leaved form *H. cordata* [6–10] is invasive, but "Chameleon" is less vigorous and colorful ground cover in dappled shade where the soil is moist. Leaves heart-shaped and variegated green, amber, yellow, and red. Spikes of tiny flowers with 4 petal-like white bracts at the base.

IMPATIENS Includes tender perennials usually grown as annuals in bedding and containers. *I.* New Guinea Group, bushy hybrids to 14in/35cm high, with dense whorls of lance-shaped leaves, often dark bronze, red or variegated yellow, sometimes with pink rib. Bright flowers.

IRIS The fan of sword leaves is an attractive feature of many bearded irises and in *I.* "Florentina" [4–9] the gray-green matches perfectly the scented white flowers. *I. pallida* [6–9] has silvery paper-like bracts around mauve-blue flowers; subsp. *pallida* has broad gray blades. Variegated "Argentea Variegata" (white stripes) and "Variegata" (yellow) have eye-catching foliage; all need sun and well-drained soil. *I. laevigata*, white and green, needs moisture. The coarseness of the beardless yellow flag, *I. pseudacorus* [5–9], reaching 4ft/1.2m at the water's edge, is mitigated by yellow striping in "Variegata;" the yellow fades in summer. *I. ensata* "Variegata" [5–8] is a shorter moisture-lover, with white-striped leaves and purple flowers.

KIRENGESHOMA A woodland plant for moist lime-free soil, *K. palmata* [5–8] makes an elegant mound up to 4ft/1.2m, quietly combining dark stems with lobed and prominently veined pale green leaves; waxy, yellow, shuttlecock flowers.

LAMIUM Deadnettle These include carpeting plants that make dense ground cover but are difficult to dislodge once established. Yellow archangel, *L. galeobdolon* [4–8], is dangerously

thuggish, the cultivar "Silberteppich," silvered and netted green, less so. *L. maculatum* [4–8], which has toothed leaves with a central silver stripe, eclipsed by forms with frosted leaves outlined in green, such as pink-flowered "Beacon Silver" and white "White Nancy;" "Aureum" has yellow leaves with white centers and pink flowers.

LIGULARIA Moisture-lovers, some with handsome leaves. *L. dentata* "Desdemona" [5–9], 4ft/1.2m high, has heart-shaped leaves, dark bronze-green with vibrant red-brown undersides; flowers orange. The fingered leaves of the taller *L. przewalskii* [4–8], irregularly lobed and toothed, topped by spires of small yellow flowers. The spluttering orange-yellow sparks of *L.* "The Rocket" [4–8] rise on dark stems above large, rounded leaves, heavily veined and serrated.

LIRIOPE Lilyturf The tuberous *L. muscari* [5–9] makes a clump of strap-shaped leaves to 18in/45cm long; spikes of violet-purple flowers in fall.

LOBELIA Some of the hybrids raised from moisture-loving, clump-forming species such as *L. cardinalis* [3–8] have richly colored foliage and spires 30–36in/75–90cm high of red, purple, or violet tubular two-lipped flowers. The stems and leaves of *L.* "Bee's Flame" [4–9], *L.* "Dark Crusader" [4–9], and *L.* "Queen Victoria" [4–9] are red-purple, the flowers red or scarlet. *L. tupa* [8–10] is very different in character, the downy leaves, up to 12in/30cm long, gray-green, the curious flowers red-brown; grows to 5ft/1.5m.

LUPINUS see Trees & shrubs

LYCHNIS Campion The short-lived dusty miller, *L. coronaria* [4–8], grows to 30in/75cm, its clump of woolly silver-gray foliage topped by wide-spreading branches carrying velvety magenta or white flowers. For full sun and well-drained soil.

LYSICHITON Skunk cabbage In boggy soil the two species produce large paddle-like leaves, preceded in early spring by arum-like flower spikes surrounded by conspicuous spathes. Yellow skunk cabbage, *L. americanus* [5–9], leaves up to 4ft/120cm long; spathes yellow. White skunk cabbage, *L. camtschatcensis* [5–9], is smaller.

LYSIMACHIA Loosestrife Golden creeping Jenny, *L. nummularia* "Aurea" [4–8], roots as it goes to make a dense yellow carpet; yellow flowers. *L. ciliata* "Firecracker"

[3–9] to 3ft 3in/1m, with pointed copper-brown leaves and heads of lemon-yellow flowers. Both for moist soil in sun or partial shade.

MACLEAYA Plume poppy Flower plumes, buff to pink, top tall plants over 6ft/1.8m, with handsome lobed leaves and running roots. *M. cordata* [3–8] and *M. microcarpa* "Kelway's Coral Plume" [3–8] with leaves white and downy on undersides.

MARRUBIUM Plants for full sun and well-drained soil, with silky leaves, the flowers of little consequence. *M. cyllenium* "Velvetissimum" [6–9], makes a sage-green mound 16in/40cm high of softest velvet. *M. incanum* [3–9], nearly twice the size, is silvery silky, the nettle-like leaves felted on the underside.

MECONOPSIS For moist, lime-free soil, ideally in woodland, the blue poppies make handsome rosettes of bristly, even spiny leaves. The blue-green basal leaves of *M. betonicifolia* [7–8] are covered with rusty hairs; stem of blue poppies up to 4ft/21.2m high.

MELISSA see **BALM** (Edible plants)

MENTHA see **MINT** (Edible plants)

NELUMBO Lotus Tropical and subtropical plants for the sunny shallow margins of pools. The leaves of the sacred lotus, *N. nucifera* [4–11], sometimes more than 30in/75cm across, are rounded, wavy edged around a central dip, and have a waxy bloom. Pink peony-like flowers followed by unusual seedpods stand 4ft/1.2m or more above the water. In frost-prone areas lift rhizomes in fall.

NYMPHAEA Water lily Aquatics often with showy flowers but the floating, sometimes mottled leaves make calming patterns on still water, and the shade they create helps to limit the development of algae. A deep cleft (sinus) divides the leaves into 2 lobes. Choose water lilies to suit the depth of water. *N.* "Aurora" [4–11], a miniature for water 12–18in/30–45cm deep, has olive-green leaves mottled purple, and flowers that pass through yellow and orange to become blood-red.

OPHIOPOGON Lilyturf Grasssy evergreens with narrow strap-shaped leaves, suitable as ground cover or as edging in partial shade where soil is moist. Small flowers followed by purple or black berries. A variegated form of white lilyturf, *O. jaburan* "Vittatus" [7–10], makes twisted tufts up to 2ft/60cm high of green leaves brightened

by cream margins. Spidery clumps of *O. planiscapus* "Nigrescens" [6–9] composed of near-black arching leaves about 12in/30cm long.

ORIGANUM Marjoram Cretan dittany, *O. dictamnus* [7–9], makes a mound about 6in/15cm high of felted, gray, rounded leaves. In summer, long-tubed pink flowers show between the purplish pink hop-like bracts. The smaller *O.* "Kent Beauty" [5–8] has rounded bright green leaves that are not felted and eye-catching rich pink bracts.

OXALIS Shamrock Among the hundreds of species are several delightful small bulbous plants with attractive flowers and foliage. *O. adenophylla* [6–8] makes a neat clump 6in/15cm high, with blue-green parasol-like leaves made of numerous pleated leaflets. Funnel-shaped pink flowers, exquisitely furled in bud. *O. enneaphylla* [6–8] similar. Leaves of *O. tetraphylla* "Iron Cross" [8–9] have 4 almost triangular leaflets meeting at their apex, where a purple band creates a dark cross; flowers pink. All for free-draining soil and full sun.

PACHYSANDRA The dark, coarsely toothed leaves of the carpeting and evergreen *P. terminalis*, 8in/20cm high, are arranged in whorls; "Variegata" with white margins. White flowers. Good ground cover in shade.

PAEONIA Peony Superb flowering plants, the compound leaves of many well above the average, as in shrubby species such as yellow-flowered *P. delavayi* var. *ludlowii* [5–8]. Purplish red young growths often highly ornamental, supremely so in the Caucasian peony, *P. mlokosewitschii* [5–8] before becoming soft gray-green at 2ft/60cm; exquisite short-lived lemon-yellow flowers. *P. cambessedisii* [7–8], 18in/45cm high, has leaves of deep green contrasting with red-purple stems, veins and undersides; deep pink flowers.

PELARGONIUM Many aromatic, shrubby perennials, much used in bedding schemes and containers for their long flowering season in summer. Also many foliage plants of exceptional quality, most 12–30in/30–75cm high, best in full sun. Rounded, lobed leaves of fancy-leaved zonal pelargoniums conspicuously banded, in *P.* "Blazonry" [8–10], *P.* "Dolly Varden" [8–10], and *P.* "Mr Henry Cox" [8–10]. Scented-leaf pelargoniums have strongly, distinctively aromatic foliage and relatively small flowers. *P. dichondrifolium* [8–10], with kidney-shaped leaves and elegant white flowers, is unusual in being lavender-scented. The compact, upright, variegated lemon-scented pelargonium, *P. crispum*

"Variegatum" [8–10], has small cream-and-green crimped leaves and pale mauve flowers. Peppermint-scented pelargonium, *P. tometosum* [7–10], is very vigorous, the velvety leaves strongly scented; flowers white. A selection from the hybrids, most highly desirable, includes: *P.* "Atomic Snowflake" [8–10], large 3-lobed leaves variegated yellow, lemon-rose fragrance, flowers pink; *P.* "Blandfordianum" [8–10], lax, much cut, lemon-scented gray-green leaves, white, red-dotted flowers; *P.* "Chocolate Peppermint" [8–10], tolerant of partial shade, dark green leaves with chocolate markings and peppermint scent, mauve flowers; *P.* Fragrans Group [8–10], compact, small, gray-green lobed leaves of finest velvet and pine-scented, white flowers; and *P.* "Gray Lady Plymouth" [8–10] rose-scented, silver-gray leaves with cream variegation, pink flowers. Ivy-leaved forms with trailing stems and fleshy leaves include the variegated *P.* "L'Elégante."

PERSICARIA Elliptic leaves of *P. virginiana* "Painter's Palette" [5–9] are an astonishing medley of green, cream, and pink, stamped with a V-shaped brown mark; to 2ft/60cm in moist soil and partial shade.

PETASITES Butterbur The rhizomatous and invasive *P. japonicus* var. *giganteus* [5–9] is ideal for heavy soils – but only for landscaping. Large rounded leaves make dense ground cover at about 3ft 3in/1m; heads of greenish yellow flowers are borne in spring.

PHLOX The border phloxes, cultivars of *P. paniculata* [4–8], 30–45in/75–115cm high, are mainly grown for their rounded heads of bright flowers. "Harlequin" and "Norah Leigh" both have white-variegated leaves and flowers in the mauve to purple range.

PHORMIUM Clump-forming, with leathery strap- or sword-shaped leaves, for full sun and moist soils. New Zealand flax, *P. tenax* [8–10], a magnificent clump of swords to 10ft/3m long, produces towering flower stalks with tubular brick-red flowers; Purpureum Group, bronze-purple; "Variegatum," cream stripes. *P. cookianum* [9–10] 6ft/1.8m high, has more lax strap-like leaves, in subsp. *hookeri* "Tricolor" with marginal cream and red stripes. Numerous hybrids, like dwarf *P.* "Bronze Baby" [9–10] and stiff *P.* "Sundowner" [9–10]), bronze-green with pink margins.

PLECTRANTHUS Includes several trailing perennials usually grown as houseplants but good as summer container plants outdoors. *P. forsteri* "Marginatus," upright then trailing, has hairy ovate leaves with white scalloped margins. *P. madagascariensis* "Variegated Mintleaf," also with white–variegated leaves and bristly, smells of mint.

PODOPHYLLUM Rhizomatous plants for moist soil and shade. Leaves of *P. hexandrum* [5–8] a fan 10in/25cm long of 3–5 toothed lobes, mottled maroon; crystalline pale pink or white flowers and red fruit. May apple, *P. peltatum* [4–9], has larger glossy leaves and conspicuous waxy flowers, followed by greenish yellow fruit.

POLEMONIUM Jacob's ladder The fanciful common name of *P. caeruleum* [4–8] refers to pinnate leaves, with leaflets ranged the length of the rib. "Brise d'Anjou" an eye-catching variegated form with blue flowers making a clump 2ft/60cm high; for shade and moist soil.

POLYGONATUM The common Solomon's seal, *P. x hybridum* [3–8], very shade tolerant, has arching stems to 3ft/90cm high, with leaves held horizontally; in spring dangles small green-tinted white bells. The leaves of "Striatum" are striped creamy white. *P. falcatum* "Variegatum" [5–8] has oval leaves with a cream edge.

PONTEDERIA Pickerel weed Marginal aquatics, *P. cordata* [3–11] edging out with a crowd of stems. The lance- or spear-shaped leaves are glossy and lightly shadowed; blue flower spikes to 18in/45cm above water.

PULMONARIA Lungwort Numerous good plants for lightly shaded ground cover in moist soils, most flowering late winter to early spring. *P. longifolia* [3–8] has narrow lance-shaped leaves with white spots on dark green; flowers blue. Jerusalem sage, *P. saccharata* [3–7], evergreen, the rough leaves dark green with silver marbling; flowers blue and pink. In **Argentea Group** the leaves are heavily silvered.

PULSATILLA Pasque flower *P. halleri* [5–7] and other species similar to pasque flower, *P. vulgaris* [5–7] in their finely cut, ferny leaves. Tuft of young leaves and large nodding purple flowers exquisitely silky, heads of seeds softly feathered; 4–8in/ 10–20cm in height. For sun and well-drained soil.

RANUNCULUS Buttercup The lesser celandine, *R. ficaria* [4–8], is a low-growing cheerful weed with lustrous yellow flowers but desirable in "Brazen Hussy," with glossy chocolate-brown leaves.

RAOULIA Mat- or cushion-forming plants with tiny, overlapping silvery leaves, often spoon-shaped, and minute flowers. For sun and well-drained soil in rock gardens and raised beds. *R. hookeri* [8–9] is a silvery creeping mat. Leaves of *R. australis* Lutescens Group [8–9] are so small that it looks like a tight gray-blue moss.

RHEUM Rhubarb The edible rhubarb, *R. x hybridum* [5–7], is itself a magnificent foliage plant. The ornamental kinds are for deep moist soil in sun or partial shade. Chinese rhubarb, *R. palmatum* [5–9], has jaggedly lobed and strongly veined leaves over 3ft/90cm long. "Atrosanguineum" and "Bowles' Crimson," leaves pink-purple when young and heavily crinkled, later green with a red underside; tall plumes of small red flowers followed by red seeds. *R.* "Ace of Hearts" [5–7], more compact, has dark green, heart-shaped leaves, red-purple on the back and heavily veined; pale airy plumes. *R. alexandrae* [6–8], with glossy dark leaves, noted for large bracts, cream then red, hiding the flowers.

RODGERSIA Moisture-loving clump-forming perennials for sun or partial shade, all with handsome leaves. The bronzed and fingered leaves of *R. aesculifolia* [5–6], conspicuously veined and crinkled, resemble those of the horse chestnut; clumps topped by plumes of white or pink flowers, 6ft/1.8m high. *R. podophylla* [5–7], of similar size, has leaves with 3–5 jaggedly lobed leaflets, bronze at first, then green, then coppery; cream flowers. *R. pinnata* "Superba" [5–7], a smaller plant, has glossy, bronzed, pinnate leaves, crinkled and veined; flowers pink.

SAGITTARIA Arrowhead Aquatics, some with decorative aerial leaves. Japanese arrowhead, *S. sagittifolia* [6–11], a marginal, has elongated arrow leaves 10in/25cm long, and white 3-petaled flowers.

SANGUINARIA Bloodroot A woodland plant for moist soils, *S. canadensis* [3–9] has blue-green leaves, up to 12in/30cm across, heart- or kidney-shaped with a scalloped edge. Beautifully folded on emerging and unfurling as the white flowers, double in "Plena," open.

SAXIFRAGA Saxifrage Numerous small, usually evergreen perennials suitable for rock gardens and some larger plants for borders. Most of the alpine saxifrages form dwarf cushions or mats composed of small leaves tightly packed in compact rosettes. An encrustation of lime whitens the leaves of many, including *S. paniculata* and

S. x irvingii "Jenkinsiae" [6–7], a dense mound, only 2in/5cm high, of tiny gray-green leaves with oversize pale pink flowers in early spring. The mossy saxifrages make small, dense hummocks of divided leaves, in the case of *S. exarata* subsp. *moschata* "Cloth of Gold" [5–7], bright yellow. The rosette of the Pyrenian saxifrage, *S. longifolia* [6–7] is 12in/30cm across, the linear leaves lime-encrusted; flowers extravagantly after 3 or 4 years, then the rosette dies. *S. fortunei* [6–8], 18in/45cm high and suitable for a shady border, has scalloped, rounded leaves, glossy and deep green with red beneath, and sprays of starry flowers in fall. The leaves of "Rubrifolia" have highly burnished bronze upper surfaces.

SEDUM Stonecrop Mainly succulent sun-loving plants for well-drained soil. Wall pepper, *S. acre* [3–9], invasive mat-forming evergreen; less vigorous "Aureum" is bright yellow. *S. spathulifolium* [5–9], also mat-forming, with tight rosettes of spoon-shaped leaves, is better behaved. "Cape Blanco" gray-white, "Purpureum" red-purple with gray. *S. sieboldii* "Mediovariegatum" [6–9], a trailing plant with coin-like leaves in threes, blue-green striped cream; stems and flowers pink. Ice plant, *S. spectabile* [4–9], and several cultivars and hybrids are border plants up to 20in/50cm high with fleshy, gray-green toothed leaves topped in fall by flat heads of pink or red flowers. A more open plant, orpine, *S. telephium* [4–9], commonly seen as the purple-leaved subsp. *maximum* "Atropurpureum." The slightly smaller *S.* "Vera Jameson" [4–9] is another good purple to mix with grays.

SEMPERVIVUM Houseleek Evergreen succulents for sun and well-drained soil with rosettes, the largest saucer-sized, of tightly packed, sometimes spoon-shaped leaves. The rosettes, which die after producing a stem of starry flowers, spawn numerous offsets. Leaves may be smooth, waxy, bristly, or covered with a web of fine hairs, often dark-tipped, mahogany, or purple. The common houseleek, *S. tectorum* [4–8], is relatively large, its elegantly tipped blue-green leaves often suffused red-purple. *S. arachnoideum* [5–8] is cobwebby, *S. ciliosum* [7–9] very hairy. Numerous cultivars and hybrids. *Jovibarba* species are similar. Suitable for rock gardens, dry stone walls, sinks or pans.

SISYRINCHIUM Several small plants with grassy leaves, such as *S. idahoense* [7–8], are suitable for rock gardens. *S. striatum* "Aunt May" [6–8] makes iris-like clump of gray-green sword leaves striped creamy yellow; zigzag spires to 2ft/60cm of cream flowers. For well-drained, sunny borders.

SOLEIROLIA Baby's tears Mind-your-own-business and mother-of-thousands are other names for *S. soleirolii* [10–11], a mat-former with tiny fresh green leaves. Ground cover for difficult corners but spreads and hard to eradicate; "Aurea," yellow-green, and "Variegata," silver, less vigorous.

SOLENOSTEMON Coleus Cultivars and hybrids of the evergreen perennial *S. scutellarioides* [A] grown as annual bedding and container plants for their brightly colored foliage. Matte ovate leaves, up to 4in/10cm long, toothed, scalloped, frilled, or bizarrely cut, conspicuously veined, and often crinkled. Colors of varying intensities include purple-black, maroon, wine red, pink, yellow, and green, in many combinations, randomly speckled, irregularly splashed, or neatly patterned, sometimes with an outline. Often raised from mixed seed or sold as unnamed hybrids, but named hybrids, about 2ft/60cm in a season, also available. They include "Black Prince," scalloped, almost black leaves; "Crimson Ruffles," bright red with purple veins and faint green frilly edge; "Kiwi Fern," red-purple with thin bright yellow edge defining finely cut, ferny outline; "Winsome," sturdy, broad heart-shaped yellow-green leaves with central red heart. Vigorous hybrids, like "Pineapple Beauty," with large lime-green and maroon leaves. Remove flower spikes.

STACHYS In sun and well-drained soil lambs' ears, *S. byzantina* [4–8], is useful ground cover or edging. Thick leaves gray-green and woolly, the non-flowering "Silver Carpet" making a dense mat of velvety foliage; "Big Ears" has large leaves and spikes of purple flowers.

SYMPHYTUM Comfrey Mainly woodland plants with fleshy roots, rough hairy leaves and coils of buds that open to tubular flowers. The leaves of *S.* "Goldsmith" [5–9], 12in/30cm high, have cream to yellow margins, and those of *S.* "Belsay" [3–8] are a fuller yellow. Taller *T.* x *uplandicum* "Variegatum" [3–9], leaves gray-green with cream margins. Flowers of both pink to blue.

TANACETUM Mainly plants of dry sunny terrain, including some good grays for rock gardens and as edging. *T. densum* subsp. *armani* [6–8] makes a low mound of silver-white, much-cut leaves like dense feathers; heads of small yellow daisies. *T. haradjanii* [8–9], similar with less rounded leaves. A

yellow-leaved feverfew, *T. parthenium* "Aureum" [4–9], about 12in/30cm high, and dwarf "Golden Moss" have finely divided yellow-green leaves and white daisies.

TELLIMA Fringe cups A woodland plant, *T. grandiflora* [4–8] is clump-forming, its mainly basal evergreen leaves hairy and scalloped, their bright green burnished in winter; spires of greenish bell flowers. Leaves of "Purpurteppich" veined and shaded maroon in summer; Rubra Group has green leaves, purple on the underside, that turn purple and bronze in winter. Makes good ground cover in moist, humus-rich soils.

THALICTRUM Meadow rue Several species for moist soil and partial shade combine sprays of elegantly divided leaves and airy, delicate flowers. *T. aquilegiifolium* [5–8], 3ft 3in/1m high, has columbine-like leaves, leaflets wavy at the margins; heads of tiny purple flowers. *T. flavum* subsp. *glaucum* [5–8], weightier and taller, has blue-gray foliage; fluffy yellow flowers.

TIARELLA Foam flower Low woodland plants making excellent ground cover in shade. Flowers of *T. cordifolia* [3–7] foam above rich green leaves, bronzed in winter, hairy and prettily lobed; spreads by creeping rhizomes. *T. wherryi* [5–9], clump-forming and leaves maple-like, in "Bronze Beauty" light green shaded red-bronze; pink flowers.

TOLMIEA Pick-a-back plant Sometimes known as thousand mothers, *T. menziesii* [6–9] makes clumps 12in/30cm high with hairy leaves, lobed, toothed, and conspicuously veined, on which plantlets form; copper-brown flowers. "Taff's Gold" has light green leaves speckled primrose.

TRADESCANTIA Several trailing perennials are useful in summer containers, especially the white-variegated wandering Jew, *T. fluminensis* "Albovittata" [10–11], *T. zebrina* "Purpusii" [10–11], a purple-leaved counterpart, and "Quadricolor," a striped mixture of green, silver, pink, and cream.

TRIFOLIUM Clover The typical leaf of these mainly meadow plants consists of 3 or 4 leaflets. In mat-forming *T. pratense* "Susan Smith" [6–9], each leaflet netted with gold veins; pink flowerheads. Shamrock or white clover, *T repens* [4–8], aggressive colonizer. Leaves of "Purpurascens" and "Purpurascens Quadrifolium" [4–8], usually with 4 crowded leaflets, purple-brown with green rim; small heads of white flowers.

TRILLIUM Trinity flower Woodland plants for shade, preferably in lime-free soil. All the parts are clearly in threes, the flowers rising from a whorl of 3 leaves. The toad-shade or wake robin, *T. sessile* [5–9], 12in/30cm high, has leaves mottled purple and wavy at the edge; stalkless maroon flowers.

TULIPA Tulip Spring bulbs with flowers in a magnificent range of colors. The dwarf *T. greigii* [A] and numerous short-growing hybrids such as *T.* "Red Riding Hood" (flowers scarlet-red) have broad, gray-green strap-like leaves, mottled and streaked purple. Another dwarf, the scarlet-flowered *T. linifolia* [A], has narrow, sickle-shaped gray leaves with wavy, almost zigzag margins. Taller tulips with creamy variegated leaves include *T. praestans* "Unicum" [A], with several red flowers to a stem.

VALERIANA The lobed basal leaves, up to 8in/20cm long, of *V. phu* "Aurea" [5–9] are fresh yellow in spring, green later; best in sun and moist soil.

VANCOUVERIA The lobed ivy-like leaflets of the creeping *V. hexandra* [5–8], smooth and bright green, form base for sprays of small white flowers. *V. chrysantha* [6–8], shield-shaped, evergreen leathery leaflets.

VERATRUM Plants needing moist fertile soil and protection from slugs and snails to reach full perfection. *V. nigrum* [3–8] makes a mound of pleated leaves up to 16in/40cm long, from which rises a tall branched stem packed with small starry maroon flowers.

VERONICA Speedwell The gray mat of *V. cinerea* [5–8] is composed of linear felted leaves from which emerge short spikes of blue flowers. Taller silver speedwell, *V. spicata* subsp. *incana* [4–8], an attractive silvered gray edging plant of silvery hairiness; spikes of blue-purple flowers. Both for well-drained soil and full sun.

VIOLA Low plants grown mainly for their flowers. *V. riviniana* Purpurea Group [5–8] is a pretty invader with lightly scalloped, almost heart-shaped leaves of greenish purple; small blue-purple flowers.

WALDSTEINIA The low, semi-evergreen carpeting *W. ternata* [3–8] has leaves consisting of 3 lobes, further lobed and toothed; yellow strawberry flowers. Useful ground cover, sun or shade.

ZANTEDESCHIA Arum lily Moisture-loving plants, most with lance- or arrow-shaped leaves and spathes of couturier elegance. *Z. aethiopica* [8–10], 3ft/90cm high, makes thick clumps of arrow-shaped leaves, glossy and dark green; the spathes are swirling white funnels.

Grasses

The herbaceous grasses have of recent years come into their own as ornamentals, many for their flowers, but some also for their foliage. The bamboos, in effect shrubby grasses with woody, usually hollow canes, have a longer history as ornamentals, particularly in the East. There are other categories of plant, including sedges, superficially resembling grasses and with similar uses, and these are all grouped here.

ALOPECURUS Foxtail grass The typical meadow foxtail, *A. pratensis* [6–9] is of little ornamental value but the gold-striped "Aureovariegatus" is a bright tufted perennial grass, 3ft 3in/1m high, with the margins joining to give the linear leaves a yellow tip. Leaves of "Aureus" completely yellow in early summer; clip over late spring.

ARUNDO Giant reed, *A. donax* [7–10], a perennial grass of river banks and similarly wet places. Bamboo-like hollow stems grow to 15ft/5m, the arching strap-shaped leaves, 2ft/60cm long, gray-green; feathery flower plumes in fall. Less vigorous var. *versicolor* [7–10] has white-striped leaves.

CALAMAGROSTIS The feather reed grass, *C.* x *acutiflora* [5–9], has purplish flower plumes that fade to pink or buff. The foliage clump, 3ft/90cm high, of "Overdam" is made up of linear arching leaves edged and striped yellow, fading to pink-tinged white.

CAREX Sedge Grass-like perennials and a few annuals, most of which require moist conditions in sun or part-shade. *C. comans* [7–9] makes a dense evergreen tussock about 14in/35cm high with hair-like leaves that are variable in color, bronze forms being favored by gardeners. The arching leaves of "Frosted Curls" turn at the tips, showing a contrast between pale and darker surfaces. *C. buchananii* [7–9] and *C. flagellifera* [7–9] are similar to *C. comans*, the plants in cultivation usually with red-brown foliage. *C. conica* "Snowline" [5–9] forms small evergreen tufts, the arching leaves, 6in/15cm long,

edged white. Bowles' golden sedge, *C. elata* "Aurea" [5–9], is a bright sedge, forming clumps of arching yellow leaves with a narrow light green edge. *C. oshimensis* "Evergold" [6–9] makes an evergreen clump with numerous arching leaves, 8–16in/20–40cm long, brightened by a central yellow stripe which pales with age. The broader, stiffer leaves of *C. morrowii* "Fisher's Form" [5–9] are margined and striped creamy yellow. One of the broadest sedges in leaf is *C. siderosticha* "Variegata" [7–9], the straps pale green with white stripes and margins, the bases tinged pink.

CHUSQUEA The glossy pith-filled canes of the bamboo *C. culeou* [8–11] are striking in the first year with their wrapping of parchment-like sheaths. They grow to 10ft/3m, arching over with the weight of the foliage. The narrow tapered leaves, mid-green and faintly checkered, carried on short twiggy branches. When leaves die the stalks persist, giving the lower part of the canes a bottlebrush appearance. Non-invasive.

CORTADERIA Pampas grass Although tarnished by a suburban reputation, *C. selloana* [7–9] carries magnificent and long-lasting flower plumes and the evergreen tussock of arching narrow leaves, as much as 8ft/2.5m long, is impressive. Variegation of "Aureolineata" gives the foliage old-gold tones. Leaves of the compact "Albolineata" [7–10] edged white, the plumes silver.

DESCHAMPSIA Hair grass The thread-like leaves of *D. flexuosa* "Tatra Gold" [4–9], gathered in arching tufts 18in/45cm high, are bright yellow-green; flowerheads bronze. For moist acid soil in sun or shade.

ELYMUS Wild rye The brilliant silver-white or blue ribbons of *E. magellanicus* [7–8] make an eye-catching feature in a hot, dry garden; evergreen perennial to 12in/30cm.

FARGESIA Evergreen clump-forming bamboos, including two outstanding species for moist conditions. The umbrella bamboo, *F. murieliae* [4–9], about 12ft/3.7m high, is fountain-like in form, the mature yellow stems arching over with the mass of lance-shaped bright green leaves. "Simba" is compact. The fountain bamboo, *F. nitida* [5–9], has purplish stems and thin dark green leaves, lustrous on the upper surface, matte on the reverse, and very mobile. It prefers light or dappled shade.

FESTUCA Fescue Evergreen perennial grasses, a number with narrow leaves that

are blue-gray or blue-green. For full sun and well-drained, even dry soil. The large blue fescue, *F. amethystina* [4–8], with gray-green, partly inrolled linear leaves forms a loose tussock about 18in/45cm high. Blue fescue, *F. glauca* [4–8], has remarkable blue-gray forms, usually growing to 12in/30cm; "Elijah Blue" has stiff inrolled leaves, needle-like and of intense metallic color. A smaller spiky plant, *F. punctoria* [4–8], only 6in/15cm high and vivid blue. *F. valesiaca* "Silbersee" [4–7] is compact, 8in/20cm high, and pale silvery blue. *F. glauca* "Golden Toupee" [4–8], with bright yellow-green tufts, provides an unexpected color shift.

GLYCERIA An aquatic perennial grass, *G. maxima* var. *variegata* [5–8], best planted in about 6in/15cm of water, restricting its roots in a basket to prevent it spreading. Elegantly arching ribbon leaves, striped cream, white, and deep green, to 2ft/60cm.

HAKENOCHLOA The deciduous perennial grass *H. macra* [4–9] has 2 remarkable variegated forms, "Alboaurea" [7–9] and "Aureola" [7–9]. Both make soft clumps of arching leaves, the narrow ribbons tapering elegantly. "Alboaurea" is striped green and yellow with hints of buff and bronze; "Aureola" has narrower leaves striped green and cream, tinted red in fall.

HELICTOTRICHON The blue oat grass, *H. sempervirens* [4–8], follows a blue-gray theme in the dense tuft of its linear leaves and its oat-like plumes. An evergreen for well-drained, preferably alkaline, soil and sun.

HOLCUS Tufts of *H. mollis* "Albovariegatus" [7–9], soft linear leaves with broad white margins; to 6in/15cm, mat-forming. Trim to prevent self-seeding: can be invasive – seedlings green-leaved.

IMPERATA The erect narrow blades of the blood grass, *I. cylindrica* "Rubra" [6–9], make clumps 16in/40cm high, purple-red staining of the upper part extending down the leaves as summer advances. For moist soil in sun; can be a weed in warm climates.

INDOCALAMUS The large, glossy leaves of *I. tesselatus* [8–10], bright green and up to 2ft/60cm long, give this bamboo a tropical appearance that can be exploited in the garden. Lax growth to about 4ft/1.2m; a rampant runner and best restricted.

JUNCUS Rush The corkscrew rush, *J. effusus* "Spiralis" [5–9], is leafless, the "foliage" consisting of cylindrical stems spiralling in a lax clump about 12in/30cm high; for moist acid soil. *J. decipiens* "Curly-wurly" [5–9] is similarly hysterical.

LEYMUS Lyme grass, *L. arenarius* [4–9] spreads aggressively but its blue-gray stems, arching leaves, and wheat-like flowerheads make a beautiful effect in full sun on dry soils.

LUZULA Woodrush Of these tufted grass-like perennials the most valuable for foliage is *L. sylvatica* "Aurea" [4–9]. Arching leaf straps lustrous yellow in winter, yellow-green in summer. For sun or partial shade in moist soil.

MILIUM Bowles' golden grass, *M. effusum* "Aureum" [6–8], a semi-evergreen perennial grass with fluttering ribbon-like leaves, rich yellow in spring, later yellow-green; shimmering gold flowers on slender stems. For moist soil and partial shade.

MISCANTHUS Perennial grasses that in the wild are found in moist habitats, the airy flowers, which appear late, and leaves highly ornamental; dead leaves attractive in fall and winter. The silver banner grass, *M. sacchariflorus* [4–8], rarely flowers in cooler regions but clumps up to 8ft/2.5m, with linear blue-green leaves up to 3ft/90cm long and with silver midribs, create a subtropical impression. *M. sinensis* [5–9] also clump-forming and similar to *M. sacchariflorus* but with hairy undersides to the leaves, has over 100 cultivars, many valued for their flowers. Capable of growing to 13ft/4m but in cooler regions about half this. "Gracillimus," fine-leaved and curling. "Grosse Fontäne" [5–9], strong growing, of fountain-like form, with extra-large ribbon leaves. Less vigorous, var. *purpurascens* [5–9] has pink flowers and purple-tinted leaves, red in fall. Two striking variegated cultivars of moderate vigor: "Variegatus" [5–9], longitudinal stripes of white and green, and "Zebrinus" [6–9], with apparently random horizontal bands of pale yellow.

MOLINIA Purple moor grass, *M. caerulea* [4–8], is a native of acid heathlands and in cultivation does best on moist, neutral to acid soil. Best form is subsp. *caerulea* "Variegata" [5–8], making a clump to 2ft/60cm high of dark green arching leaves striped creamy white; flowers purple.

PHALARIS The white-variegated gardeners' garters, *P. arundinacea* var. *picta* [4–9], a striking evergreen perennial grass to 3ft 3in/1m high, with ribbon-like leaves; tolerant of most conditions and invasive. "Feesey" has more white on paler green; spreads slowly.

PHYLLOSTACHYS Bamboos of medium to large size, including the largest growing, the giant timber bamboo, *P. bambusoides* [6–10], which in favorable conditions can exceed 30ft/9m. The splendid *P. viridiglaucescens* [6–10] easily grows to 20ft/6m, its tall green stems carrying many glossy, lance-shaped leaves, blue-green on the underside. Invasive in moist conditions.

PLEIOBLASTUS Evergreen bamboos including 2 variegated species suitable for moist soil and best cut back annually in late winter to get fresh growth. *P. variegatus* [5–10] has downy linear leaves, striped white; it grows to 3ft/90cm. The slightly taller *P. auricomus* [5–10], strap-shaped leaves 8in/20cm long, pale green striped yellow if grown in sun. Both tend to run.

SASA Evergreen bamboos of moderate height with running rhizomes forming large thickets. *S. palmata* f. *nebulosa* [6–9], with purple-streaked canes, forms dense canopy at 6ft/1.8m, the large fingered leaves deep blue-green; margins wither in winter to give a variegated effect. *S. veitchii* [6–9], smaller deep green leaves, grows to 4ft/1.2m; leaf edges whiten with the first frost. Landscape plants for moist soil, in sun or shade.

SEMIARUNDINARIA Narihira bamboo, *S. fastuosa* [6–9], narrowly upright to 26ft/8m and suitable for hedging. Canes, first green, become purplish brown; glossy green leaves, gray-green on undersides, lance-shaped and borne high on the plant. For moist but well-drained soil in sun or dappled shade.

SHIBATEA Evergreen bamboos, *S. kumasasa* [7–9], making a bushy clump 2–3ft/60–90cm high; dark green lance-shaped leaves taper abruptly to a point. Spreads slowly in moist soil in sun or shade; plant thickly to make ground cover.

UNCINIA Hook sedge Tufted evergreen perennials for moist but well-drained soil in sun or partial shade. The tuft of *U. rubra* [8–11] 14in/35cm high, the shiny grass-like leaves, narrowing abruptly to a point, reddish green or red-brown. *U. uncinata* [8–11] is slightly larger, the leaves purplish brown.

ZEA Maize or sweetcorn, *Z. mais* [A] is an upright grass with lance-shaped leaves up to 3ft/90cm long with wavy margins. There are several ornamental forms. "Harlequin," up to 4ft/1.2m high, has leaves striped green, red, and white, and cobs with purplish red grains. Leaves of slightly smaller "Variegata" striped white and green.

Annuals & biennials

True annuals go through their whole life cycle, from germination to setting seed, in a year. Biennials germinate and make leaf growth one year and the next year flower before dying. Many plants grown as annuals are in reality perennials that are quick to reach flowering maturity. There are also plants that are usually biennial but may live longer, especially if prevented from flowering.

ALTERNANTHERA Tropical and subtropical plants, including the calico plant, *A. bettzichiana*, a short-lived perennial sometimes used in bedding. Leaves narrow, spoon-shaped, and yellow-green with bronze, red, and purple shading; flowers insignificant. Parrot leaf, *A. ficoidea* var. *amoena*, is a multi-colored mat-forming perennial.

BASSIA Burning bush, *B. scoparia* f. *trichophylla*, is an annual that forms a dense cone of narrow leaves, turning from light green to intense red or purple in late summer or fall. Usually 2–4ft/60–120cm high and suitable for bedding in full sun.

BRASSICA see Cabbage (Edible plants)

ERYNGIUM Sea holly The fierce bracts of *E. giganteum* "Miss Willmott's Ghost", a biennial to 3ft/90cm, surround cones of steel-blue flowers; a nearly-white plant in "Silver Ghost."

GLAUCIUM Horned poppy A biennial or short-lived perennial growing to 20in/50cm. The yellow horned poppy, *G. flavum* [6–9], forms a rosette of deeply cut and ruffled blue-gray leaves; yellow to orange flowers.

HELICHRYSUM see Trees & shrubs

IMPATIENS see Perennials

IRESINE Two tender plants often used for summer bedding, needing full sun to give best foliage color. Beefsteak plant, *I. herbstii*, a short-lived perennial capable of growing to 5ft/1.5m but generally much smaller. Commonly seen forms are "Aureoreticulata," ovate leaves heavily veined yellow, and "Brilliantissima," leaves often twisted, rich red with deeper markings. Bloodleaf, *I. lindenii*, is a perennial sometimes grown as an annual; grows to 3ft/90cm high, the stems and leaves vibrant, the veins red and very conspicuous.

LUNARIA Honesty The self-seeding biennial *L. annua* [5–9] has roughly heart-shaped leaves, in "Alba Variegata" with toothed fringes picked out in white, the topmost leaves most strongly frosted. White flowers followed by flat and circular silvery seedpods; grows to 30in/75cm. Only true from seed if grown in isolation.

ONOPORDUM Cotton thistle Biennial *O. acanthium* makes a large rosette of cobwebby gray-green leaves armed with spiny teeth. In the second year a gauntly branched stem, felted and prickly, towers to 10ft/3m, bearing pale purple thistle flowers.

PELARGONIUM see Perennials

PERILLA The red-purple foliage of *P. frutescens*, to 2ft/60cm high, is useful in summer bedding. Aromatic leaves ovate, pointed, and deeply toothed; in var. *crispa* they are bronzed and frilled.

SALVIA Sage The biennial or short-lived perennial, *S. argentea* [5–8] forms a soft rosette silvered by a cobwebby fleece. Candelabra to 3ft/90cm of white flowers. Biennial *S. sclarea* var. *turkestanica*, to 4ft/1.2m, with purple-pink bracts.

SILYBUM Deeply lobed and ruffled leaves, glossy rich green netted with white, form the spiny basal rosette, up to 3ft/90cm across, of the biennial Blessed Mary's thistle, *S. marianum* [6–9]. Topped in second year by purple-pink thistle flowers surrounded by sharp-spined bracts. Needs sun and good drainage on neutral to alkaline soil.

SOLENOSTEMON see Perennials

TROPAEOLUM Mainly trailing and climbing plants, including annuals derived from nasturtium, *T. majus*, a vigorous climber or scrambler with usually spurred flowers in red, orange, and yellow. Smooth, mid-green, rounded leaves with waved edges up to 3in/8cm across. "Empress of India" is bushy, 10in/25cm high, with purple-tinged leaves and semidouble scarlet flowers. The leaves of dwarf "Alaska" are light green, speckled, and streaked creamy white. Moisture, fertility, and partial shade increase luxuriance of foliage.

VERBASCUM Mullein Several biennials or short-lived perennials for dry, sunny gardens make large woolly rosettes, from which in the second year rise dramatic flower spikes.

Magnificent overwintering rosette and spike, up to 8ft/2.5m, of *V. bombyciferum* [4–8] are silver-felted; flowers yellow. *V. olympicum* [5–9] similarly tall and woolly.

ZEA see Grasses

Ferns, palms, & cycads

Ferns are among the most primitive and beautiful of foliage plants and they are represented in most regions of the world. They do not flower but bear spores in clusters on the under-surfaces of the fronds, usually visible as rusty patches. New ferns develop from an intermediate generation of tiny organisms. Palms, predominantly tropical, vary greatly in character, many being tree-like with a crown of large leaves. Cycads superficially resemble palms, but represent a much earlier stage in the development of seed-bearing plants.

ADIANTUM Maidenhair fern The genus contains more than 200 ferns, most tropical and subtropical. The true maidenhair fern, *A. capillus-veneris* [7–10], widely grown under glass, has fronds making light green showers of pretty segments from glossy dark stems. The deciduous *A. pedatum* [3–8], growing to 18in/45cm, has wiry dark stems contrasting with delicate bright green fronds. The arrangement of the pinnae, springing from a single point on each stem, can give the fern a curiously angular look. The Aleutian maidenhair fern, *A. aleuticum* [3–8], similar but semievergreen, young fronds often tinged pink. The evergreen Himalayan maidenhair fern, *A. venustum* [3–8], rarely over 8in/20cm, has lacy triangular fronds on black stalks; new fronds tinted bronze-pink. All for moist soil and partial shade.

ASPLENIUM Spleenwort The terrestrial ferns described need moisture and partial shade but do best on lime. Evergreen hart's-tongue fern, *A. scolopendrium* [6–8], makes light green shuttlecock tufts up to 2ft/60cm high of strap-shaped, leathery fronds. Several forms, including **Crispum Group**, have fronds with wavy and crinkled edges. The maidenhair spleenwort, *A. trichomanes* [5–8], semievergreen,

8in/20cm high, with tapering fronds composed of dark green segments paired along black stems.

ATHYRIUM Lady fern Terrestrial deciduous ferns for shady moist conditions and neutral to acid soil. The lady fern, *A. filix-femina* [4–8], is a model of refined laciness, the fresh green arching fronds making a clump up to 3ft 3in/1m high; "Minutissimum" is a delightful dense miniature of the species. Japanese painted fern, *A. niponicum* var. *pictum* [3–8], spreads slowly but worth cherishing for its silvered green fronds, made more conspicuous by midribs flushed purple; deciduous, grows to 18in/45cm.

BLECHNUM Hard fern Mainly evergreen ferns for moist acid soil and shade. The creeping rhizomes of *B. penna-marina* [9–10] produce dense tufts of fronds, the segments on the fertile ones more widely spaced than those of the sterile fronds. Fertile fronds of the hard fern, *B. spicant* [5–8] often stand erect in the center of a rosette of sterile fronds. A much larger fern than these, *B. chilense* [10–11] grows to 3ft 3in/1m; the dark green sterile fronds arch out from the central tuft of rather rusty fertile fronds.

CHAMAEROPS The stiff gray-green "fans" of the dwarf fan palm, *C. humilis* [9–11], to 3ft 3in/1m long, are composed of up to 15 narrow leaflets. In frost-free conditions thorny stems can be 20ft/6m high, the leaves gathered in rounded clusters. Pot-grown specimens are almost trunkless.

CYCAS Fern palm In frost-free conditions the Japanese sago palm, *C. revoluta* [9–11], slowly attains a height of 10ft/3m or more and produces a number of stems, from the top of which radiate stiff herringbone leaves.

CYRTOMIUM The Japanese holly fern, *C. falcatum* [6–10], has the appearance of a low shrub about 2ft/60cm high, the dark, shiny frond segments looking a bit like holly leaves. For a sheltered, moist position in shade.

DICKSONIA The man or woolly tree fern, *D. antarctica* [9–10], the most widely grown of tree-like ferns. Can grow to over 20ft/6m; the fronds, with 2 or 3 divisions and up to 10ft/3m long, radiate from the top of the dark stem. Often seen as a much smaller plant and can be container-grown. Best in filtered light and moist acid soil.

DRYOPTERIS Buckler fern Several species are valuable plants for moist conditions and varying degrees of shade. Semievergreen golden male fern, **D. affinis** [5–8], makes a rich green shuttlecock but fronds unfurl pale green contrasting with scaly golden-brown midribs. Variable in height and can attain 5ft/1.5m. "Cristata" is a handsome cultivar with crested segments.

D. erythrosora [5–8], usually deciduous, is desirable for the pink-brown young fronds; grows to 18in/45cm. The male fern, **D. filix-mas**[4–8], tolerates a wide range of conditions and its much divided fronds, about 4ft/1.2m high, are sometimes evergreen in sheltered sites; crested forms include "Cristata". The most handsome species is deciduous **D. wallichiana** [6–8], the fronds yellow-green when unfurling and contrasting with very dark green hairy scales, 3ft/90cm long when fully developed.

MATTEUCCIA The ostrich plume fern, **M. struthiopteris** [3–8], deciduous species for permanently moist ground, but invasive. Makes a slight stem, the base for a pale green shuttlecock of delicately lacy fronds, which unfurl from elegant fiddle-necks.

ONOCLEA The deciduous sensitive fern, **O. sensibilis** [4–9], has a running rootstock and covers a lot of ground in the permanently moist conditions it requires. The fresh green fronds, produced throughout the growing season, are broadly triangular, the individual segments usually wavy edged.

OSMUNDA The flowering or regal fern, **O. regalis** [4–7], is a luxuriant deciduous species for permanently moist conditions, making a magnificent clump about 4ft/1.2m high at the waterside. Young fronds tinted copper brown – and after their summer green elegance turn yellow and tan.

PHOENIX In a frost-free climate the Canary Island date palm, **P. canariensis** [9–11], can grow to 50ft/15m or more and is topped by a fountain of arching deep green fronds as much as 20ft/6m long, composed of numerous narrow leaflets. Even as a much smaller container plant it is dramatic, with a wide crown. In containers use a loam-based potting mix and water sparingly in winter.

POLYPODIUM The common polpody, **P. vulgare** [6–8], is one of the most successful ferns in dry conditions; can be epiphytic or terrestrial. Narrow lance-shaped fronds dark green and leathery; those of "Cornubiense Grandiceps" are crested or branched.

POLYSTICHUM Shield fern A large genus of mainly evergreen ferns, including some highly ornamental terrestrial species. The hard shield fern, **P. aculeatum** [3–7], forms a shuttlecock of narrowly lance-shaped fronds, which seem to throw themselves backwards as they unfurl. When fully developed the clumps are 30in/75cm high, the fronds leathery and glossy. **P. munitum** [5–7] has leathery, lance-shaped fronds up to 3ft/90cm long; matte dark green, slightly hairy on the underside, the leaflets spine-toothed. The pick of the species, the soft shield fern, **P. setiferum** [5–7], tolerates dry conditions; soft-textured dark green fronds on shaggy buff stems make lax shuttlecock up to 3ft/90cm wide. Selected forms include the feathery Plumosum Group and Divisilobum Group "Herrenhausen," which forms a large lacy rosette.

TRACHYCARPUS The Chusan palm, **T. fortunei** [8–10], which in favorable conditions grows 70ft/22m, throws out fan-like pleated leaves up to 3ft/90cm across from the top of an upright stem covered with the fibrous remains of dead leaves. The ends of the pleats are split, the fans jagged. This and the similar **T. wagnerianus** [9–10] for sheltered positions and well-drained soil.

Edible plants

This section covers a wide range of plants that are grown as herbs, vegetables, and fruit, but at the same time have foliage that is ornamental. The selection includes annuals and biennials, perennials, and woody plants: what groups them together is the use to which they are put. There are plants here for the ornamental kitchen garden, but most of them are adaptable enough to be used more generally, with a wide range of other plants.

ANGELICA The herb *Angelica archangelica* [4–9] is a biennial or short-lived perennial with ridged stems and light green, deeply cut leaves up to 2ft/60cm long; rounded heads of small yellow-green flowers can take the height to 6ft/1.8m or more. For full sun or partial shade and moist but well-drained soil; it is also a fine foliage plant for a container. *A. gigas* [5–8], also biennial, has thick purplish stems and heads of beet-colored flowers.

BALM, LEMON The bushy perennial *Melissa officinalis* [3–7] grows to 3ft 3in/1m and needs full sun and well-drained soil. Aromatic light green leaves wrinkled and attractively notched; pale yellow flowers attractive to bees. Leaves of "Aurea" dark green splashed with gold; "All Gold" yellow.

BASIL, SWEET The annual *Ocimum basilicum* [9–10], growing to 3ft/60cm, has large, strongly aromatic leaves. Cultivars of special ornamental value include "Green Ruffles" and "Purple Ruffles," both with leaves curled and gathered at the edges, the former rich green, the latter red-purple. For a warm, sheltered position, well-drained soil.

BAY LAUREL The evergreen *Laurus nobilis* [8–10], a tree or large shrub with dark green, lance-shaped, glossy leaves, strongly aromatic. For a sheltered, sunny position in well-drained soil; suitable for a container and tolerates regular trimming.

CABBAGE Cultivars of *Brassica oleracea* [A] are biennials cultivated as annuals; the culinary versions often highly ornamental on account of the leaves' rosette arrangment. Savoys particularly beautiful because of their wrinkled, prominently veined leaves, often with a heavy waxy bloom. Red cabbages, also with a waxy bloom, are tightly folded and purple-red. Some, such as "Osaka Red" and "Osaka White," are grown specifically for their ornamental value, the leaves, red or gray-green, waved and curled at the edges and often handsomely variegated. Kale, also cultivar of *B. oleracea*, is widely grown as winter greens. Leaves usually very tightly curled, some cultivars blue-green in color, others purple-red.

CARDOON see *Cynara cardunculus* (Perennials)

CHARD Cultivars of the biennial *Beta vulgaris* [A], as is beetroot, but grown as annuals for their often highly ornamental leaves. In the most familiar version they are glossy dark green, with prominent white leaf stalks and midribs; rainbow mixtures include plants with red and yellow stalks.

CORN SALAD A modest little plant, *Valerianella locusta* [A], also known as lamb's lettuce, is an annual that tolerates most conditions; much used for winter and early spring salads; leaves tongue-shaped.

DILL Aromatic annual, *Anethum graveolens* [A], to 12in/30cm, with feathery foliage, the compound blue-green leaves consisting of thread-like leaflets; flat-topped heads of tiny yellow flowers. Foliage and seeds used as flavoring. For full sun and well-drained soil.

FENNEL Aromatic perennial *Foeniculum vulgare* [4–9], an aniseed-flavored herb growing to 6ft/1.8m, with hazy blue-green foliage consisting of finely cut leaves; tiny yellow flowers. Thread-like foliage of **"Purpureum"** is bronze, fading to green-purple. For full sun and well-drained soil.

FIG Common fig, *Ficus carica* [7–9], a large shrub or small tree grown for its brown, purple, or green fruit and as an ornamental for its hand-like lobed leaves, yellow-green and glossy. Full sun and well-drained soil.

KALE see Cabbage

LETTUCE Cultivars of *Lactuca sativa* [A] are favorite salad crops and there is great variety in form and color. Some of the most ornamental are **Salad Bowl** types with very crinkled leaves, often colored rich bronze. **"Lollo Rosso"** is an example of a very frizzy kind, with red-purple edges to the leaves. **"Oakleaf Red"** is a bronzed lettuce with deeply lobed leaves. The rosette form is more obvious in crisp head lettuces, with the heart surrounded by frilly leaves.

MARJORAM, WILD The rounded or ovate paired leaves of *Origanum vulgare* [5–9] are dark green and very aromatic. A less vigorous yellow-leaved form, **"Aureum,"** grows to 12in/30cm. For full sun and well-drained soil.

MINT Several species of *Mentha* grown for their freshly aromatic foliage, the most interesting ornamentally being variegated. Pineapple mint, *M. suaveolens* **"Variegata"** [6–9], grows to 18in/45cm, its leaves a bright mixture of ivory and green. The contrast of yellow and green in *M. x gracilis* **"Variegata"** [6–9] is strongest in full sun. The Corsican mint, *M. requienii* [6–9], a creeping miniature with minute bright green leaves. All need moist conditions.

ORACH Sometimes also known as mountain spinach, *Atriplex hortensis* [A] is an erect annual to 4ft/1.2m; succulent, almost triangular leaves. The foliage is gray-green or, in **var. rubra**, purple-red. For full sun and moist soil; bolts in dry weather.

PARSLEY The herb *Petroselinum crispum* [5–8], used for flavoring and garnishing, has 2 distinct forms, one with foliage that is curled and moss-like, the other with flat leaves divided into toothed segments. For full sun or partial shade, preferably moist.

RHUBARB see *RHEUM* (Perennials)

ROSEMARY Upright or bushy *Rosmarinus officinalis* [6–9] grows to 5ft/1.5m, clothed with linear, almost needle-like leaves. They are dark green, gray-white on the underside and strongly aromatic when lightly bruised; flowers usually blue. **"Miss Jessopp's Upright"** very erect; **Prostratus Group** sprawling. For full sun and well-drained soil.

SAGE The shrubby culinary herb *Salvia officinalis* [5–9] grows to 2ft/60cm; has gray-green, rather wrinkled ovate leaves; flowers violet-blue. Several forms grown for their colored foliage: **"Purpurascens"** has red-purple young leaves; **"Icterina,"** variegated yellow and green, and **"Tricolor,"** leaves gray-green with cream, purple, and pink zones, are less vigorous. For full sun and well-drained soil.

SEAKALE see *CRAMBE* (Perennials)

STRAWBERRY Cultivated strawberries are derived from woodland species of *Fragraria* [5–9], spreading by stolons and with leaves consisting of three-toothed leaflets. Alpine strawberries, such as **"Baron Solemacher"** [5–9], thrive in moist, neutral to alkaline soils and are a pretty underplanting in dappled shade in beds, and attractive in containers.

THYME Garden thyme, *Thymus vulgaris* [4–9], is a bushy shrublet with gray-green, finely hairy, aromatic leaves; flowers usually bright purple. **"Silver Posie"** is a bright cultivar with white variegated foliage. Mat-forming thymes include: *T. x citriodorus* **"Bertram Anderson"** [6–9], with yellowish leaves; *T. x citriodrus* **"Silver Queen"** [6–9], leaves variegated cream; *T.* **"Doone Valley"** [6–9], dark green with yellow splashes; and *T. serpyllum* **"Minimus"** [4–9], moss-like with minute woolly leaves. All for full sun and well drained soil.

plant care

Pests and diseases that can mar the ornamental quality of foliage may cause problems in any garden. Disasters are, however, rare and you can minimize the risk of disappointments and failures by the way you garden.

• By preparing the ground well, paying particular attention to drainage, soil structure, and fertility you give plants the best chance of making strong vigorous growth and developing foliage that is truly ornamental. Although some plants are adapted to living in permanently wet ground, in general even plants that require a plentiful supply of moisture do not like stagnant conditions. If the garden as a whole is regularly waterlogged it may be necessary to lay drains. If, however, the problem is confined to a small low-lying area it might be worth developing this as a special garden for plants that relish boggy conditions. Most soils benefit from the addition of generous quantities of well-rotted organic matter, which can be dug in when flowerbeds and borders are being prepared and added subsequently in the form of mulches. It will help improve the soil's structure, make free-draining soils more water retentive, and some kinds, such as garden compost, will boost the soil's fertility.

• Many plants are very adaptable but to get the best results you need to choose plants that suit the growing conditions. Ardent sun lovers will look sickly in shade and are likely to become spindly and untypical in their growth. Many plants that thrive in partial shade will also do well in sun provided they get plenty of moisture. Dense planting has the advantage of leaving little room for weeds but you can find bumptious plants elbowing out milder-natured companions. One solution is to begin with dense planting, including a proportion of quick-maturing plants that can be dispensed with after a couple of years. In a dry garden you could use biennials such as some of the verbascums and even the easy-going shrubby lupine, *Lupinus arboreus*. When choosing plants you have to weigh up how much you value those that are particularly vulnerable to disease or appetizing to

pests. If you cannot or will not protect your hostas from slugs and snails it may be better not to grow them at all.

• Weeds compete with garden plants for nutrients and moisture and therefore should be controlled. Dense planting is one way of keeping them out. Another is the use of mulches. Organic kinds include bark chippings and garden compost. Inorganic mulches can also be highly effective. Stone chippings go well with dwarf plants in containers and raised beds. Black plastic sheeting is more utilitarian but is a useful mulch if, say, you are planting ground cover. Make slits through which to plant. The plastic can be hidden under a decorative mulch such as bark chippings. Always water the ground well before applying a mulch.

• Good garden hygiene will help to minimize the risk of disease. You should think of dead, diseased, and damaged growths as potential reservoirs of infection. As a general rule, keep the garden tidy and burn anything that you think is diseased. Scrupulously tidy gardeners miss out, however, on some of the real delights of winter. The dead leaves of deciduous leaves should be raked up in autumn (they take time but eventually will rot down to make superb leaf mold) but you can enjoy the dead leaves and flowerheads of grasses standing in the garden until late winter or early spring. It is a time of the year when many plants benefit from having old growth tidied away or cut back to encourage new shoots.

• Your sound practise must include responses to problems as they arise. "Green" gardeners are usually willing to tolerate some degree of damage in preference to using chemical pesticides, fungicides and herbicides. Those who decide to rely at least in part on chemical controls must use them responsibly, following the manufacturer's instructions closely.

Disease control

There are three main kinds of disease that can cause damage. Virus infections, caused by microscopic virus particles in the plant tissue, give rise to a variety of symptoms, including stunted and distorted growth and yellowing of the foliage, which can be streaked, mottled, ring-spotted, or marked by a mosaic pattern. There is no way of treating affected plants, which should be removed and burned. Viruses can be transmitted in a variety of ways, particularly by sap-feeding pests such as aphids. Keeping potential carriers under control limits the risk of infection.

Fungal infections of plants are usually caused by microfungi attacking particular parts of a plant and may show on the leaves in the form of spots, mildew, or rust. Some but by no means all of these can be controlled reasonably effectively with the use of fungicides such as Bordeaux mixture, carbendazim, mancozeb, and penconazole. An adequate measure of control is usually achieved by removing and burning infected leaves or whole plants at the end of the season.

Bacterial infections are less common than fungal diseases but in the case of leaf spots the symptoms are superficially similar. Prompt removal of infected parts is the best control but the presence of bacterial infections often indicates a more serious underlying problem.

Pest control

The leaves of plants can be attacked by a wide range of pests. Infestations of sap-feeders such as aphids can cause distortion of the leaves and there is the more serious risk of virus diseases being transmitted from infected plants. Aphids can be controlled by the insecticide pirimicarb, which has the advantage of posing little risk to beneficial insects. Pests that eat leaves include the larvae of insects that feed inside the leaves as leaf miners, caterpillars of various moths and butterflies, slugs and snails, and adult vine weevils. Great damage can also be done by rabbits, hares, and deer. If the larger pests are a serious problem, it may be necessary to keep them out with fencing.

Picking off pests such as caterpillars and destroying them often gives an adequate measure of control. Slug and snail numbers can be controlled with the use of poisoned baits. Pellets based on metaldehyde or methiocarb give good results but these are toxic to cats and dogs. Slug killers based on aluminum

sulfate do not pose the same threat. The use of the nematode *Phasmarhabditis hermaphrodita* as a biological control is mainly effective against underground slugs and not snails or slugs that attack leaves. An alternative to chemical controls is the beer trap, consisting of a container half-filled with beer and set in the ground. The smell attracts slugs, which fall in and drown.

Pruning and trimming

All pruning should be carried out with sharp clean tools. Basic equipment includes secateurs, loppers, hand shears, and a pruning saw. Powered hedge trimmers are invaluable, provided they are used with proper attention to safety. Always wear protective goggles when operating powered equipment and, if the trimmer is electrically powered, use an adaptor or plug fitted with a residual current device (RCD). This circuit-breaker giving protection should the flex be accidentally cut.

Pruning cuts should be clean and correctly positioned. Rough cuts and the jagged remnants of broken limbs can be points of entry for fungal diseases. A clean cut gives the plant the opportunity to respond to the wound by developing a protective callus. If the plant has alternate buds or shoots, make the cuts just above and sloping back from a shoot or bud so that the new growth does not clutter the center of the plant. If the plant has opposite shoots or buds, cut straight across just above a pair. Avoid making cuts that would leave a stub extending beyound a bud or shoot. The stub will die and become a likely entry point for disease.

Many trees, shrubs, and climbers will give good value as foliage plants with very little pruning other than the removal of dead, diseased, and damaged wood. Drastic pruning is all too often a desperate measure when growth from badly positioned plants overwhelms part of the garden. It often initiates a tiresome cycle, for pruning encourages growth; hard pruning stimulates more vigorous growth than light pruning. Once the cycle has been started it is difficult to break.The moral is to plant trees and shrubs where they can develop their natural shape unimpeded. Drastic pruning is fully justified when variegated

plants produce shoots with plain leaves. Because they are more vigorous than the variegated growths and will eventually take over, they should be cut out as soon as they are noticed.

Formative pruning

The aim of formative pruning is to encourage a sound, well-balanced shape. Deciduous trees such as *Liquidambar styraciflua* that naturally develop a strong central leader need little attention. However, any lateral that competes with the leader should be cut out. In a garden it is often sensible to remove the lower branches of a central-leader tree. This allows light in to lower levels of the garden and makes working and mowing round the base much simpler. Some central-leader trees, especially oaks (*Quercus*) eventually develop a branched crown. No pruning is necessary for this but the same kind of shape can be encouraged in smaller trees by cutting back the leader to encourage the development of branches to form the head. This formative pruning is often used on fruit trees and can be applied to ornamentals such as *Crataegus persimilis* "Prunifolia." Trees of pendulous habit, such as the weeping silver pear (*Pyrus salicifolia* 'Pendula'), often need to have the leader and even the topmost lateral above it trained up to form an upper tier. As these trees mature, the weeping growths get rather tangled and warrant an occasional winter clearing out.

With shrubs, formative pruning may be necessary to remove surplus or badly placed shoots. The pruning regimes of many established shrubs are intended to promote a good show of flowers. Some shrubs, such as forsythias, that produce flowers on growths made the previous year, are pruned immediately after flowering. Others, like buddlejas, flower on growth made in the current season and are cut back in spring.

Hard pruning for large leaves

Several deciduous shrubs and trees can be pruned hard in spring and then fed generously to produce unusually large leaves. Shrubs such as the plain and purple-leaved forms of the smoke bush (*Cotinus*), the gold- and purple-leaved forms of hazel (*Corylus*) and *Sambucus racemosa* "Sutherland Gold" can be coppiced, that is cut to near ground level. The tree of heaven (*Ailanthus altissima*), the Indian bean tree, especially its yellow-leaved form (*Catalpa bignonioides* "Aurea") and the foxglove tree (*Paulownia tomentosa*) lend themselves to pollarding, the growths being cut back to a point on the main stem or stems. A consequence of maintaining rigorous pruning regimes is that plants do not produce flowers, which might be considered a disadvantage, for example, in the case of the smoke bushes. Eucalypts also tolerate hard pruning. In their natural habitat these evergreen trees are often badly burned by naturally occurring fires but sprout again from the base. A severe pruning regime takes advantage of their tremendous resilience and is a way of perpetuating the juvenile phase, which can be of remarkable beauty in species such as *Eucalyptus gunnii*. These evergreens are best cut back a little later than deciduous trees and shrubs and not before mid-spring where there is a strong possibility of late frosts. Eucalypts can be coppiced, pollarded, or maintained in bush form by cutting back the leader at a suitable height and subsequently taking out upright growths and lightly shaping the shrubby form.

Trimming evergreens

Most of the larger evergreens need very little pruning, except for the removal in spring of any growths that have died back during winter. Some small evergreen shrubs that are grown for their foliage and flowers became straggly if not clipped over in spring. This is the way to keep lavender (*Lavandula*) and cotton lavender (*Santolina chamaecyparissus*) compact and is also advisable for most heaths and heathers (*Calluna* and *Erica*).

Hedges and topiary

Windbreaks and informal hedges require little pruning other than some cutting back at an early stage to encourage bushy growth and, as the plants mature, some light trimming. Hedges and specimens of topiary require much more rigorous training and trimming, topiary plants being treated very much as isolated hedge plants. Topiary specimens with large leaves such as bay laurel (*Laurus nobilis*) are best gone over with secateurs so that whole leaves are removed.

Some young hedging plants need to be cut back to encourage bushy growth. These include several deciduous trees and shrubs such as hawthorn (*Crataegus*) and some evergreens, notably box (*Buxus sempervirens*). Hornbeam (*Carpinus*

betulus) and beech (*Fagus sylvatica*) need less severe pruning and with most conifers, including yew (*Taxus baccata*), it is enough to trim back the laterals. From an early stage, the sides should be clipped with a batter, that is sloping, with the base of the hedge thicker than the top. This allows reasonably even distribution of light across the surface of the hedge and reduces the risk of damage by snow. Hedges of beech, hornbeam, and yew are among those that keep a well defined shape with a single annual trim, in the second half of summer. Fast-growing hedging plants such as privet (*Ligustrum ovalifolium*) may need to be cut three times in the growing season.

Foliage for cutting

Many gardens yield plenty of foliage for cutting from plants grown ornamentally. If you are going to make heavy demands on your plants and have a large enough garden it is well worth lining out a selection of plants in a spare piece of ground for cutting foliage. Your selection could include coppiced or pollarded eucalypts, *Pittosporum tenuifolium*, large perennials such as the cardoon (*Cynara cardunculus*), and also numerous ferns and grasses.

index

Page numbers in *italics* indicate an illustration. There may be text on these pages as well

acknowledgments

1 Marianne Majerus; 2-3 © IPC Syndication/Andrea Jones/New Eden; 4-5 Jerry Harpur; 6-7 Bruce Coleman Collection; 8-9 Bruce Coleman Collection/Stephen J Krasemann; 10-11 Marianne Majerus/designer Pat Wallace; 11 Andrew Lawson/Beth Chatto gardens, Essex; 12-13 Marianne Majerus; 14 above Garden Picture Library/John Glover; 14 below Andrew Lawson; 15 above Andrew Lawson; 15 below Garden Picture Library/Christi Carter; 16 S & O Mathews; 17 above Jonathan Buckley; 17 below John Glover; 18 Mark Bolton; 19 below S & O Mathews; 20 above Mark Bolton; 20 below Jerry Harpur; 21 Andrew Lawson; 22 above Garden Picture Library/David Cavagnaro; 22 below Andrew Lawson; 23 Andrew Lawson; 24 S & O Mathews; 25 above Andrew Lawson; 25 below Marcus Harpur; 26 Marianne Majerus; 27 above Jonathan Buckley; 27 below Garden Picture Library/Ute Klaphake; 28 above Jörgen Schwartzkopf; 28 below Andrew Lawson; 29 Andrew Lawson; 30 Mark Bolton; 31 above S & O Mathews; 31 below Jean-Pierre Gabriel; 32 Anne Hyde; 33

Garden Picture Library/Sunniva Harte; 34 S & O Mathews; 35 above Marianne Majerus; 35 below Mark Bolton; 36 Andrew Lawson; 37 above Marcus Harpur; 37 below Marianne Majerus; 38 above Jonathan Buckley; 38 below Marianne Majerus; 39 Jonathan Buckley; 40 Jonathan Buckley; 40-41 Garden Picture Library/J S Sira; 41 Clive Nichols; 42 above Jerry Harpur; 42 below S & O Mathews; 43 Marianne Majerus; 44-45 Mark Bolton; 46 S & O Mathews; 47 above Marcus Harpur; 47 below Marianne Majerus; 48 Jerry Harpur; 48-49 Garden Picture Library/Howard Rice; 49 S & O Mathews; 50-52 Jonathan Buckley; 53 Mark Bolton; 54 above S & O Mathews; 54 below Andrew Lawson; 55 Jonathan Buckley; 56 Clive Nichols; 57 above Clive Nichols; 57 below Mark Bolton; 58 above Andrew Lawson; 58 below John Glover; 59 Andrew Lawson; 60 Anne Hyde; 61 above Mark Bolton; 61 below Jonathan Buckley; 62 above Mark Bolton; 62 below Anne Hyde; 63 Jonathan Buckley; 64-65 Marianne Majerus; 66 Andrew Lawson; 67 above S & O Mathews; 67 below Marcus

Harpur; 68 Andrew Lawson; 69 above Jonathan Buckley; 69 below Andrew Lawson; 70 Jonathan Buckley; 71 Andrew Lawson; 72 above Anne Hyde; 72 above Andrew Lawson; 72 below Jerry Harpur; 73 Clive Nichols; 74 above Andrew Lawson; 74 below Marcus Harpur; 75 Anne Hyde; 76 above Marcus Harpur; 76 below Mark Bolton; 77 above Marianne Majerus; 77 below Marianne Majerus; 78 S & O Mathews; 78-79 Andrew Lawson; 80 S & O Mathews; 81 Andrew Lawson; 82 above Mark Bolton; 82 below Andrew Lawson; 83 Marianne Majerus; 84 Andrew Lawson; 85 John Glover; 86 Marianne Majerus; 87 above Andrew Lawson; 87 below John Glover; 88-89 John Glover; 90 Garden Picture Library/Christopher Gallagher; 91 S & O Mathews; 92 Clive Nichols; 93 Clive Nichols/Hillier Gardens; 94 above Garden Picture Library/Jerry Pavia; 94 below Marcus Harpur; 95 Clive Nichols/The Manor House, Walton-in-Gordano; 96 Garden Picture Library/Howard Rice; 97 above Andrew Lawson; 97 below S & O Mathews; 98 above Andrew Lawson; 98

below Garden Picture Library/Roger Hyam; 99 John Glover; 100 John Glover; 101 above Clive Nichols; 101 below Anne Hyde; 102 Jonathan Buckley/designer Christopher Lloyd; 103 above S & O Mathews; 103 below Mark Bolton; 104 Andrew Lawson; 105 Jerry Harpur/designer Christopher Bradley-Hole; 106 Jonathan Buckley; 107 Clive Nichols; 108-109 Marianne Majerus/designer Will Giles; 110 Marianne Majerus; 111 Clive Nichols/designer Sarah Hammond, US; 112 above Anne Hyde; 112 below S & O Mathews; 113 Jerry Harpur/Jason Payne, London; 114-115 Andrew Lawson; 116 Andrew Lawson/designer Christopher Holliday/Charney Well; 117 Andrew Lawson/designer Penelope Hobhouse; 118 above Marcus Harpur; 118 below S & O Mathews; 119 Jerry Harpur; 120 Jonathan Buckley; 121 Garden Picture Library/Michele Lamontagne; 122 above Clive Nichols; 122 below Andrew Lawson; 123 Robert O"Dea; 124 Jean-Pierre Gabriel; 125 above Andrew Lawson; 125 below S & O Mathews; 126 Andrew Lawson.

Author's acknowledgments

I am indebted to many gardeners and writers on gardening who have helped form my view on plants and gardens and who has enriched my knowledge. I am particularly grateful for the help I have received from the following in the research and writing of this book: George Debbage (Fairhaven Garden Trust, Norfolk), Margot di Menna, John Elsley, David Hatfield and Phil Parker (Dibley's Nurseries).
In thanking Carole McGlynn and Paul Welti for their contributions as editor and designer, I am conscious that there are many other people who have also played an important role in the production and promotion of this book.